NAPOLEON'S CAVALRY

Napoleon's Cavalry

EMIR BUKHARI

Colour plates by
ANGUS McBRIDE

PRESIDIO PRESS
SAN RAFAEL, CALIFORNIA
LONDON, ENGLAND

Edited by Martin Windrow
© Copyright 1979 Osprey Publishing Limited
ISBN 0 85045 339 9

Published simultaneously with Osprey Publishing
Limited of London, England, by Presidio Press of
San Rafael, California and London, England, with
editorial offices at 1114 Irwin Street, San Rafael,
California 94901.

Library of Congress Cataloging in Publication Data

Bukhari, Emir.
    Napoleon's Cavalry.

    'Originally published as five separate monographs
in the renowned Men-at-Arms series.'
    Bibliography: P.
    Contents: Introduction. – Cuirassiers and
Carabiniers. – Dragoons and Lancers. – Line
Chasseurs. (Etc.)
    1. France. Armée. Cavalerie – History – 18th
Century.   2. France. Armée. Cavalerie – history –
19th Century.   I. McBride, Angus.   II. Title.
UA704, A6B84   357'1.1'0944   79-10364
ISBN 0-89141-090-2

Printed in Hong Kong

ACKNOWLEDGEMENTS

The author would like to express his gratitude for the
assistance rendered him by the following persons in
the preparation of this book: the staff of the Musée
de l'Armée, Paris; the Musée Royale de l'Armée,
Bruxelles; the Victoria and Albert Museum, and the
National Army Museum, London; Jean and M. le
Baron de Gerlache de Gomery; Massimo da Luigi
Lucchesi; Michel Risser; Gerry Embleton; Richard
Hook; Martin Windrow; Chris Brennan; Sue
Armitage; Mary Parker; Blaise Morgan; John
Andow; Sharon Massey and Caroline Lederer. The
author would also like to acknowledge the works of
Comndt. Bucquoy and M. Lucien Rousselot, in
particular, whose meticulous researches have proved
invaluable in the writing and illustrating of this book.

Contents

SELECT BIBLIOGRAPHY

Anon., *Manoeuvres de la Cavalerie*

H. Bouchot, *L'Epopée du costume militaire française*

Commandant Bucquoy (ed.), *Les uniformes et les armes des soldats 1ᵉʳ Empire*

French Ministry of War (pub.), *Historique des corps de troupe de l'armée française*

Dr. Hourtouille (ed.), *Soldats et uniformes du 1ᵉʳ Empire*

Job, *Tenues des troupes de France*

H. Lachouque, *The Anatomy of Glory*

Marx, *Tableaux synoptiques des manoeuvres de la Cavalerie*

J.C. Quennevat, *Atlas de la Grande Armée*

J.C. Quennevat, *Les vrais soldats de Napoleon*

J. Regnault, *Les aigles perdus*

Col. H.C.B. Rogers, *Napoleon's Army*

Lucien Rousselot, *L'armée française*

Various issues of the periodicals *La Giberne*, *Le Passepoil*, *Le Sabretache*, *Les Fiches Documentaires*, and *Tradition*

Introduction

By the close of the Napoleonic Wars the names of Murat, Bessières, Lasalle and Kellermann, together with those of the regiments they led, had charged into legend. Even the Duke of Wellington indirectly paid homage to Napoleon's cavalry when in 1826 he admitted in a letter to Lord Russell that in battle the order and handling of the French formations were unsurpassed; indeed, the greater the numbers involved, the better the discipline told. But Napoleon, as First Consul, did not inherit from the Directorate the crack regiments with which he set Europe aflame.

Although the Royal cavalry suffered less than any other branch of the army from the upheavals and purges which ushered in the fledgling Republic, the desertions among both officers and men were sufficient to undermine seriously the morale and leadership of the regiments. Rebuilding the ranks proved far simpler than inculcating tactical knowledge, however. Such was the state of affairs that generals such as Marmont, St. Cyr and Napoleon himself were forced openly to concede that the cavalry's performance during the campaigns of 1793, 1794 and 1795 was little better than worthless. But the experience gained in these initial campaigns was to tell in the following year when, following a spectacular charge of *chasseurs* led by Murat, Napoleon was at last able to say: '*This was the first time that the French cavalry, seeing the state in which it had been, measured itself to advan-* *tage against the Austrian cavalry.*' From these humble beginnings emerged the formidable bludgeon that was to make Waterloo '*...a near run thing.*'

Hoche, commanding the Army of the Sambre and the Meuse, set the pattern for Napoleon's Imperial Army in 1797 when he organized his cavalry on a higher level than that previously employed. Prior to this date, the cavalry regiments had been distributed piecemeal among the infantry divisions, with only a few retained in reserve; now, however, Hoche appointed a single regiment of *chasseurs* to each division, and amassed the balance of his cavalry in a massive reserve, sub-divided into divisions according to class. This provided him with a strong and highly mobile reserve corps, of a kind which Napoleon was to employ brilliantly.

The Emperor conceived of this cavalry reserve as being integral part of his war machine, fully incorporated in the tactical dispositions of the infantry and artillery. Its function was principally two-fold: firstly, it acted as a screen to mask the movements of the main army, concealing both the strength and direction of the various advancing corps (the most notable example of this application being the preliminaries to the Austrian campaign of 1805); secondly, it acted on a tactical basis on the battlefield by administering the *coup de grace* to an already closely-engaged enemy line, the best example being the charge at Eylau and the most unsuccessful the *chevauchée* at Waterloo. At no time did Napoleon utilize his cavalry as a separate, self-sufficient arm, free to go its own way on large-scale raids on the rear of the enemy, disrupting communications and pillaging supply depots; individual units were, however, gainfully employed on reconaissance sorties. As to his attitude towards this most dashing and colourful arm of his forces, perhaps his own cold words neatly dispel illusions one might harbour that there existed a difference between a commander's relationship with men and beasts, and his attitude towards mechanical instruments of war:

'*The use of cavalry demands boldness and ability, above all it should not be handled with any miserly instinct to keep it intact...I do not wish the horses to be spared if they catch men...Take no heed of the complaints of the cavalry, for if such great objects may be obtained as the destruction of a whole hostile army, the State can afford to lose a few hundred horses from exhaustion.*'

Originally produced as a series of five separate monographs, this present compilation volume is an exploration – necessarily tentative, at this distance in time – of the organization, dress, equipment, and campaign record of all the colourful cavalry regiments of Napoleon's *Grande Armée*. Its preparation involved the generous help and advice of many institutions and individuals, who are thanked by name elsewhere in this book.

———❋———

1

Cuirassiers and Carabiniers

‘ It is surely in the heavy cavalry that the art and science of the mounted man is exemplified to the highest order. ’

(Napoleon to Eugéne, 13 March 1806)

‘ The cuirassiers are of greater value than any other type of cavalry. ’

(Napoleon to Bessières, 16 April 1808)

Organisation

The entire French army was reorganised in 1791, and all old regimental titles were abolished. Regiments were once more commanded by colonels and included the following officers: two lieutenant-colonels, a *quartier-maître trésorier* (paymaster quartermaster), a surgeon major, a chaplain, two adjutants, a trumpet-major and five *maîtres-ouvriers*. The two regiments of carabiniers were composed of four squadrons each and the 27 *cavalerie* regiments of three squadrons, each of two companies which included: a captain, a lieutenant, two second-lieutenants, a *maréchal-des-logis-chef*, two *maréchaux-des-logis*, a *brigadier-fourrier*, four *brigadiers*, 54 troopers and a trumpeter. In 1792, the *cavalerie* regiments were reduced to 25 and, in 1793, had the number of squadrons brought up to four. Also in 1793 colonels were renamed as *chefs de brigade* and lieutenant-colonels as *chefs d'escadron*.

Upon becoming First Consul, Bonaparte restored the title of colonel and introduced that of major. In September of that same year, 1802, he wrote to General Berthier, Minister of War: 'I desire you, citizen minister, to submit to me a scheme for reducing the regiments of heavy cavalry to twenty – two of which should be carabiniers – all four squadrons strong. The last six of the now existing regiments should be broken up to furnish a squadron to each of the first eighteen proposed regiments. Of the eighteen regiments, the first five are to wear the cuirass, in addition to the eighth, which is already equipped in this manner, making in all, six regiments with, and twelve regiments without cuirasses'. The 1st regiment of *cavalerie* had, on 10 October 1801, already been converted to the 1st Cavalerie-Cuirassiers and, on 12 October 1802, the 2nd, 3rd and 4th regiments followed suit; shortly thereafter, on 23 December 1802, the 5th, 6th and 7th did likewise. Within a

year the 9th, 10th, 11th and 12th regiments were also transformed, bringing the new arm to a strength of twelve cuirassier regiments. This situation remained static until, in 1808, the 1st Pro-

A trooper of the 12th Cuirassiers, October 1804. Formed in late 1803, this regiment remained without cuirasses until 1804. Although issued with a short-tailed tunic from 1803, the cuirassiers were obliged to continue wearing their cumbersome long-tailed *cavalerie* tunics until they wore out; this particular *habit-veste* is interesting in that it is of 1803 cut but complete with lapels, of which the 1803 pattern was devoid. Reconstructed after an inspection report, it demonstrates how frequently the reality of uniform differed from the official orders. The 5th Cuirassiers are also reported as having had lapels of the regimental colour. Just visible is the single-section *cavalerie* swordbelt which was found to hold the sabre too high for an armoured horseman and was duly replaced by the 'AnXI' pattern of three sections, which suspended the sabre at wrist height. The sabre is the 'AnIX' model soon to be replaced by the guttered 'AnXI' pattern (*Illustration by L. Rousselot, courtesy of the De Gerlache de Gomery Collection*)

11

visional Regiment of Heavy Cavalry became the 13th Cuirassiers, followed by the 2nd regiment of Dutch cuirassiers who, in 1810, were renamed the 14th Cuirassiers.

As we have seen, the regiments were composed of four squadrons, raised to five in March of 1807, each of two companies of two troops apiece. In 1806 the regimental staff in theory consisted of a colonel, a major, two *chefs d'escadron*, two *adjutant-majors*, a paymaster-quartermaster, a surgeon-major, an *aide-major*, two *sous-aide-major*, two

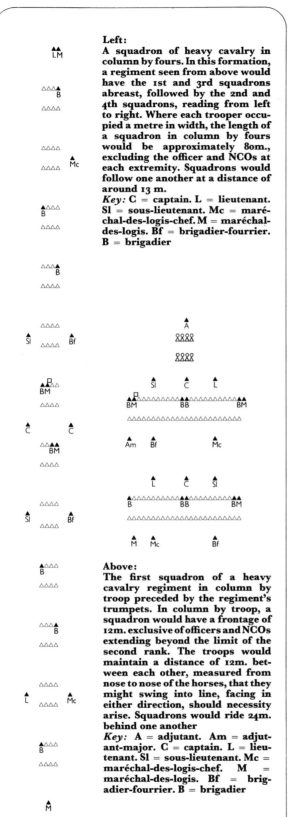

Left:
A squadron of heavy cavalry in column by fours. In this formation, a regiment seen from above would have the 1st and 3rd squadrons abreast, followed by the 2nd and 4th squadrons, reading from left to right. Where each trooper occupied a metre in width, the length of a squadron in column by fours would be approximately 80m., excluding the officer and NCOs at each extremity. Squadrons would follow one another at a distance of around 13 m.
Key: C = captain. L = lieutenant. Sl = sous-lieutenant. Mc = maréchal-des-logis-chef. M = maréchal-des-logis. Bf = brigadier-fourrier. B = brigadier

Above:
The first squadron of a heavy cavalry regiment in column by troop preceded by the regiment's trumpets. In column by troop, a squadron would have a frontage of 12m. exclusive of officers and NCOs extending beyond the limit of the second rank. The troops would maintain a distance of 12m. between each other, measured from nose to nose of the horses, that they might swing into line, facing in either direction, should necessity arise. Squadrons would ride 24m. behind one another
Key: A = adjutant. Am = adjutant-major. C = captain. L = lieutenant. Sl = sous-lieutenant. Mc = maréchal-des-logis-chef. M = maréchal-des-logis. Bf = brigadier-fourrier. B = brigadier

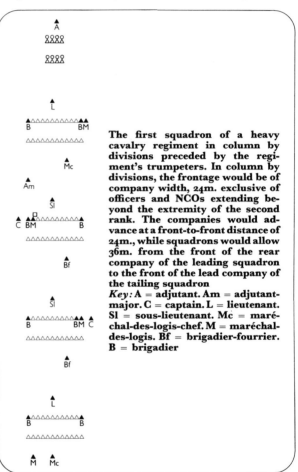

The first squadron of a heavy cavalry regiment in column by divisions preceded by the regiment's trumpeters. In column by divisions, the frontage would be of company width, 24m. exclusive of officers and NCOs extending beyond the extremity of the second rank. The companies would advance at a front-to-front distance of 24m., while squadrons would allow 36m. from the front of the rear company of the leading squadron to the front of the lead company of the tailing squadron
Key: A = adjutant. Am = adjutant-major. C = captain. L = lieutenant. Sl = sous-lieutenant. Mc = maréchal-des-logis-chef. M = maréchal-des-logis. Bf = brigadier-fourrier. B = brigadier

adjutants, a *brigadier-trompette*, a veterinary surgeon and six *maîtres* (i.e. cobblers, tailors, armourers and saddlers).

Each company supposedly boasted a captain, a lieutenant, a second-lieutenant, a *maréchal-des-logis-chef*, four *maréchaux-des-logis*, a *fourrier*, eight *brigadiers*, 82 troopers and a trumpeter. That this was the exception and not the rule is certain. Consider the following returns of the two divisions of heavy cavalry in the reserve cavalry corps of the

12

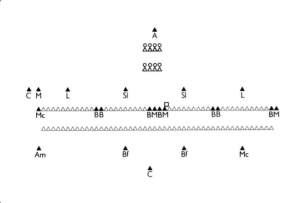

The first squadron of a heavy cavalry regiment in formation of *colonne serré* preceded by the regiment's trumpeters. The *colonne serré* comprised of the squadrons extended to total length, 48m. exclusive of officers and NCOs extending beyond the extremity of the second row, and formed up one behind the other at a distance of 16m. from the front of the lead squadron to the front of the following squadron. The total depth of such a formation would be 54m., excluding officers, NCOs and trumpeters

Key: A = adjutant. Am = adjutant-major. C = captain. L = lieutenant. Sl = sous-lieutenant. Mc = maréchal-des-logis-chef. M = maréchal-des-logis. Bf = brigadier-fourrier. B = brigadier

Grande Armée of 1805:

Nansouty's First Division:	*Officers*	*Men*	*Horses*
2nd Cuirassiers	22	510	469
9th Cuirassiers	22	491	513
3rd Cuirassiers	20	500	475
12th Cuirassiers	24	566	590
D'Hautpoul's Second Division:			
1st Cuirassiers	32	498	500
5th Cuirassiers	32	468	367
10th Cuirassiers	32	551	475
11th Cuirassiers	32	539	443

Official policy and reality should never be confused; and this should be borne in mind when considering the dress and equipment of the heavy cavalry, the subject of the next section.

Dress and Equipment

As we have all too briefly noted, the cuirassiers and carabiniers had something of a common history and this was reflected in their dress. It was only after the Austrian campaign of 1809 that any great fundamental change was wrought and, paradoxically, this in many ways accentuated their resemblance.

Owing to the heavy casualties suffered by the carabiniers in the 1809 campaign, the Emperor determined to protect these élite cavalrymen better and, in an edict dated 24 December 1809, he decreed that they should be armoured to the same advantage as the cuirassiers while still maintaining their separate identity. This last was provided by changing the basic colour of their uniforms from dark blue to white which contrasted bril-

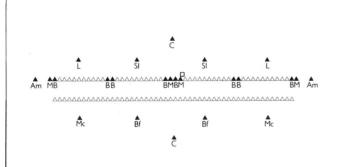

A squadron of heavy cavalry drawn up in battle order. Battle order, like the *colonne serré*, involved the squadron presenting its full double-row length of 48m., excluding officers and NCOs beyond the extremities of the second rank. A regiment so developed could either have all its squadrons in line, running from 1st to 4th from right to left, or one behind the other with 9m. between the back of the leading squadron and the front of the trailing one, reading 1st, 3rd, 4th and 2nd from the front backwards

Key: A = adjutant. Am = adjutant-major. C = captain. L = lieutenant. Sl = sous-lieutenant. Mc = maréchal-des-logis-chef. M = maréchal-des-logis. Bf = brigadier-fourrier. B = brigadier

A trooper of the 5th Cuirassiers in campaign dress, post 1812. Here, a little removed from the pomp of the paradeground, this trooper has made several concessions to the realities of the march: his tall scarlet plume has been encased in an oilskin envelope and left atop the helmet; and the long horsehair mane of the helmet has been plaited along its entire length (designed to control it in high winds or devised to dispel the boredom of irksome guard-duty?) He carries a spare pair of boots strapped to the top of his portemanteau, suggesting that he is either very fortunate or has just left a rather unfortunate comrade lying in the grass; he wears linen overalls over his hide breeches to protect them from the elements; and, finally, has tied his horse's tail into a knot to avoid it becoming tangled in the undergrowth (*Illustration by Job, courtesy of the National Army Museum*)

liantly with the copper-plated armour with which they were issued. In this way the two corps drew together in being the only troops of the Grande Armée who were armoured, while at the same time they diverged in breaking away from their traditionally similar dress.

ARMOUR

Headgear

The cuirassier helmet consisted of an iron cap surrounded by a fur turban and with a copper crest surmounted by a horsehair mane. Helmets differed, however, in points of detail, for each regiment purchased its own: thus the height of the cap, the shape of the peak, the degree of curve and type of ornament of the crest, and the socket of the horsehair aigrette varied considerably. In 1811, an attempt was made to rationalise the situation by producing a universal pattern. Unfortunately, from an urge to simplify grew a desire to economise and the new model was far from popular owing to its shoddy manufacture: the low quality of the iron, copper and horsehair, the absence of a metal edge to the peak which resulted in its losing shape, and the removal of the heavy embossing which had given the crest its solidity, made it a poor substitute for the old patterns. Indeed, the troops were so unhappy with them that many retained their old helmets, patching them up as best they could, trusting to their greater strength. Despite protest, the helmet continued to be issued without modification to the chagrin of all: '. . . [the helmet] thought to be so good in principle is so defective that we ought to hasten to replace almost all those currently in use,' lamented General Saint-Germain in 1814.

Cuirassier officers' helmets were essentially the same although of better quality. There was, however, a more marked and distinctive evolution of shape in their patterns: while at first very similar to the troopers', around 1808 a subtle change became apparent in the angle of inclination of the crest towards the front and the degree to which the increasingly high dome of the cap slouched towards the rear; this was the first step towards the so-called 'Minerva-style' helmet with its neo-Grecian profile. This change was not born out of any desire to emulate classical elegance, but rather from a vain craving to look as smart as the armoured dragoons of the Imperial Guard.

Both officers and men sported a plume inserted in a holder just forward of the left-hand chinstrap rose. These were scarlet, except those worn by senior officers and staff, which were white.

Musicians' helmets were identical with those of the men excepting for a white horsehair mane, an occasional scarlet aigrette and the use of a non-scarlet plume. Here are a few recorded plume colours:

1st Cuirassiers – white tipped scarlet, 1805–10 (after Wurtz).

– white, 1811 (after Col. Jolly).

2nd Cuirassiers	–	white with scarlet tip and base, 1804–7 (after Marckolsheim).
5th Cuirassiers	–	scarlet tipped white, 1808 (after Marckolsheim).
7th Cuirassiers	–	yellow, 1810 (after Martinet).
9th Cuirassiers	–	white, 1804–5 (after Marckolsheim).
	–	black tipped yellow, 1805–6 (after Marckolsheim).
10th Cuirassiers	–	pink, 1811 (after de Ridder).
	–	yellow with white base, 1810
	–	(after Marckolsheim).
	–	scarlet tipped white, 1809 (after Marckolsheim).
13th Cuirassiers	–	scarlet tipped white, 1810 (after Marckolsheim).
14th Cuirassiers	–	scarlet with white base, 1810 (after Suhr).

The carabiniers' helmet was of yellow copper with iron chinstrap scales and roses, and headband. The crest had a scarlet comb in place of a mane. The officers' version was similar but made of red copper and silver, where a trooper's would be yellow copper and iron; further, the crest was much more extensively embossed and boasted a more voluminous scarlet comb.

The trumpeters wore troopers' helmets, complete with scarlet (in accordance with the 1812 Regulations) or light blue combs.

Cuirasses
The 'MkI cuirass' dated back to 1802 and was that year issued to the 1st Cuirassiers. The following year the 2nd, 3rd, 6th, 7th and 8th Cuirassiers were given theirs, while the 4th, 9th, 10th, 11th and 12th Cuirassiers waited until 1804 and the 5th Cuirassiers until 1805 to be armoured. The breastplate of this model was not very rounded and formed a blunt angle at the bottom; a total of 34 copper rivets were driven into the perimeters of both breast and back plate. The cuirass was put on by first hooking the ends of the metal-scaled, cloth-covered, leather shoulder straps to the spherical copper buttons riveted to the breastplate, lifting the ensemble over the head, then fastening the two halves together at the waist by means of a copper-buckled leather belt which was secured to the back plate by twin copper rivets at each end. Though shoulder straps were normally covered in brass scales, those of the 9th Cuirassiers were armoured with twin yellow-copper chains along their length, and those of the 8th Cuirassiers were devoid of any metal, being merely unadorned black leather.

After 1806, a 'MkII cuirass' came to be issued but it differed from the 'MkI' only in that the bottom of the breastplate had been rounded-off. As of 1809 the 'MkIII cuirass' made its appearance, differing only in having a more rounded profile and being slightly shorter.

The officers' pattern of the 'MkI cuirass' was more stylish; a deeply engraved single line, placed 3cm from the edge, described a margin about the perimeter of the breast and back plates into which 32 gilded copper rivets were driven. Though at first resembling those of the men but with gilded scales and silver lace down their lengths, the shoulder straps of the officers later tended to be armoured with two or three lengths of gilded chain. The officers' waistbelt was of red leather, embroidered with silver thread and secured by means of a gilded buckle. Their 'MkII' and 'MkIII' pattern cuirasses were only slightly modified versions of the 'MkI', becoming rounder, longer and heavier, and acquiring 34 gilded rivets.

The carabiniers' iron cuirass was covered overall by a thin sheet of brass which left but a 25mm.-margin of white metal about the edge, into which the yellow copper rivets were inserted. The cuirass was otherwise essentially no different from the cuirassier version save for the natural leather waistbelt and shoulder straps, both of which had copper fittings.

The carabinier officers' model was very distinctive, with a red copper 'skin' in place of brass, a silver sunburst at the centre of the breast, light blue silver-edged cloth on the shoulder straps, and a light blue waistbelt embroidered with silver thread and secured by a silver buckle. Where the troopers' visible lining was edged in white lace, subalterns adopted twin rows of silver lace while superior officers enjoyed the privilege of a silver laurel leaf repeat-pattern embroidered directly on to the dark blue cloth.

TUNICS

The Cuirassiers

The 1803 habit-surtout: The inconvenient, long-tailed habit worn by the *cavalerie* was, by order of the *Ier Vendémiaire An XII*, to be replaced by a single-breasted, shorter-skirted *habit-surtout* provided from the funds of each individual regiment. The facing colours and their disposition were to remain the same as under the 1791 regulations, that is:

TABLE OF FACING COLOURS, 1791-1810

Facing colour				Position
Scarlet	Jonquil			
1	4	7	10	Collar, cuffs, cuff-flaps and turnbacks
2	5	8	11	Cuffs and turnbacks
3	6	9	12	Collar, cuff-flaps and turnbacks
H	V	H	V	
(Direction of pockets)				

Where the facings remained dark blue, they would be piped in the regimental colour and *vice versa* where the facings were of the regimental colour. The simulated tail pockets were contrived with piping of the distinctive colour and three pewter buttons stamped with the regimental number.

A letter dated 20 September 1803 from the War Ministry to the administrative board of the 9th Cuirassiers informs us that the *habit-surtout* was to have had shoulder-straps of dark blue, piped in the regimental colour, and to have been devoid of emblem on the turnbacks. We can be sure, however, that by this date all regiments had adopted all the symbols of élite status: plumes and epaulettes of ·scarlet, and dark blue grenade devices on the turnbacks.

Dismounted cuirassiers in Hamburg, 1813. These dismounted cuirassiers wear the updated *habit-veste* specified by the 1812 Regulations, with its waist-fastening, lapelled breast and short skirt. On the right is a trumpeter dressed in the Imperial Livery of 1811 with the unusual, for this date, headdress of a colpack. The figure on the far left is wearing black gaiters, a more usual form of legwear for foot duty than the heavy riding boots of his comrades (**Illustration by Job, courtesy of the National Army Museum**)

The 1806 habit-veste: Though the 1803 *habit-surtout* was worn throughout the Bavarian campaign, it would seem that the Prussian and Polish campaigns of 1806 and 1807 saw the use of an identical tunic embellished with lapels of the regimental colour. There would seem to be no logical or practical reason for the readoption of squared lapels and we must assume the motivation to have been to render the *habit-surtout* more French in appearance or simply more colourful when worn without the cuirass.

The 1809 habit-surtout: In 1809, a new *habit-surtout* was devised which differed considerably from the 1803 pattern: the tunic had ten pewter buttons in a single row down the breast and mid thigh-length tails without pockets or turnbacks. This garment immediately presented problems for, without pockets, the 1st and 4th, 2nd and 5th, 3rd and 6th, 7th and 10th, 8th and 11th, and 9th and 12th regiments were seemingly indistinguishable. As a consequence, late in 1810, a new system of facing colours was devised on the following lines:

TABLE OF FACING COLOURS, 1810-1812

Facing colour				Position
Scarlet	Aurore	Jonquil	Pink	
1	4	7	10	Collar and cuffs
2	5	8	11	Cuffs only
3	6	9	12	Collar only

Until late 1810, therefore, we can only assume that the regiments took on the above colours unofficially, sewed on directional pocket piping, attached a colour patch to the collar of the tunics or, simply, were unrecognisable except by the stamped number on their buttons.

At this stage, two new regiments were created, the 13th and 14th Cuirassiers, and they were assigned the facing colour of *lie de vin*. The 13th regiment displayed the colour on collar and cuffs while the 14th carried it only on the cuffs.

The 1812 habit-veste: As early as 1810, much criticism had been levelled at the 1809 *habit-surtout* on account of the length of the tails which, though shorter than those of the old *cavalerie* habits, were still so long as to be rucked up by the cuirass and come between trooper and saddle. A new pattern of *habit-veste* was therefore designed, single-breasted with nine pewter buttons and very short-skirted, with turnbacks and vertical simulated pockets. The regimental colour was used on the collars and turnbacks of all regiments, leaving the problem of identification to the cuffs and cuff-flaps as shown in the table below:

TABLE OF FACING COLOURS, 1812–1815

	Facing colour			Position
Scarlet	Aurore	Jonquil	Pink	
1	4	7	10	Cuffs and cuff-flaps
2	5	8	11	Cuffs only
3	6	9	12	Cuff-flaps only

This garment marked the last change in the development of a suitable tunic for troops wearing a cuirass and it was worn throughout the rest of the reported period.

A brief note on the dress of officers would not be out of place. Although they wore tunics basically identical with those of the troopers, with the exception of silver buttons, grenade patches and epaulette loops, there was a considerable latitude in dress which bears examination. In day-to-day wear the officers favoured the old *cavalerie* habit, with its long skirt and coloured lapels; having retained this garment, they took to wearing it again in service dress in 1806, when the troopers acquired their short-skirted lapelled *habit-vestes*. With the introduction of the 1809 *habit-surtout*, the *cavalerie* habit resumed its place in purely everyday wear alongside a *surtout* tunic identical with the *habit-surtout* but without piping down the breast. The 1812 Regulations prescribed a dark blue undress *surtout* with scarlet turnbacks and piping, edging collar, cuffs and breast; but they also specified that a long-tailed habit was to be worn in society and this garment was undoubtedly a modernised *cavalerie* habit, identical but for the fact that it was cut slimmer and fastened to the waist.

The Carabiniers

The 1791 habit-veste: Prior to 1810, the carabiniers wore a modernised *cavalerie habit-veste* of dark blue with scarlet lapels, cuffs and turnbacks

Trumpeter of carabiniers, 1790–1807. The rather baggy cut of the tunic, the primitive aspect of the bearskin and the powdered and queued hair of this individual suggest that he dates from the Directory, Consulate or early Empire. As the years rolled by, so the increasingly slim cut of civilian dress began to make itself felt in military tailoring and uniforms towards 1807 are distinctly 'sharper' than those of the first years of the *Grande Armée*. Modernisation is equally apparent in the headdress if the reader compares this figure with that wearing almost identical uniform in the colour plates: the bearskin became squarer and more highly polished and finished in later years. Queued hair was worn by the carabiniers as late as 1809 (*Illustration by Job, courtesy of the National Army Museum*)

piped in dark blue, and dark blue collar piped in scarlet. The two regiments were distinguished solely by the cuff-flaps which were scarlet piped in dark blue for the 1st regiment, and dark blue piped in scarlet for the 2nd. Interestingly, Martinet depicts troops of the first regiment wearing tunics with scarlet collars: could this have been an attempt to identify each regiment more readily? If so, it was unofficial and certainly of very short duration. The *habit-veste* had scarlet epaulettes, edged in white lace, pewter buttons and, prior to 1809, dark blue grenade devices on the turnbacks; as of 1809, these last were white.

The 1805 surtout: A single-breasted *surtout* tunic was more frequently worn on service than the habit. Save for the scarlet turnbacks, the garment was entirely dark blue with scarlet piping about the collar, cuffs and down the breast. Between six and eight pewter buttons ran down the front, while two were worn in the small of the back, one was sewn on each shoulder and a pair were worn on each cuff.

The 1810 habit-veste: The white, single-breasted *habit-veste* issued at the time the carabiniers were armoured was of the same pattern as that worn by the cuirassiers after 1812. The collar, cuffs and turnbacks were light blue, piped in white, and light blue piping ornamented the breast and contoured the false pockets of the skirt. Again, the regiments were identified by the cuff-flaps: those of the 1st regiment were white piped in light blue and those of the 2nd were the reverse; this situation was altered only slightly in 1812, when the 1st regiment was given scarlet cuffs in place of light blue.

Officers wore basically the same pattern of *habit-veste* as the men, both before and after 1810,

but made of finer cloth and with silver buttons, epaulette loops and grenade devices. After 1810, they were issued with a new long-tailed *surtout* of light blue with white piping down the breast and about the collar and cuffs; the turnbacks were white with silver grenades. The 1812 Regulations specified the turnbacks to be henceforth light blue but it is extremely unlikely that this was ever brought about. For ball dress, a long-tailed white *surtout* with facings and ornaments identical to the *habit-veste* was worn.

LEGWEAR

The Cuirassiers
The sheep or deer-hide breeches of the cuirassiers were reserved for parade dress and, on the march and when campaigning, they would be replaced by overalls. No official mention of these exists prior to 1812. They were manufactured of linen or hide varying in colour from light grey through grey-brown, sometimes with and sometimes without cloth-covered or bone buttons down the outer seams, for lack of official prescription. For town or society dress, linen breeches and stockings or gaiters were worn; these would be white in summer and dark blue, with dark blue or black woollen stockings, in winter. The 1812 Regulations made no adjustment to town dress but did describe an official pattern of overalls: grey linen with cloth-covered buttons down the length of the outer seams.

Officers' breeches were of deer or chamois-hide, but these too would be replaced on active service with dark blue linen ones. Officers' society dress would include white linen breeches and white cotton stockings in summer, and dark blue linen or cashmere breeches with dark blue or black woollen stockings in winter.

The Carabiniers
Before 1810, the carabiniers wore sheep's-hide breeches under overalls of dark blue linen or unbleached cloth; this last variety would have twelve bone buttons down the outer seam of each leg. After 1810, linen overalls of grey-brown with buttons down the leg were used, conforming to the pattern later set out in the 1812 Regulations. White

A trumpeter of carabiniers, 1812. There were eight such trumpeters per regiment, one for every company. Between 1810 and 1812 the trumpeters wore a sky blue tunic with white lace, but from 1812 they adopted the Imperial Livery along with the rest of the musicians of the line; in their case with sky blue collar and turnbacks, and cuffs of scarlet, for the 1st regiment, and sky blue for the 2nd. The trumpet banner illustrated here is of the 1812 pattern, but it is highly unlikely that these expensive items were ever manufactured (*Illustration by Job, courtesy of the National Army Museum*)

linen breeches, replaced prior to 1810 with dark blue pairs in winter, were worn in town dress with white cotton stockings in summer and dark blue or black stockings in winter.

The officers wore deer-hide breeches beneath dark blue or unbleached cloth overalls in the same manner as the men. Similarly, in society dress, white linen or cashmere breeches and white cotton stockings were carried in summer and, before 1810, dark blue or black breeches and black stockings in winter.

COATS AND CAPES

The Cuirassiers
The cuirassiers at first received a three quarter-length, sleeveless cape with a short shoulder cape attached, made of white mixed with a dash of blue cloth. The insides of the front opening and the back vent of this rather shapeless cloak were edged with serge of the regimental colour. The 1812 Regulations ordered the manufacture of a slimmer, sleeved version of the cape, giving it the smarter appearance of a greatcoat. In 1813 a small modification was made in the removal of the coloured serge from the interior edges of the front and back openings.

The officers' patterns of the troopers' capes were identical save that they were in finer cloth and dark blue in colour. Officers also wore a dark blue overcoat which reached to approximately mid calf; this garment was double-breasted, seven silver buttons to the row, and had a large fold-down collar.

The Carabiniers
The carabiniers' capes were the same as those of the cuirassiers except for the serge lining: at first scarlet, it then became sky blue in 1810, only to be dropped altogether the following year; with the advent of the sleeved cape, the sky blue lining was

21

Officer of the 6th Cuirassiers in full dress, 1807. This dashing fellow is either a rich staff officer or a superior officer of some means, since only they wore white rather than scarlet plumes, and such a saddle was certainly not regulation issue. The leopard-skin shabraque, covering a natural leather French or English saddle, has a scarlet fringe and silver lace edging. It is a little unlikely that even the most flamboyant dandy – and the cuirassiers boasted not a few – would go into battle so dressed and accoutred, and we might more readily expect to meet this character at a full-dress parade (*Illustration by Benigni after Vernet, courtesy of the De Gerlache de Gomery Collection*)

A trooper of the 13th Cuirassiers, 1811–13. The 13th Cuirassiers were formed in 1808 from the *1er Régiment Provisoire de Grosse Cavalerie* and saw lengthy service in the Peninsula. It was there that this fellow acquired his brown trousers, manufactured, like so many overalls and jackets in this theatre of war, of confiscated monks' habit fabric. Of further interest is his black gourde, strung on a light blue cord; his striped swordknot, contrived from a fragment of rag; and the net of fodder attached to his saddle, a vital reserve in so inhospitable a land (*Illustration by Benigni, courtesy of the De Gerlache de Gomery Collection*)

resurrected, but removed again in 1813.

Prior to 1810, officers wore capes and overcoats of precisely the same colour and pattern as those of cuirassier officers, with the addition of a strip of silver lace to the short shoulder cape of the three quarter-length cape. After 1810 a sky blue sleeved cape, again with silver lace about the shoulder cape, was adopted, essentially no different from the model worn by the men. A sky blue overcoat was also sported, of identical cut to that worn previously.

WEAPONS

Sabres

From 1803 through 1805 the cuirassiers were issued with the flat and straight-edged 'An IX' pattern sabre with a plain iron scabbard. At this period the regulation swordbelt was of the old *cavalerie* design, as worn by carabiniers prior to 1810, which held the sabre at an angle at waist height; this was a rather impractical arrangement for armoured troops since the cuirass impeded the drawing of the sword and emitted an unmilitary 'clang' at the least movement of the wearer. The situation was resolved by the adoption of the 'An XI' pattern waistbelt which suspended the sabre from a pair of slings, the hilt at wrist level. This improvement was soon followed by the distribution of the 'An XI' pattern sabre with its 97cm. twin-guttered blade and more robust iron scabbard. The standing height of this sword, sheathed, was 120cm.

Cuirassier officers were armed with a '*sabre de bataille*' with either a straight or lightly curved blued steel blade engraved along a third of its length. Both types of sabre fitted into the same variety of scabbard and these were either of black leather with gilded copper fittings or of browned sheet iron reinforced with gilded copper. The sabre was at first carried in a three-section swordbelt much like the troopers' 'An XI' model, but as the years wore on a slimmer single-section belt tended to be favoured; both varieties were secured with a gilded copper buckle bearing a grenade emblem. For town and society dress, officers carried a short épée in a waistbelt.

Before 1810, the carabiniers were issued either the 'An IV' or 'An IX' pattern sabre. The 'An IV' model stood 115cm. tall when sheathed and had a copper guard with a grenade device stamped upon it; the blade was straight and flat and the scabbard was of black leather with brass fittings. The 'An XI' pattern differed only in that the guard had an additional branch and the scabbard fittings were of red copper. These were sheathed at first in the

1801 pattern single-section swordbelt which had the frog suspended at an angle by two straps sewn directly to the belt. This was replaced by the three-section 'An XI' pattern which hung the frog from the two copper rings which linked the belt together. In both cases, the bayonet frog was sewn directly to the belt at a perpendicular angle and the belt fastened by a brass buckle with grenade device. A peculiarity of carabiniers of this period was their black leather swordknot with scarlet tassel: although all mounted troops were strictly required to have swordknots through which to slip their hands before drawing their sabres, carabiniers were the only ones accorded the privilege of black leather straps in place of cloth.

Upon becoming armoured in 1810, the cara-

23

Troopers of the 13th Cuirassiers, 1812. These battle-weary veterans are dressed for the long haul back to France from the Peninsula. In their bundle and portemanteau are either the tattered remains of their habits or a few souvenirs of the hospitality of the pillaged churches and monasteries they leave behind. They are wearing the equivalent of stable dress, comprising a dark blue shell jacket and fatigue cap. The trousers and sandals were no doubt acquired while on campaign, for lack of supplies of regulation issue (*Illustration by Benigni, courtesy of the De Gerlache de Gomery Collection*)

A chef d'escadron of the 5th Cuirassiers in service dress, 1812. This officer wears regulation dress for the march: a helmet without plume and dark blue breeches in place of those of deer- or chamois-hide. His saddle is also of regulation pattern, though a half-shabraque of black sheepskin with 'wolves' teeth' edging of the regimental colour was more frequently employed than the cloth holster covers seen here. Note that the tail of his horse has been clubbed (*Illustration by Benigni, after Adam, courtesy of the De Gerlache de Gomery Collection*)

biniers were obliged to acquire sabres with a curved blade '*à la Montmorency*'. While awaiting these however, they retained their old straight sabres but housed them in the iron 'An XI' dragoon pattern scabbards. It would seem that the carabiniers were rather attached to their old sabres with the prestigious grenade symbol upon the guard and, having received the Montmorency blades, they had the hilts soldered to the new sabre rather than lose them. The dragoon pattern scabbards were now discarded and replaced by either a curved iron or a black leather version, with copper fittings. The distinctive black leather swordknots also had to go and these were exchanged for white buff models with scarlet tassels.

Carabinier officers also carried a sabre with a grenade device on the guard; the hilt would be

brass, red copper or gilded copper and the blade straight or lightly curved. It appears that after 1810 officers still carried a straight-bladed sabre if they so chose. The scabbards would be of black leather with gilded copper fittings, and the swordknots were gold. Like cuirassier officers, officers of carabiniers at first wore a three-section swordbelt but later opted for the single-section variety.

FIREARMS

Despite the official directive to arm the cuirassiers with muskets looted from the Vienna arsenal in 1805, they were only equipped with pistols until 1812. The pistols issued were of the 'An IX' and 'An XIII' patterns of which the 'An XIII' model had the following characteristics: *total length*, 35·2cm.; *length of barrel*, 20·7cm.; *weight*,

24

1·269kg.; *calibre*, 17·1mm. Most contemporary illustrations therefore show cuirassiers without cartridge-pouches, and indeed inspection reports for 1805 and 1807 list the following regiments as having none: the 3rd, 4th, 7th and 8th regiments in 1805, and the 4th, 6th, 7th and 8th regiments in 1807; just what the 6th Cuirassiers did with theirs during 1806 I leave to the reader's imagination. For those troops who were equipped with a cartridge-pouch, it would conform to the 1801 pattern and be of black leather with a buff button-holed strap by which to secure it from flapping about by fastening it to a tunic button.

Further to the Imperial Decree of 24 December 1811, the cuirassiers were equipped with the 'An XI' pattern cavalry musketoon complete with crossbelt and bayonet, in early 1812. The musketoon was approximately 115cm. long with an 85cm. barrel and the bayonet, sheathed in a scabbard inserted in a frog sewn to the middle section of the swordbelt, had a blade 46cm. long. The musketoon was slung on a crossbelt, thrown over the left shoulder and fixed to the cartridge-pouch belt by means of a spherical button. It incorporated a steel clip, through which a ring on the left side of the musketoon was passed, and a buff strap, which was wound once about the lock and then buckled. The cartridge-pouch was of the 1812 pattern, 23cm. by 14cm., and of black leather with the securing strap now moved to the top and with the addition of two buff straps beneath it for carrying the rolled-up fatigue-cap. Neither officers or musicians were armed with muskets, consequently neither carried cartridge-pouches.

The carabiniers not only carried the 'An IX' and 'An XIII' pistols but were additionally armed with muskets. Contemporary illustrations depict carabiniers with long and short muskets and, for lack of any official information, we can only hazard that these are probably the 'An IX' and 'An XIII' dragoon patterns, standing at 1·463m. and 1·415m. respectively, and the 'An IX' artillery pattern at 1·305m. The bayonet was hung in a frog stitched to the swordbelt but, unlike the sabre, at the perpendicular. The cartridge-pouch in use prior to 1812 was of black leather, approximately 24cm. by 16cm., with a brass grenade badge and a strap by which to secure it to a button on the tunic.

Early in 1812, the carabiniers were also issued the 'An IX' cavalry musketoon and bayonet complete with cartridge-pouch and musket crossbelt. Note however that these were no idle replacement for their old muskets and equipment, since these had been surrendered with their old uniforms in 1810. Like the cuirassiers, the officers and musicians of carabiniers were not equipped with muskets or musketoons and therefore did not wear a cartridge-pouch.

SADDLES AND HARNESS

The Consulate decree of 26 October 1801 (*4 Brumaire An X*) fixed the basic colour of *cavalerie* regiments' saddles as dark blue edged in white lace, and so it was to remain for cuirassiers throughout the Empire period, and for carabiniers' until 1810.

Dismounted cuirassiers, 1812. The Russian campaign was a nightmare for the cavalry; at Borodino, no less than 6,000 horses were killed, but many thousands more died through malnutrition and lack of veterinary care. After only 20km. of the retreat from Moscow, the cuirassiers were obliged to walk their starving mounts and, within five days of the first snow, the staggering loss of 30,000 horses had been reached. Following this campaign, the 1st Cuirassiers, to a man, found themselves serving on foot (*Illustration by Benigni, after Guesse, courtesy of the De Gerlache de Gomery Collection*)

25

The sabre in action. This ink drawing demonstrates firstly the manner in which the sabre was wielded in the charge, and, secondly, what became of the well-dressed lines once the charge got under way. The heavy cavalry sabre was a thrust weapon and, though sharp of edge, was never used to cut; the troopers therefore leaned well forward in the saddle, right arm thrust out as far as it would stretch with sabre continuing the plunge towards the enemy; in this illustration, the troopers' elbows are bent to a rather marked degree whereas, in fact, they would be trained never to bend the sword arm lest the enemy's edged weapon slide off their sabre guard and amputate the elbow. During a charge, enemy fire would be constantly eroding the most forward line of troopers, who, falling, would bring down men of the second row attempting to plug the gaps; the net result of this and the gradual loss of the riders' control over their mounts as they careered forward, would be a disintegration of the strict spacing and uniformly even lines so vital to the success of a charge; in effect, the only manner of maintaining a wall of horseflesh and steel was to cram too many men and horses into far too little space (*Illustration by Job, courtesy of the National Army Museum*)

The cuirassiers' natural leather saddle had dark blue saddle-cloth, portemanteau and holster covers (though these last were rare), all laced in white. In place of the holster covers, the troopers usually employed a half-shabraque of white sheepskin edged with 'wolves' teeth' of the regimental colour. Some idea of the rarity of the use of holster covers or *chaperons* is demonstrated by the fact that, in 1807, the 12th Cuirassiers had only 85 pairs and the 7th Cuirassiers only 65 pairs; in 1808, the 3rd, 4th, 7th, 8th, 9th and 10th regiments are known to have acquired some, but whether they had sufficient numbers and whether these were

ever repaired or replaced as they wore out, is unknown. The saddle-cloth originally had the number of the regiment in white in the angle, but as time passed this was replaced by a white grenade in most cases (that of the 7th Cuirassiers was yellow while those of the 6th and 10th regiments had the regimental number cut out of the body of the grenade). The portemanteau usually bore the regimental number in white at each end, though those of the 6th and 11th Cuirassiers had (*c.* 1810), grenades.

Attached to the top of the portemanteau was the folded cape displaying the serge of the regimental colour uppermost. In an effort to decrease the height of the pack, three black leather straps were added to the saddle, one to the pommel and two about the holsters, by which the rolled cape might be secured; this served a second purpose in that it made the cape more readily accessible in bad weather. The portemanteau was held in place by three white Hungarian leather straps.

Officers of cuirassiers had a dark blue French saddle, edged in blue lace; a cloth girth; red leather stirrup-leathers; bronzed stirrups; black leather martingale, false-martingale, crupper, bridle and reins, and stable-halter; silver parade-halter and reins; silvered buckles; and silver-

26

tipped holsters. The saddle-cloth was dark blue, piped in the regimental colour and edged in silver lace of the following widths: second-lieutenants, 35mm.; lieutenants, 40mm.; captains, 45mm.; and majors, *chefs d'escadrons* and colonels, 50mm. Those of colonels and majors also had a 15mm.-wide secondary strip of lace on the inside of the wider strip. The holster covers were identical but officers tended to prefer a black sheepskin half-shabraque, edged with 'wolves' teeth' of the regimental colour.

For everyday use, the officers employed a dark

Maréchal-des-logis-chef, standard-bearer, of the 7th Cuirassiers, 1813–14. This senior NCO carries the regimental standard of 1812 pattern. Prior to this date, each squadron of cavalry had its own guidon marked with both its and the regiment's number; but this practice led to a good many losses and it was therefore determined that each regiment should have but one eagle. The bearer's rank is indicated by his mixed silver and scarlet epaulettes and the twin strips of silver lace on scarlet ground sewn on each forearm (here invisible). Only four cuirassier standards were lost in the course of the wars: that of the 1st Cuirassiers at Taroutina, 18 October 1812; that of the 14th Cuirassiers at the Berezina, 26–29 November 1812; that of the 4th Cuirassiers on the retreat towards Vilna in 1812; and, finally, that of the 9th Cuirassiers on that same road (*Illustration by Benigni, courtesy of the De Gerlache de Gomery Collection*)

blue saddle-cloth, with dark blue holster covers, edged in blue goat's hair and without ornament in the angle. Officers were also frequently mounted on English saddles equipped in the same manner as the French; neither variety having a cantle, they were both devoid of portemanteaux.

Before 1810, the carabiniers sat a natural leather French saddle with Hungarian leather stirrup-leathers and portemanteau straps, blackened iron stirrups, black leather martingale, false-martingale, crupper and boot for the musket, and a grey cloth girth. The saddle-cloth was dark blue with white grenade and lace, of which there were two strips after 1808. Again, the holster covers were rarely used as against a white sheepskin half-shabraque with scarlet 'teeth'. Bridle, reins and parade-halter were of black leather, while the stable and feed-halters were of Hungarian leather. The portemanteau was dark blue with white lace and grenade patch.

After 1810, the carabiniers were assigned a French saddle with natural leather holsters, girth, seat and stirrup-leathers; blackened iron stirrups; and black leather crupper, martingale, musket boot and portemanteau straps. The saddle-cloth and portemanteau were light blue with white grenades and strips of lace. The sheepskin shabraque was given teeth of light blue. The 1812 Regulations made only minor modifications in removing the inner, narrow strip of white lace from the saddle-cloth and adding three black leather straps to the pommel and holsters to which the cape could be tied.

Prior to 1810, officers of carabiniers had a dark blue saddle with silver-tipped holsters and bronzed stirrups. The saddle-cloth was piped in red and had silver lace, regulated in width in the same manner as for cuirassier officers, and silver grenade. The holsters had covers either identical with the saddle-cloth or fashioned of bearskin. After 1810, the saddle had Hungarian leather stirrup-leathers and bronzed stirrups. The saddle-cloth became light blue, as did the holster covers. The martingale, false-martingale, headstall and stable-halter were of black leather, while the parade-halter was in silver. The 1812 Regulations amended the above to a light blue saddle, edged in blue silk lace, and added a second strip of 15mm.-wide lace to the saddle-cloths and holster covers, in gold for majors

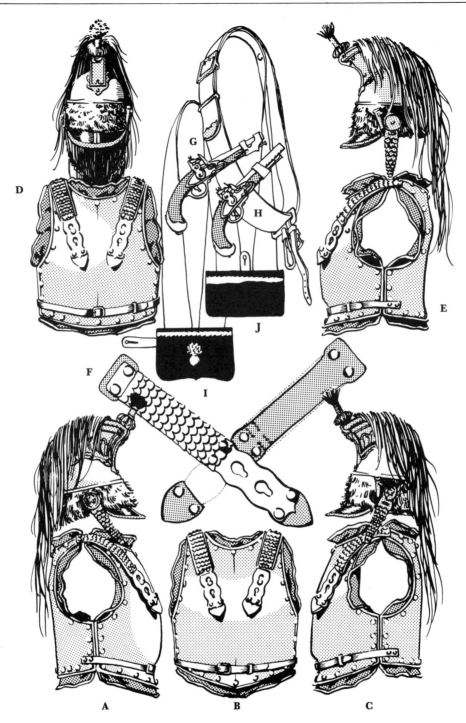

Equipment of cuirassier troopers: *A & B:* The MkI pattern cuirass issued from 1802–5. *C:* The MkII pattern, with which troopers were equipped from 1806–8. *D & E:* The MkIII pattern, in service from 1809–15. *F:* The copper-scaled shoulder strap in detail, from above and below. *G:* The 'AnIX' pattern cavalry pistol with which both cuirassiers and carabiniers were armed. *H:* The 'AnXIII' model cavalry pistol, used in conjunction with the above model again by both carabiniers and cuirassiers. *I:* The 'AnXI' pattern cartridge-pouch and crossbelt complete with horizontal securing strap, by which it would be fastened to a tunic button, and brass grenade badge. *J:* The 1812 Regulations model of cartridge-pouch, crossbelt and musketoon belt and sling. Note the difference in size and shape of this pattern of cartridge-pouch to that carried prior to 1812

and silver for colonels.

For everyday and campaign, officers employed saddle-cloth and portemanteau of light blue with a 40mm.-wide strip of light blue goat's hair about the edge, both devoid of silver grenade devices.

★　　★　　★

It should be borne in mind, however, that neither carabiniers or cuirassiers were as well turned out and homogenous in dress as regulations imply and artists and writers express. In reality, most regiments were in a continual state of chronic disrepair, of which the following report, from Marshal Davout to the Emperor, concerning General Doumerc's inspection of the 4th Cuirassiers on 25 January 1812 at Hamburg, speaks most eloquently:

'Dress . . . I perceived to be very bad, not through lack of good will between officers and men, but by reason of the terrible state which all members of this regiment are in.

'I noticed that the entire regiment had *surtouts* instead of *habit-vestes;* being unaquainted with any order on this subject, I am at a loss as to which is considered uniform dress. What is certain, however, is that two-thirds of cuirassier regiments are dressed in short tunics and that the other third is in *surtouts;* it would be desirable to come to some decision on this matter so that we might, by that means, get a little uniformity into this item of dress. . . . The surtouts are quite good but their cut is terrible.

'Waistcoats – There are only 247 in use, 530 are required. . . .

'Stable jackets – This regiment uses worn-out habits as stable jackets. In truth, the *chef d'escadron* has received news that we were going to perpetually despatch without delay this item of dress for the years 1810 and 1811. . . .

'Hide breeches – All the cuirassiers have a pair but at least half of them are mediocre. . . .

'Boots – The boots are by-and-large in fairly good condition.

'Helmets – This regiment's helmets are in the most pitiful state imaginable; all the turbans need to be replaced; they are atrocious, and much the same can be said for the peaks; a total overhaul of this item is needed, only the caps and the crests are capable of being used. . . .

'Cuirasses – These are generally good, but they need considerable repairs such as having them rebored, which entails great expenditure since the rivets will all have to be removed and then replaced. Further, the waistbelts are too short or worn in some cases and these need replacing; the shoulder-straps are also in need of a lot of attention.

'Sabres – Two-thirds of the sabre scabbards are of iron and two-thirds are of leather, it so pleased some to have their iron scabbards covered in leather. . . .

'Swordbelts – These are in general bad, there are about a quarter which cannot be worn over the shoulder.

'Cartridge-pouches – One thing which surprised me was to see this regiment without cartridge-pouches and without anything in which they might store their cartridges. The *chef d'escadron,* acting commander of the regiment, informed me that these have been lacking since the formation of this corps of cuirassiers. The crossbelts having, he added, been useful for repairing the swordbelts. As to the cartridge-pouch proper, no one knows what these might have been used for.

'Saddles – these are in fairly good condition. . . .

'Shabraques – these are all terribly bad. . . .

The 1804-pattern squadron eagle of the 2nd squadron of the 3rd Cuirassiers. The staff is dark blue with a brass eagle on top. Total height of the staff was 2·1m., while the eagle and socket measured 31cm. and the flag itself, 60cm. by 60cm. This standard would also have been carried by a *maréchal-des-logis-chef*

'Portemanteaux – There are 777 currently in use of which 400 deserve to be taken out of service. . . .

'Capes – Of 776, there are 300 good ones, 376 mediocre ones and 100 which should be destroyed.

'. . . I cannot close this report without informing Your Excellency that fifty men despatched from the depot some ten days since, arrived without other clothing than an old short tunic for use as stable jacket, a pair of hide breeches, gaiters and a pair of shoes. It is inconceivable that anyone should have allowed men to set off so badly protected against the weather of this season.'

The generalisations relating to dress and equipment quoted above therefore provide only a thumb-nail sketch of the *principles* behind the dress of the troops. Inspection reports and contemporary illustrations throw up fascinating anomalies which, along with specific details of the dress of the different ranks, are too lengthy to be quoted here; the reader is referred instead to the illustrations which, we trust, speak for themselves.

There remains only to return to the regiments in order to examine their individual histories and war records. Their number and busy service records regretably oblige us to restrict ourselves to the barest mention of their campaigns and battles, leaving the stirring tales of individual feats of arms for another occasion.

War Service of Individual Regiments

1st Cuirassiers

Regimental history:
1635: Admitted into French service from the Army of the Duke of Saxe-Weimar.
1657: Named Colonel-Général.
1791: Became 1er Régiment de Cavalerie.
1801: Renamed 1er Régiment de Cavalerie-Cuirassiers.
1803: Renamed 1er Régiment de Cuirassiers.
1814: Renamed the Cuirassiers du Roi.
1815: Renumbered as the 1er Régiment de Cuirassiers, only to be disbanded on 16 July at Loches.

War record:
1805: With the Grande Armée at Wertingen, Ulm, Hollabrünn, Raussnitz and Austerlitz.
1806: With the Grande Armée at Jena and Lübeck.
1807: With the Grande Armée at Hoff and Eylau.
1809: Part of the Armée d'Allemagne at Eckmuehl, Ratisbonne, Essling, Wagram, Hollabrünn and Znaïm.
1812: With the Grande Armée at La Moskowa and Winkovo.
1813: With the Grande Armée at the Katzbach, Leipzig, Hanau and the defence of Hamburg.
1814: Fought at La Chaussée, Vauchamps, Bar-sur-Aube, Sézanne and Valcourt.
1815: Fought at Ligny, Genappes and Waterloo.

2nd Cuirassiers

Regimental history:
1635: Created from Cardinal Richelieu's ordnance company and named Cardinal-Duc.
1643: Renamed Royal-Cavalerie.
1791: Became 2eme Régiment de Cavalerie.
1802: Renamed 2eme Régiment de Cavalerie-Cuirassiers.
1803: Renamed 2eme Régiment de Cuirassiers.
1814: Became the Régiment de Cuirassiers de la Reine.
1815: Renamed 2eme Régiment de Cuirassiers and disbanded later the same year.

War record:
1805–7: With the Grande Armée at Wertingen, Austerlitz, Glottau and Friedland.
1809: Part of the Armée d'Allemagne at Eckmuehl, Ratisbonne, Essling and Wagram.
1812: With the Grande Armée at Ostrowno, La Moskowa and Stakov.
1813: With the Grande Armée at Reichenbach, Dresden and Wachau.
1814: Fought at La Rothière, Rosnay, Champaubert, Vauchamps, Athies, La Fère-Champenoise and Paris.
1815: Fought at Quatre-Bras and Waterloo.

3rd Cuirassiers

Regimental history:
1645: Created from three new and three old cavalry companies.
1654: Named Commissaire-Général.
1791: Became 3eme Régiment de Cavalerie.
1802: Renamed 3eme Régiment de Cavalerie-Cuirassiers.

Equipment of cuirassier officers: *A:* Early model of officers' helmet, 1804–6. *B:* Helmet of senior officer of the 11th Cuirassiers, 1807–9. Of interest is the large number of differences between this and the previous model despite their chronological proximity. *C:* Helmet of a superior officer of the 13th Cuirassiers 1809–12. At this point we can perceive the near-fruition of the neo-classical style of officers' helmet: the cap is swept perceptibly higher and farther back, while the crest has become taller and farther forward than on either of the preceding models. *D:* The culmination of the Grecian-influenced helmet style, the 'Minerve', 1810–15. *E:* The officers' version of the MkI troopers' cuirass, 1804–9. *F:* Another version of the above cuirass, curiously missing the engraved line about the bottom. *G:* Cuirass of a superior officer with laurel leaf motif ornament, 1804–9. *H:* The MkIII officers' cuirass, 1809–15. *I:* The straight bladed officers' sabre worn throughout the wars. *J:* The same sabre hilt mounted on a curved 'Montmorency' blade

1803: Renamed 3eme Régiment de Cuirassiers.
1814: Became the Régiment de Cuirassiers du Dauphin.
1815: Renamed 3eme Régiment de Cuirassiers and disbanded on 25 November.

War record:
1805: With the Grande Armée at Austerlitz.
1806–7: With the Grande Armée at Jena, Heilsberg and Friedland.
1809: With the Armée d'Allemagne at Eckmuehl, Essling and Wagram.
1812: Fought at La Moskowa.
1813: Fought at Dresden and Leipzig.
1814: Fought at Champaubert.
1815: Fought at Fleurus and Waterloo.

4th Cuirassiers

Regimental history:
1643: Formed of twelve volunteer companies of cavalry and named La Reine-Mère.
1666: Renamed La Reine.
1791: Became 4eme Régiment de Cavalerie.
1802: Renamed 4eme Régiment de Cavalerie-Cuirassiers.
1803: Renamed 4eme Régiment de Cuirassiers.
1814: Became the Régiment de Cuirassiers d'Angoulême.
1815: Renamed 4eme Régiment de Cuirassiers and disbanded at Fontenay on 21 December.

War record:
1805: With the Armée d'Italie at Caldiero and the crossing of the Tagliamento.
1807: With the Grande Armée at Marienwerder and Heilsberg.
1809: Part of the Armée d'Allemagne at Essling and Wagram.
1812: With the Grande Armée at Polotsk, Smoliany, Borisov and the crossing of the Berezina.
1813: With the Grande Armée at Bautzen, Dresden, Wachau, Leipzig and the siege of Hamburg.
1814: Fought at Brienne, La Rothière, Champaubert, Vauchamps, Laon, La Fère-Champenoise and Paris.
1815: Fought at Ligny and Waterloo.

5th Cuirassiers

Regimental history:
1653: Creation of the regiment.
1725: Named Stanislas-Roi.

1737: Renamed Royal-Pologne.
1791: Became 5eme Régiment de Cavalerie.
1803: Renamed 5eme Régiment de Cuirassiers.
1814: Became the Régiment de Cuirassiers de Berry.
1815: Renamed 5eme Régiment de Cuirassiers and later disbanded.

War record:
1805: With the Grande Armée at Hollabrünn, Brunn and Austerlitz.
1806–7: With the Grande Armée at Jena, Lübeck, Hoff, Eylau, Wittenberg and Königsberg.
1808: The 1st squadron was on service in Spain.
1809: Part of the Armée d'Allemagne at Rohr, Eckmuehl, Ratisbonne, Essling and Wagram.
1812: With the Grande Armée at La Moskowa and Winkovo.
1813: With the Grande Armée at Leipzig and Hanau.
1814: Fought at Montmirail, Bar-sur-Aube, Troyes, Nogent and Saint-Dizier.
1815: Fought at Ligny and Waterloo.

6th Cuirassiers

Regimental history:
1635: Formed and named the Dragons du Cardinal.
1638: Renamed the Fusiliers à Cheval de son Eminence.
1643: Renamed the Fusiliers à Cheval du Roi.
1646: Renamed the Régiment du Roi.
1791: Became 6eme Régiment de Cavalerie.
1803: Renamed 6eme Régiment de Cuirassiers.
1815: Became the Régiment du Colonel-Général on 16 January, renamed 6eme Régiment de Cuirassiers on 20 March and disbanded later the same year.

War record:
1805: With the Armée d'Italie at Verona and Caldiero.
1807: With the Grande Armée at Heilsberg.
1809: With the Armée d'Allemagne at Eckmuehl, Essling and Wagram.
1812: With the Grande Armée at La Moskowa, Winkovo and Malojaroslavetz.
1813: With the Grande Armée at Dresden, Wachau and Leipzig.
1814: Fought at Champaubert.
1815: Fought at Waterloo.

7th Cuirassiers

Regimental history:
1659: Formed and named the Royal-Étranger.

1 Trooper of the 9th Cuirassiers in full
  dress, early 1804
2 Trumpeter of the 9th Cuirassiers in full
  dress, 1804-1805
3 Officer of the 3rd Cuirassiers, 1804–1805

A

1 Trumpeter of the 7th Cuirassiers, 1805–1809
2 Marechal-des-logis of the 2nd Cuirassiers, 1806
3 Superior officer of the 7th Cuirassiers, 1807

B

ANGUS McBRIDE

1 Trooper of the 5th Cuirassiers, 1807–1809
2 Officer of the 10th Cuirassiers, 1807–1809
3 Officer of the 4th Cuirassiers, 1804–1809

1 Trooper of the 12th Cuirassiers, 1813
2 Trumpet-Major of the 6th Cuirassiers, 1813
3 Trumpeter of the 1st Cuirassiers
  (ex-Cuirassiers du Roi), beginning of
  the Hundred Days, 1815

D

ANGUS McBRIDE

1 Carabinier in full dress, 1808–1810
2 Officer of the 2nd Carabiniers, 1809
3 Trumpeter of the 2nd Carabiniers in full dress, 1807–1810

1 Marechal-des-logis of the 1st Carabiniers,
  1808–1810
2 Trumpeter of the 1st Carabiniers, early 1810
3 Officer of carabiniers in full dress, 1807–1810

1 Marechal-des-logis of the 2nd Carabiniers,
  1812–1814
2 Officer of carabiniers, 1811–1814
3 Trumpeter of the 2nd Carabiniers, 1812

1 Trooper of the 1st Carabiniers, 1812
2 Officer of carabiniers in overcoat
3 Trumpeter of the 1st Carabiniers, 1813–1815

ANGUS McBRIDE

1791: Became 7eme Régiment de Cavalerie.
1803: Renamed 7eme Régiment de Cuirassiers.
1815: Disbanded.

War record:
1805: With the Armée d'Italie at the crossing of the Tagliamento.
1806: Part of d'Espagne's division of the Grande Armée.
1807: With the Grande Armée at Heilsberg.
1809: With the Armée d'Allemagne at Essling and Wagram.
1812: With the Grande Armée, Doumerc's division of Oudinot's corps, at Polotsk and the crossing of the Berezina.
1813: Fought at Reichenbach, Dresden and Leipzig.
1814: Fought at Champaubert and Vauchamps.
1815: Fought at Ligny and Waterloo.

8th Cuirassiers

Regimental history:
1665: Created from the Mestre-de-Camp company of the Régiment de Villequier in 1638, the regiment was now named the Cuirassiers du Roi.
1791: Became 8eme Régiment de Cavalerie.
1803: Renamed 8eme Régiment de Cuirassiers.
1815: Disbanded at Saumur on 5 December.

War record:
1805: With the Armée d'Italie at Caldiero and the crossing of the Tagliamento.
1807: With the Grande Armée at Heilsberg.
1809: With the Armée d'Allemagne at Essling and Wagram.
1812: With the Grande Armée at La Moskowa.
1813: With the Grande Armée at Leipzig and Hanau.
1814: Fought at Vauchamps.
1815: Fought at Quatre-Bras and Waterloo.

9th Cuirassiers

Regimental history:
1684: Formed from the volunteer company of the old Régiment de Villars (created in 1666).
1686: Named the Régiment d'Anjou.
1753: Renamed the Régiment d'Aquitaine.
1761: Renamed the Régiment d'Artois.
1791: Became 9eme Régiment de Cavalerie.
1803: Renamed 9eme Régiment de Cuirassiers.
1815: Disbanded at Poitiers on 16 July.

War record:
1805: With the Grande Armée at Austerlitz.
1806-8: With the Grande Armée at Jena and Friedland.
1809: With the Armée d'Allemagne at Eckmuehl, Ratisbonne and Essling.
1812: With the Grande Armée at Ostrovno, La Moskowa and Winkovo.
1813: With the Grande Armée at Lützen, Bautzen, Dresden and Leipzig.
1814: Fought at Saint-Dizier, Brienne, La Rothière, Champaubert, Vauchamps, Craonne and La Fère-Champenoise.
1815: Fought at Ligny and Waterloo.

10th Cuirassiers

Regimental history:
1643: Created from the remainders of the Croatian regiments in French service which had been disbanded at the time of Louis XIII's death and named the Royal-Cravates.
1791: Became 10eme Régiment de Cavalerie.
1803: Renamed 10eme Régiment de Cuirassiers.
1815: Disbanded at Angers and Fontenay-le-Comte.

War record:
1805: With the Grande Armée at Austerlitz.
1806–7: With the Grande Armée at Jena, Eylau and Hoff.
1809: With the Armée d'Allemagne at Eckmuehl and Wagram.
1812: Fought at La Moskowa.
1813–14: With the Grande Armée at Leipzig and Hamburg.
1815: Fought at Waterloo.

11th Cuirassiers

Regimental history:
1665: Created from the Mestre-de-Camp company of the Régiment de Montclar.
1668: Named the Royal-Roussillon.
1791: Became 11eme Régiment de Cavalerie.
1803: Renamed 11eme Régiment de Cuirassiers.
1815: Disbanded.

War record:
1805: With the Grande Armée at Austerlitz.
1806–7: With the Grande Armée at Eylau and Friedland.
1809: With the Armée d'Allemagne at Ratisbonne and Essling.

Brigadier of the 4th and trooper of the 11th Cuirassiers 1810. These unarmoured cuirassiers are wearing the 1809 *habit-surtout* which was to present serious problems of identification. The reason for this lay in the fact that several regiments would share the same facing colour but were hitherto identifiable by the positioning of the colour and the direction of the tail pockets. The 1809 *habit-surtout*, being devoid of both cuff-slashes and tail pockets, therefore required a re-organisation of the facing colours which, though known to historians, are of uncertain specific origin

1812: With the Grande Armée at La Moskowa, Winkovo and Tholoschinn.
1813: With the Grande Armée at Dresden and Leipzig.
1814: Fought at Laon.
1815: With the Armée du Nord at Ligny and Waterloo.

12th Cuirassiers

Regimental history:
1668: Created from various companies of reformed regiments and one company of the Chevau-Légérs du Dauphin. Named Le Dauphin.
1791: Became 12eme Régiment de Cavalerie.
1803: Renamed 12eme Régiment de Cuirassiers.
1815: Disbanded at Niort.

War record:
1805: With the Grande Armée at Wertingen, Elchingen, Hollabrünn and Austerlitz.
1806-7: With the Grande Armée at Jena, Heilsberg and Friedland.
1809: With the Armée d'Allemagne at Eckmuehl, Ratisbonne, Essling and Wagram.
1812: With Valence's Division of the 1st Reserve Corps of the Grande Armée at Mohilev, La Moskowa and Winkovo.
1813: With Bordesoulle's Division of the Grande Armée at Bautzen, Reichenbach, Jauer, Dresden, Wachau and Leipzig.
1814: Fought at La Rothière, Rosnay, Champaubert, Vauchamps, Valjouan, Athies, Reims, La Fère-Champenoise and Paris.
1815: With Milhaud's 4th Corps of the Reserve Cavalry at Ligny and Waterloo.

13th Cuirassiers

Regimental history:
1807: Formed, in December, at Libourne from detachments of existing regiments of cuirassiers and carabiniers★. Named the 1er Régiment Provisoire de Grosse Cavalerie.
1808: Became 13eme Régiment de Cavalerie having been amalgamated with most of the 2eme Régiment Provisoire de Grosse Cavalerie★★.
1814: Disbanded in July at Colmar.

War record:
1808–13: Fought in Spain at Tudela, the siege of Saragossa, the battle of Saragossa, Villareal, the siege of Lerida, Margalef-Lerida, the siege of Tarragona, Sagonte, Castalla and the Ordal pass.
1814: Fought at Lyon.

★The regiment was composed of men from the 1st and 2nd Carabiniers and the 1st, 2nd and 3rd Cuirassiers.
★★This second provisional regiment consisted of men from the 5th, 9th, 10th, 11th and 12th Cuirassiers who had survived the Baylen catastrophe.

A third provisional regiment was created in 1808 of detachments of the 4th, 6th, 7th and 9th Cuirassiers but was disbanded in 1809.

14th Cuirassiers

1810: The Dutch 2nd Regiment of Cuirassiers were incorporated in the French army and named 14eme Régiment de Cuirassiers.

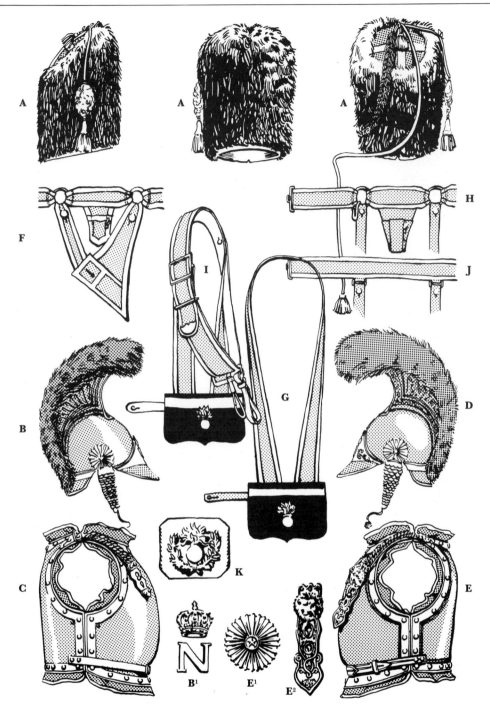

Equipment of carabinier officers and troopers: *A:* The carabiniers' bearskin as described by the 'AnX' Regulations, originally 318mm. but rarely below 350mm. towards 1810. *B & B¹:* Helmet and front decoration as worn by troopers from late 1810. *C:* The troopers'-pattern cuirass. *D:* The officers' model of post 1810 helmet. Note that the crest is rather larger than that of the troopers' version. *E, E¹ and E²:* The officers' model cuirass, sunburst device from its breast and shoulder-strap detail. *F:* The 'AnIX'-pattern troopers' swordbelt. *G:* The troopers' cartridge-pouch prior to 1810. *H:* Troopers' swordbelt and bayonet frog, post 1809. *I:* Troopers' cartridge-pouch and musketoon crossbelt as carried post 1811. *J:* Officers'-pattern swordbelt, worn before and after 1810. *K:* Officers' swordbelt buckle

43

Unarmoured cuirassiers of (from left to right) the 3rd, 9th and 5th Cuirassiers, 1805. On the left, a cuirassier in town dress: the *surtout* has replaced the *habit-veste* and a chapeau, the helmet; the breeches would be exchanged for a pair in dark blue, worn with dark blue or black stockings, in winter. The centre figure demonstrates the continued use of the old *cavalerie* habits, with their long ungainly skirt, until the arrival of the short-skirted 1803 *habit-surtout*. On the right, a cuirassier in off-duty wear, including the *surtout*, stable trousers, buckled shoes and fatigue-cap; note his queued hair (*Illustration by Benigni, courtesy of the De Gerlache de Gomery Collection*)

1809: With the Armée d'Allemagne at Eckmuehl, Ratisbonne, Essling and Wagram.
1812: With the Grande Armée at La Moskowa, Winkovo and Viasma.
1813: With the Grande Armée at Dresden, Leipzig and Hanau.
1814: Fought at Montmirail, La Guillotière, Troyes, Craonne, Laon and Reims.
1815: Fought at Quatre-Bras and Waterloo.

A *chef d'escadron* in ball dress, 1806–10. For full ball dress, the helmet would be replaced by a felt bicorn and the short-skirted habit by a long-tailed, lapelled tunic reminiscent of, and frequently actually, the old *cavalerie* habit. Notice the use of an épée in lieu of the *sabre de bataille* (*Illustration by Benigni, courtesy of the De Gerlache de Gomery Collection*)

The Carabinier Regiments

Regimental histories:

1693: Formed of an amalgamation of all seven existing carabinier companies and named the Royal-Carabiniers.
1758: Renamed the Carabiniers de M. le Comte de Provence.
1774: Renamed the Carabiniers de Monsieur.
1791: Become 1er and 2eme Régiments de Carabiniers.
1815: Disbanded and then reformed as the Carabiniers de Monsieur.

War record:

1805: With the Grande Armée at Nuremberg and Austerlitz.
1806–7: With the Grande Armée at Prentzlov, Lübeck, Ostrolenka, Guttstadt and Friedland.

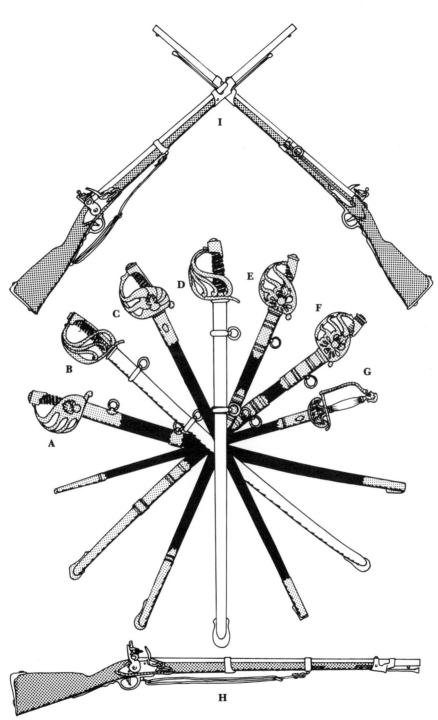

Weapons of cuirassiers and carabiniers: *A:* **Carabinier troopers' 'AnIX'-pattern sabre.**
B: **Iron scabbarded carabinier troopers' sabre post 1810.** *C:* **Carabinier troopers'
'AnIV'-pattern sabre.** *D:* **Cuirassier troopers' 'AnXI'-pattern sabre.** *E:* **The 'AnIV'-
pattern carabinier officers'-pattern sabre.** *F:* **Carabinier officers' sabre with the 'AnIV'
hilt remounted on a Montmorency blade.** *G:* **Typical épée carried by officers of carabiniers and cuirassiers in walking-out dress.** *H:* **The short, 1·20m., artillery model
'AnIX'-pattern musket carried by troopers of carabiniers prior to 1810.** *I:* **The 'AnIX'-
pattern cavalry musketoon used by troopers of cuirassiers and carabiniers after 1811**

Cuirassiers in capes, 1813. Before 1813, a long, sack-like cloak was issued for use in bad weather, as worn by the left-hand figure. The 1812 Regulations altered this garment to include sleeves, thereby making it more of a greatcoat than a cape, as worn by the figure on the right. Unlike that carried by dragoons, the post-1812 cuirassier cape was seemingly without buttons on the body or shoulder cape with which it might be secured closed (*Illustration by Benigni, courtesy of the De Gerlache de Gomery Collection*)

The Plates

A1   Trooper of the 9th Cuirassiers in full dress, early 1804.

This cuirassier wears the first full dress uniform of the new cuirassier heavy cavalry arm. Beneath the armour, a single-breasted tunic with short skirt now replaced the old *cavalerie habit-veste*. Although a letter from the Ministry of War, dated 20 December 1803, to this regiment specified that the new tunic was to have shoulder-straps and no ornaments on the turnbacks, it is likely that the 9th regiment opted for the scarlet epaulettes and dark blue grenade insignia by 1805. Similarly, the official black plume topped with the regimental colour would be swapped for a red one. Of interest is this fellow's powdered and queued hair,

a hallmark of all those regiments which formed a part of Nansouty's Division as late as 1809.

A2   Trumpeter of the 9th Cuirassiers in full dress, 1804–1805.

This reconstruction of the trumpeter's uniform from official regulations would at first appear to contradict other references, notably the Marckolsheim MS, which indicate that a pink tunic was carried at this period. In fact, the oft-quoted pink garment's origin lies in the Consulate's Decree of 31 December 1802 which, in eliminating those regiments of *cavalerie* numbered 19 through 22, incorporated fresh troops into regiments 9 through 18 to bring them up to strength; the 9th regiment thereby received a company of both the 19th and 22nd regiments whose troops retained the uniforms of their old regiments of which the distinctive colour was pink. From 1805, the colours of the tunic was reversed, that is dark blue facings on a yellow tunic, until the advent of the dark green Imperial Livery issued from 1811.

A3   Officer of the 3rd Cuirassiers, 1804–1805

Officers' no. 2 riding dress consisted of the *surtout*, a single-breasted long skirted jacket, worn with a white waistcoat of linen or cashmere and riding breeches. These last were generally white for summer wear and dark blue for winter. Equipment was as that for full dress with the exception of the slimmer swordknot and the option of wearing helmet or bicorn. Note also that short gloves replace the cuffed variety. In these early years, the *cavalerie* tunic was frequently worn for walking-out dress, but, in this particular instance, the Colonel of the regiment specified that the *surtout* tunic as shown here was to be worn for both riding and society dress.

B1   Trumpeter of the 7th Cuirassiers, 1805–1809

This full dress figure illustrates one of several variations in uniform at this period. While an inspection report dated October 1805 maintains that there were as many cuirasses as men, including trumpeters, in this regiment, only one source, the Marckolsheim MS, shows a trumpeter so armoured. Martinet and Valmont insist on the other hand that no cuirass was worn. In their depictions of the tunic, they complicate the issue still further, for,

Officer of the 3rd Cuirassiers 1805 and officer of the 10th Cuirassiers, 1806. They wear the double-breasted overcoat popular with officers both before and after 1812. This garment, in conjunction with a fatigue-cap, was used for both morning and undress wear on foot (*Illustration by Benigni, courtesy of the De Gerlache de Gomery Collection*)

Officers of the 4th and 5th Cuirassiers, 1813. These officers wear the undress *surtout*, as prescribed by the 1812 Regulations, for full dress on foot. Note the use of short gloves in place of the cuffed variety employed for riding (*Illustration by Goichon, courtesy of the De Gerlache de Gomery Collection*)

while the basic yellow colouring of the garment is not disputed, they disagree as to whether the lace was white or light blue and the turnbacks yellow, white or dark blue. Perhaps it might be best to let the Marckolsheim MS have the last word on the matter; it insists on white lace, and, for good measure, throws in that the epaulettes were scarlet.

B2 *Maréchal-des-logis of the 2nd Cuirassiers, 1806*
As of 1806, all new cuirassier tunics were made with the addition of old-style lapels of the regimental colour, but this NCO, his grade indicated by the single silver stripe on scarlet ground on each sleeve, still wears the *habit-surtout* with the popular though unofficial fringed epaulettes. Further, despite the fact that the 2nd Cuirassiers were supposedly issued cuirasses of French manufacture in 1803, this individual has the dubious distinction of having received a captured Prussian cuirass

which, though handsome, consisted only of a breastplate. The single silver chevron on his left sleeve denotes his completion of between eight and ten years of military service, while the absence of the tall scarlet plume on his helmet and his wearing button-up overalls indicate that he is on active service. Although here invisible, his hair would be queued.

B3 *Superior officer of the 7th Cuirassiers, 1807*
This rather elegant figure in campaign dress has heavy silver bullion epaulettes and a richly ornamented cuirass as symbols of rank. Officers' cuirasses were normally only decorated with a deeply engraved single line about 3cm. from the edge and 32 gilded copper rivets on both breast and backplate. The shoulder-straps were made of leather covered in red cloth and had a strip of silver lace down the sides; their ornament at first consisted of

gilded copper scales, but these were eventually replaced by two or three lengths of gilded chain. The waistbelt of the cuirass was of red leather with silver lace and embroidery and a golden buckle. Of interest is the fact that this officer still wears what appears to be, judging from the length of the skirt, the old *cavalerie* tunic which would have had yellow lapels. It would seem that officers had retained these old tunics for off-duty wear and, when the troopers again adopted a lapelled *habit-veste* in 1806, had reintroduced them for service dress.

C1   Trooper of the 5th Cuirassiers, 1807–1809
In anticipation of the rigours of the road ahead, this trooper has thoughtfully encased the plume of his helmet in oilskin and adopted hard-wearing button-up overalls in place of his hide breeches. An inspection report dated 27 July 1805 reveals that this regiment alone persisted in having their *habit-surtouts* manufactured with lapels identical to those reintroduced for all regiments in 1806. A

tenuous connection might perhaps be made between this and the fact that this regiment was the last to receive its cuirasses at the late date of early 1805. The iron cuirass had 34 copper rivets on both breast and backplate, excluding the two which held each end of the waistbelt to the backplate; the shoulder-straps were of leather, sheathed in scarlet fabric and embellished with copper scales.

C2   Officer of the 10th Cuirassiers, 1807–1809
This officer wears the standard uniform of the commissioned ranks for the greater part of the Empire period, with the exception of his interesting cuirass. The officers' pattern breastplate, summarized briefly under B3 above, had an engraved line around the perimeter forming a margin into which rivets were struck, whereas in this instance the line is clearly absent. Further, the waistbelt is of plain black leather instead of the red leather decorated with silver embroidery which one might expect. We can only conclude either that the source – Weiland – is inaccurate; or that for lack

Officer and men of the 3rd Cuirassiers, 1804–5. These figures are dressed for riding instruction, that is in stable dress with the use of riding boots in place of clogs, and overalls in lieu of trousers. Note that the troopers' harness consists only of stable-halter and stirrup-less saddle (*Illustration by Benigni, courtesy of the De Gerlache de Gomery Collection*)

Officer in undress uniform of the 3rd Cuirassiers, 1804–5. In undress, the officers' saddlery consisted solely of a natural leather English or French saddle with dark blue saddle-cloth edged with a 40mm.-wide band of blue goat's hair (*Illustration by Benigni, courtesy of the De Gerlache de Gomery Collection*)

of officers' armour this gentleman has pressed that of a trooper into service – surely the more likely explanation. If this were the case it is entirely feasible that the 'salvageable' parts of the old armour would be added to the new, thus the officers' pattern shoulder-straps and officers' pattern lining with silver lace.

C3   Officer of the 4th Cuirassiers, 1804–1809

This unarmoured officer permits us to examine the *habit-veste* in more detail. This single-breasted tunic, fastened by between seven and ten silver buttons, was the forerunner of the *habit-veste* of 1812 in that it fitted to the waist and had a short skirt. The grenade devices on the turnbacks were embroidered with silver thread and the epaulette loops were also silver. Around 1808, the cut was modified somewhat: the waist tended to be cut higher and the turnbacks were frequently extended all the way round the front of the tunic, ending about an inch wide and joining up with the narrow strip of piping down the front.

In 1809, a new *habit-surtout* was issued to the cuirassiers but, although officers were required to equip themselves with one for wearing with the cuirass, it seems likely that they retained the more practical 1803 tunic for riding, leaving the *habit-surtout* for walking-out and no. 2 dress. With the introduction of the 1812 Regulations, the situation was clarified: officers were attired in a waist-length, lapelled and short-skirted tunic differing from that of the rank and file only in its ornamentation and quality.

D1   Trooper of the 12th Cuirassiers, 1813

After 1812, several changes were made in the equipment of cuirassiers. Having been issued a musketoon and bayonet in early 1812, they now also carried a second crossbelt over the left shoulder, from which the firearm was suspended, and a bayonet frog stitched to the centre section of the swordbelt. The cuirass was of the third pattern, issued from 1809, rounder and shorter, but otherwise identical with previous models.

The helmet, distributed as of 1811, was also of a new pattern, much simplified and most unpopular: the band of copper normally edging the peak was absent, causing the peak to warp out of shape once wet; the crest was devoid of the extrava-

Trumpeter of the 13th Cuirassiers, 1808–9. This trumpeter wears the familiar reversed-colour habit of musicians, in this case *lie de vin* with dark blue facings. The epaulettes are white, as is his helmet's mane (*Illustration by Benigni, courtesy of the De Gerlache De Gomery Collection*)

gant decorations which had hitherto given it great strength, and the absence of a plate of copper on the very top did little to increase its solidity; for lack of this last, water tended to seep into the crest and rot the roots of the horsehair mane which was itself of dubious quality; finally, the copper and iron utilised in the construction of the helmet were of inferior grades. Such was the dislike of this headgear that many cuirassiers departed for Russia in their old helmets, repaired and patched up as well as possible, rather than trust to the new pattern. In 1814, General Saint-Germain opined that the helmet was so defective that nearly all those at that time in service were in dire need of replacement.

D2   Trumpet-Major of the 6th Cuirassiers, 1813

This uniform is a reconstruction of the full dress

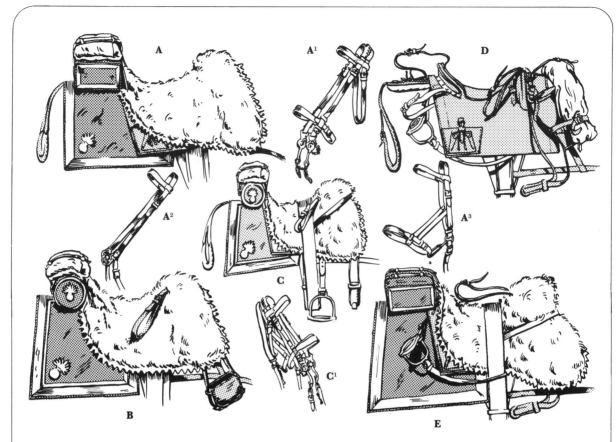

Saddles and harness of troopers of cuirassiers and carabiniers: *A:* Cuirassiers' saddle before 1812. The regimental number would be entered on the ends of the portemanteau in white. A^1; A^2 & A^3: Headstall of the bridle, stable halter and parade halter of cuirassiers. *B:* Carabiniers' saddle before 1810. *C:* The carabiniers' saddle after 1810. C^1: Carabiniers bridle, post 1810. *D:* Basic saddle, after Bardin, 1812. *E:* The same saddle but dressed for cuirassiers after the 1812 Regulations

specifications of the 1812 Regulations. The Imperial Livery was an attempt to rationalise the dress of musicians throughout the Grande Armée; hitherto left to the discretion of the colonels, their costume had become so excessive and multi-coloured as the regiments vied with one another for the most striking heads of column, that the situation bordered on chaos.

The new green tunic had facings and piping of the regimental colour, green grenade devices on the turnbacks, white metal buttons and a specially developed lace. This lace, which edged the collar, cuffs, turnbacks, false back pockets, five of the nine buttons down the front and the two in the small of the back, came in two varieties: the one for vertical and the other for horizonal positioning. The design consisted of alternating Imperial 'Ns' and eagles, in green on a yellow base, separated by black thread. Needless to say, official prescriptions were ignored and specimens survive with Imperial 'Ns' in yellow on a green ground, dark green but crowned 'Ns' on a yellow ground, and Imperial eagles facing right or left, with due human disregard for orderly precedent. A 5mm. width of white lace was supposed to be sewn between the double strips of Imperial lace on the button-holes of the cuff-flaps and on the two hooks and eyes of the collar, ending in tiny white tassels as a finishing touch to all this embellishment; there is, however, no trace of this elusive white lace in evidence.

50

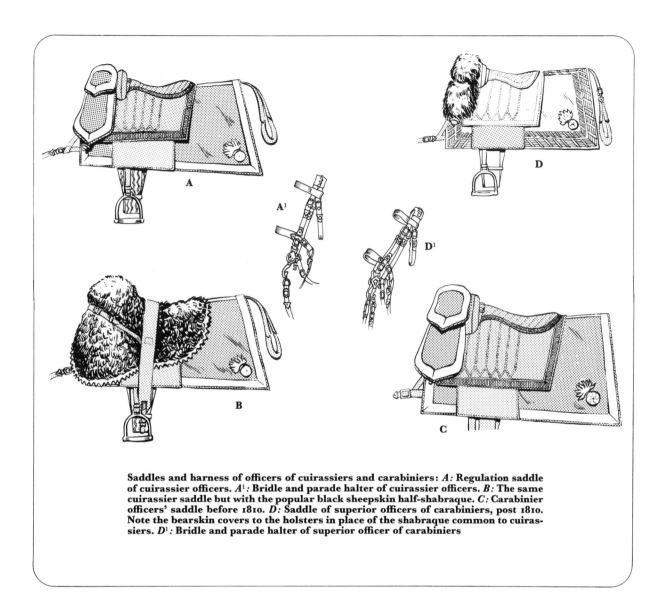

Saddles and harness of officers of cuirassiers and carabiniers: *A:* Regulation saddle of cuirassier officers. *A¹:* Bridle and parade halter of cuirassier officers. *B:* The same cuirassier saddle but with the popular black sheepskin half-shabraque. *C:* Carabinier officers' saddle before 1810. *D:* Saddle of superior officers of carabiniers, post 1810. Note the bearskin covers to the holsters in place of the shabraque common to cuirassiers. *D¹:* Bridle and parade halter of superior officer of carabiniers

The rank of this *brigadier* (corporal) is indicated by the twin strips of white lace on scarlet ground visible on each forearm. Note also the replacement of the plume by an *aurore* lentil-shaped pompon which denotes that he is a member of the first company of the third squadron of this regiment.

D3 Trumpeter of the 1st Cuirassiers (ex-Cuirassiers du Roi), beginning of the Hundred Days, 1815

With the abdication of the Emperor in 1814, all traces of his reign were suppressed and, where possible, eradicated. The Imperial Livery was replaced with this dark blue tunic, bearing the white and crimson lace of the Bourbon dynasty and buttons stamped with the royal fleur-de-lys. Upon the return of Napoleon for the brief Belgian campaign, not all souvenirs of France's fleeing monarchy could be erased in time for the coming campaign: and this fellow, assuming his survival, would have found himself mercifully well dressed for the reappearance of the deposed Louis XVIII later in the year.

E1 Carabinier in full dress, 1808–1810

The two carabinier regiments were indistinguishable except for the colour of the cuff-flaps: red with blue piping for the 1st Carabiniers and the reverse for the 2nd. The tunic was essentially identical to that prescribed in 1791 bar the grenade devices on the turnbacks which, now white, were

Wagram, however, the troops were equipped with either copper or white metal scaled chinstraps.

E2 Officer of the 2nd Carabiniers, 1809

This officer in marching order, his plume packed along with his fine white breeches in his porte-manteau, has had armoured jugulars fitted to his headdress. His uniform differs from that of the rank and file only in its finer quality cloth and its silver ornaments in place of white. Officers carried only a sabre as armament (excluding the twin pistols holstered at the front of the saddle), of identical shape to that of the men but sheathed in a more extravagantly fitted scabbard.

E3 Trumpeter of the 2nd Carabiniers in full dress, 1807–1810

Trumpeters wore a tunic of reversed colours with the addition of white lace to the facings. Prior to 1808 the grenade devices were red, but these subsequently became white in line with those of the troopers. A trumpeter of the 1st regiment would be dressed in exactly the same manner but with dark blue epaulettes, edged in white lace, in place of white. Like the officers, trumpeters were armed only with a sabre, but in their case it would be identical with that of the troopers. Before 1807, the plume would have been entirely red. The horse furniture would be the same in all respects as that of the troopers save for a black sheepskin shabraque in place of white. Trumpeters rode greys.

F1 Maréchal-des-logis of the 1st Carabiniers, 1808–1810

This sous-officier, his rank indicated by the single silver stripe on each forearm and the mixed silver and red threads of his epaulettes and swordknot, wears the popular surtout tunic in lieu of the more formal, and consequently less frequently used, habit. A report to the Emperor dated 5 July 1808 gives us the following insight into the use of the two tunics: '. . . the carabiniers have owned surtouts for the last three years, the uniform habit has been worn but once. . . .'. The garment was fastened by between six and eight pewter buttons. Note that the service chevron on the left upper-arm was silver on a red ground for sous-officiers as against red for other ranks.

Trumpeter of the 4th Cuirassiers, 1805–9. He wears a single-breasted scarlet habit with white lace loops, a common practice. His epaulettes and horsehair mane are white, and his plume and trumpet cords are scarlet. Trumpeters always rode greys and employed a black sheepskin shabraque in place of the troopers' white ones (*Illustration by Benigni, courtesy of the De Gerlache de Gomery Collection*)

dark blue prior to 1808. The distinctive bearskin headdress of these two regiments was, according to regulations dated 21 October 1801, 318mm. tall, but became markedly taller as the years passed, certainly never less than 350mm., such being the vanity of man. This headgear had no jugulars but was maintained in place by a leather strap, which passed under the queue of the hair, and a white cord which descended from the top of the bearskin, passed under the left epaulette and was looped about a tunic button. Interestingly, when, in early 1809, the carabiniers were required to wear their hair short, no steps were taken to issue them chinstraps and many men were consequently wounded or killed owing to being hit on the skull, their bearskins trailing behind them and tangling them up in the cord; by the time of the battle of

52

F2 Trumpeter of the 1st Carabiniers, early 1810
With the approaching change-over to armour, the old-fashioned lapelled habit fell still further into disuse in favour of the *surtout*, itself soon to be replaced with a similar but shorter skirted habit. In this instance, the trumpeter's tunic has been decorated with loops of white lace, terminating in tassels, passing about the ventral buttons and anchored to two extra rows of buttons on each breast. This embellishment lasted throughout 1810, even to its use on a short-skirted red tunic, until the arrival of the light blue habits. At one point during the period of adaptation, this same tunic with the addition of lace to the turnbacks

Trumpeter of the 7th Cuirassiers, 1813. After 1812, musicians of all troops of the line were required to wear the Imperial Livery of dark green, an attempt to rationalise the chaotic situation created by leaving the uniforms of the heads of column to the vagaries of the individual regiments' colonels. Although this trumpeter's livery lace has a 5mm.-strip of tasselled white lace between its loops, as prescribed by the Regulations of May 1810, no trace of this exists on garments or on tailors' returns of 1812 or 1813 and it is likely that, in the same manner as the trumpet banners described in the 1812 Regulations, it was never manufactured or issued (*Illustration by Benigni, courtesy of the De Gerlache de Gomery Collection*)

was employed in conjunction with a cuirass. It seems that the regiments were attempting to use up all their existing stocks of red fabric while acquiring those items of equipment of the new uniform as and when they arrived; the short-skirted version of this tunic, mentioned above, was worn with the new white-crested trumpeters' helmet.

F3 Officer of carabiniers in full dress, 1807–1810
Full dress for officers consisted of habit, waistcoat, deer hide breeches, stiff or soft leather boots complete with bronzed spurs, buff swordbelt with gilded copper buckles, cuffed gauntlets and bearskin embellished with full cords and plume. The sabre could be either straight or lightly curved with red or gilded copper hilt; the leather scabbard had gilded copper fittings. Officers utilised a *surtout* as frequently as the men, of identical pattern but of finer materials and with silver decorations. In walking-out dress either of the tunics could be employed, with linen breeches and white stockings in summer, or dark blue or black breeches and black woollen stockings in winter. The outfit was completed by black shoes with silver buckles and a bicorn chapeau with silver tassels in the angles.

G1 Maréchal-des-logis of the 2nd Carabiniers, 1812–1814
The carabiniers suffered such considerable losses during the 1809 campaign that, on 24 December, the Emperor decreed that they were to be armoured in such a manner as to afford them the same protection as the cuirassiers while at the same time maintaining a distinct visual difference between the two types of élite heavy cavalry. To this end, Napoleon selected a yellow copper helmet and an iron cuirass covered in a thin sheet of brass. Although the Emperor desired the tunic to be madder red, he was overruled by the war office which, probably for reasons of economy, opted for a white tunic with sky blue facings. This *sous-officer* wears such a tunic: the sky blue cuff-flaps piped in white distinguished the second regiment from the first; the silver chevrons and single stripe on sky blue ground, and the mixed silver and scarlet epaulettes denoted his rank. He wears a pair of button-up *surculottes* to protect his breeches. Note the mixed silver and scarlet swordknot on his

Trumpeter of the 9th Cuirassiers, 1814. This illustration permits us to examine the rear of the Imperial Livery. Although decreed 23 May 1810, described in the Journal Militaire of 30 December 1811 and detailed in the 1812 Regulations, the livery can only be sure to have been issued from early 1813 (*Illustration by Rousselot, courtesy of the De Gerlache de Gomery Collection*)

copper-hilted sabre, a further indication of his near-officer status.

G2 Officer of carabiniers, 1811–1814

Officers wore a tunic identical with that of the men but of finer quality and with silver ornaments and buttons. Armour was essentially of the same pattern, but with red copper replacing the yellow copper of the rank and file, and silver replacing the iron. The cuirass was embellished with a silver sun symbol with a gilt star at its centre and had sky blue shoulder-straps edged in silver and ornamented with three silver chains. The dark blue padding of the cuirass was decorated with two strips of silver lace for junior officers and a single strip and laurel leaf border for senior officers. Officers' sabres had hilts of yellow, gilded or red copper, and black leather scabbards with gilded fittings. The swordbelt was ochre edged in silver with a gilded buckle bearing a silver grenade and laurel leaf motif.

G3 Trumpeter of the 2nd Carabiniers, 1812

Trumpeters were dressed in precisely the same manner as the men, bar the usual practice of reversing the colours. This trumpeter, drawn from the Marckolsheim MS, has several unusual features: while trumpeters were supposed to wear a trooper's helmet, it appears that musicians of the 2nd Carabiniers affected a sky blue crest, and those of the 1st Carabiniers a white one. The tunic has been duly reversed, leaving the turnbacks and collar white and prompting a query as to the point of then lacing the collar in white when this would be far from readily visible. Lastly, again on the point of facing colour, another musician of this same regiment is shown as having sky blue cuffs and cuff-flaps, edged with white, contrary to the reversed colour principle and highlighting the white collar/white lace question. As can be seen, trumpeters were equipped with neither cuirass nor cartridge-pouch. The lack of cuirass led to frequent instances of the musicians' tunics being decorated with white lace about the buttons of the breast.

H1 Trooper of the 1st Carabiniers, 1812

The iron cuirass, ornamented with copper rivets, had a skin of brass overall, bar a 25mm. margin which revealed the iron base. The waistbelt was brown leather with a copper buckle, while the shoulder-straps were plain leather (unlike those of the cuirassiers) and covered with two copper chains. The black leather cartridge-pouch was suspended on a white-edged, ochre shoulder-belt worn over the left shoulder over which was hung the musketoon crossbelt which was of the same colouring and construction but marginally wider, ending in a steel clip from which the firearm was hung. The yellow buff waistbelt was composed of three sections linked by copper rings. The middle section had a bayonet frog sewn to it. The slings were of ochre buff with copper buckles and were attached to the two rings of the iron scabbard.

H2 Officer of carabiniers in overcoat

This cape was the standard officers' issue after 1811, although versions without sleeves were not uncommon. The 1812 Regulations specified that the silver lace was to be dropped from the short cape about the shoulders, but it seems unlikely that this order was ever implemented. The troop-

54

ers' version was a three quarter-length coat of white cloth (with just a touch of blue thread) until 1813. As of that date, a new overcoat called the *manteau-capote* came into use; it had sleeves, but, unlike the preceding model, was devoid of the sky blue lining cloth on each side of the interiors of the front and back vents.

*A trooper of the 7th Cuirassiers, 1812. This cuirassier wears, during the Russian campaign, the final uniform of the arm which was to carry them through 1815. We must assume that this individual dates to the very beginning of the campaign since, as we have seen, his horse would be unlikely to look anything like so fit after a few months on the march. The saddle has an unbleached fodder bag tied to it in which feed would be stored. Note the boots wrapped in fur to protect the feet from frostbite (**Illustration by Benigni, courtesy of the De Gerlache de Gomery Collection**)*

H3   Trumpeter of the 1st Carabiniers, 1813–1815
This trumpeter is dressed as prescribed by the 1810

Regulations: a tunic of Imperial Livery pattern, with sky blue facings bar the cuffs of scarlet (to dis-

55

Cuirassiers after the restoration of Louis XVIII. During the First Restoration, the dress of cuirassiers remained precisely that of the 1812 Regulations, save that all Imperial emblems were deleted in favour of the fleur-de-lys. With the return of Louis XVIII after the Hundred Days began a very testy period for the army, with the suppression of all things Imperial – from the changing of the regiments' names to the altering of their uniforms (these were to undergo no less than five major changes in ten years). The resentment caused by the monarchy's denial of recent glories went deep, and grew and festered through the whole of the French people until the Empire was recalled as a 'golden age' with which the current monarchy compared badly (*Illustration by Job, courtesy of the National Army Museum*)

tinguish the regiment from the 2nd Carabiniers who had sky blue cuffs); a trooper's helmet; breeches; boots; and a sabre. Although the Decree establishing the Imperial Livery is dated 23 May 1810, it would appear that no musicians actually acquired the uniform before 1813. As to the dark green trumpet banners described by the 1812 Regulations with their yellow fringes and embroidery, it is certain that they were never manufactured.

On the other hand, the Schmidt Collection contains a drawing of a trumpeter whose instrument is ornamented with a square trumpet banner of sky-blue fabric, trimmed in white fringe and embroidered in white thread with an Imperial eagle motif. Unfortunately, no other contemporary document corroborates this evidence. Finally, all details of the lace of his Imperial Livery is identical to those referred to in the caption to figure D2, the trumpeter of *cuirassiers*.

2

Dragoons
and Lancers

‘ The dragoons are vital to support the light cavalry in advance guard, rear guard, and on the flanks of the army. ’

(Napoleon, undated)

The Men

From the great victories of Marengo and Hohenlinden in 1800 to the terrible defeat of Waterloo in 1815, France was to call up a total of 1,600,000 men of whom a mere 600,000 were to survive. Little, perhaps, in comparison to the giant levies and losses of the wars of this century, but what matter cold statistics to the man who has to do the soldiering? Whether armed with pike, musket or anti-tank gun, the grisly reality remains the same.

In 1803, undeclared war was renewed between the principals of the near-farcical Peace of Amiens, France and Great Britain, and the Frenchman once again found himself liable to be called up. Conscription had existed for some while in post-revolutionary France. Introduced originally by decree of the Convention on 14 February 1793, the law had been both modified and extended by order of the Directory on the 8th Fructidor An VIII. A bachelor aged between twenty and twenty-five, our potential conscript was now obliged to present himself at his local depot for the draw, a 'lucky dip' designed to select which out of every seven prospective candidates would actually join the ranks. Let us suppose that our man was unlucky.

This young Frenchman, along with the other seventh of the conscripts, was now destined to serve under the nation's banner indefinitely: until old age, crippling wounds, death or the cessation of hostilities culled him from the ranks. Prospects were therefore far from bright, since all Europe was ranged and pledged to destroy the young republic of France. But it was this same democracy so feared by France's neighbours that had reinforced her soldiers with the necessary idealism and had maintained her inviolate for the last eleven years. Our conscript was fired with the revolutionary notion that France belonged to her people and was no longer the plaything of a jaded aristocracy, and

it was this that gave him the will to win.

This was no army of embittered conscripts. Born under the Monarchy, raised during the turbulence of successive revolutionary régimes, this generation had a sense of freedom—a possession worth dying for. To them, neighbouring rulers were prepared to go to any lengths to preserve their thrones from the free-thinking philosophies which had so recently stemmed from the Americas; and Great Britain's

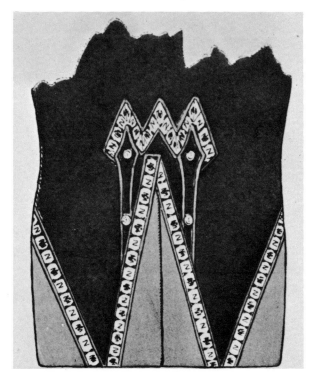

The skirt of the Imperial Livery as worn by the French line lancers, showing the decoration of the small of the back and the turnbacks. Unlike the rear of the dragoon trumpeters' tunic, the lancers' is devoid of false pockets and all the attendant piping and lacing. Instead, it has only slim piping of regimental colour forming points above each of the waist-height buttons, the Imperial lace decorating the rear of the tunic proper, and further lengths of the same lace along the turnbacks. In this case plain, the turnbacks might easily bear yellow or green eagle patches (depending on the colour of the facings) or the flaming grenade device if the owner was trumpeter to an élite company. (National Army Museum)

59

renewed hostility was proof that the misguided peoples of all Europe were being slowly coerced into obliterating the fledgling republic that could provide them their own salvation. What might have been dull resignation to military service was, in fact, more a dogged determination to preserve both the motherland and the freedom which was the birthright of France's oppressed neighbours.

Having been inoculated against smallpox, the conscripts next presented themselves at their barracks for roll call and food hand-out. The following day they would be issued their equipment and, soon after, their uniforms.

The pay book of one Claude Defrère itemizes the issue as follows: one tunic; one fatigue jacket and cap; one chemise; one pair of linen trousers; one white and one black collar; four handkerchiefs; two pairs of cotton and one of woollen stockings; three pairs of shoes; one grey and one white pair of gaiters; one cloth bag and a hide haversack; and finally, two cockades. Equipment would include a cover for the cartridge-pouch, a screwdriver, a needle for piercing cartridges and clearing the touch-hole of the musketoon, and an instrument for extracting musket balls; as well as a helmet, cartridge-pouch, sabre, bayonet and musketoon. All these items were the conscript's personal and absolute responsibility; were any article lost or damaged, he was obliged to repair or replace it out of his pay. The durability of such things as the webbing being no less than twenty years, it was clearly very difficult to serve without having to pay the army for the pleasure, as the following extracts from the army record of Trooper Clavieux of the 28th Dragoons attest:

One of the many slightly different types of copper helmet worn by the rank and file of the chevau-légers lanciers. Basically no more than a dragoon helmet, it does, however, boast a rear peak and large horsehair crest. On this model we note a strap and buckle with which to secure the chinstraps under the jaw, rather than the more common lengths of leather thong. **(National Army Museum)**

01.1.1810:	—Boot repairs	0.90F
19.1.	—One pair of shoes	6.00F
10.2.	—One pair of overalls	6.50F
18.2.	—Leather wax & harness buckles	0.85F
25.2.	—One pair of gaiter straps	0.60F
26.2.	—One harness buckle, a tin of grease and a grease brush	1.29F
07.3.	—One sponge	0.80F
16.3.	—One copper brush & boot repairs	0.75F
24.3.	—One pair of scissors	0.98F
03.4.	—One pair of grey gaiters	2.20F
04.4.	—Boot repairs	0.75F
11.4.	—One pair of shoes	6.00F
27.5.	—One horse brush & a scabbard	6.25F
26.5.	—One headband for helmet	0.35F
	—One tin of grease and a brush	0.79F
	—One plume holder, two scales and a rosace for the chinscales	0.95F
	—One feed bag	2.00F
	—Repairs to bed linen	0.10F
	—Repairs to musketoon	0.37F
	—Soldering of new guard to sabre	1.25F
10.7.	—One chemise	4.00F

14.7.   —Resoling of shoes.....................2.50F
        —Grease, shoe repairs and an
            attachment to the horsecloth 0.70F

Thus, in twenty-six weeks, Trooper Clavieux was down 46.08F in equipment alone; add to this his punishment fines and he was out of pocket a total of some 126 francs as against an earning of approximately 54.60 francs!

The list below, drawn from Trooper Defrère's pay book, indicates the official estimate as to the durability of items of dress and equipment:

Dress:

Habit-veste:	2 yrs	Shakos:	4 yrs
Gilet à manches:	2 yrs	Greatcoat:	3 yrs
(stable jacket)		Fatigue-cap:	2 yrs
Trousers:	1 yr	Bearskin:	6 yrs

Equipment:

Swordbelt:	20 yrs	Musket-sling:	20 yrs
Cartridge-pouch:	20 yrs	Drum and sticks:	20 yrs
Crossbelt:	20 yrs	Horns and trum-	
		pets:	20 yrs

Poor indeed was Clavieux and his like among the conscripts, but theirs was one great redeeming consolation: they were cavalrymen.

The barracks (or stables as they were more aptly called) were cold, damp and drab establishments, as likely as not converted church properties confiscated following the repudiation of direct Papal authority by the Constituent Assembly's Act of 1790. At least a quarter of their total area was confined to the stables proper, where the all-important mounts were housed, whose care and maintenance were entrusted to the dragoons.

An NCO of the 3rd Lancers in action. His medium-green tunic and overalls would have pink facings and lace respectively. The red epaulettes inform us that he is a member of the élite company while the red chevrons on his left upper sleeve denote a period of between sixteen and twenty years service. His helmet appears to have a leopard skin turban, which would suggest he has lost his own and has made do with an officer's retrieved from the field. (National Army Museum)

A trumpeter of a centre company of the 1st Lancers in the uniform decreed by the 1812 Regulations. His tunic is the Imperial Livery adopted by all musicians of line regiments after 1812. The facings are scarlet, as is the piping on the shoulder-straps, and the trumpet cord. There were two such trumpeters in every squadron of lancers, bringing the regimental effective to a total of eight under the command of a trompette-brigadier or trompette-major. (National Army Museum)

The horses were acquired by each regiment independently in one of two fashions: by direct purchase from bloodstock merchants or local farmers, or by requisition against a promise of future settlement. By the latter means, up to 500 head of four years or less were frequently stripped from individual *départements*, ruining many citizens who were left with but a paper pledge that the authorities would one day pay them as much as 400 francs per horse—if and when ... At such cost, albeit often unpaid, these animals were rightly considered more valuable than the men who rode them and therefore, when not being instructed as to how to remain seated upon them, the recruits were obliged to lavish considerable care on the grooming of the beasts and the mucking-out of their stalls. However, no amount of care makes up for substandard horseflesh and, by and large, the Flemish and Norman breeds ridden by dragoons, though of great strength, were both too slow and too heavy.

These, then, were the men and their responsibilities. But they were not just any band of individuals sorted and labelled cavalrymen; they were mounted infantrymen, trained to be equally adept with musket and sabre, and proud of that distinction. Though their role was to become increasingly similar to that of heavy cavalry, theirs was a distinguished heritage. Originally mounted for the sake of mobility but generally fighting on foot, they evolved into an army equally at home sabring at the charge as firing dismounted, becoming neither light nor heavy but medium cavalry by the time of the Revolution.

Dragoon Uniform

Of the sixty-two regiments of cavalry inherited from the *ancien régime*, only eighteen were dragoon regiments, but the re-organizations of 1791 and 1792 raised the number to twenty, then to twenty-one. Only in 1803 did Napoleon Bonaparte, as First Consul, bring the number to thirty: thirty on paper that is, for the additional nine regiments were dragoon in name only. Formed of six of the old 'cavalry' regiments and three of hussars, the men remained for some while dressed and equipped as though their old units had never been disbanded; as late as 1805 the three former hussar regiments (the *7eme(bis)*, *11eme* and *12eme Hussards*) had still not received their full quota of dragoon uniforms and accoutrements. Thereafter, however, all regiments were more or less uniformly dressed and equipped. The regiments were distinguished not only by their number but also, more readily, by the colours adopted for the facings of their tunics.

Tunics

The middle-green tunic or 'habit' of dragoons was contrasted by areas of cloth of a distinctive colour. These regimental colours, their position and the direction of the false pockets on the skirt of the habits distinguished the regiments, as the table below portrays:

Pockets:	Table of regimental facings					Position:
	Scarlet	Crimson	Pink	Yellow	Orange	
Horizontal	1	7	13	19	25	Lapels, turnbacks, cuffs & flaps, collar
	2	8	14	20	26	Lapels, turnbacks & cuffs
	3	9	15	21	27	Lapels, turnbacks, cuff-flaps & collar
Vertical	4	10	16	22	28	Lapels, turnbacks, cuffs & flaps, collar
	5	11	17	23	29	Lapels, turnbacks & cuffs
	6	12	18	24	30	Lapels, turnbacks, cuff-flaps & collar

Wherever the facings were of one of the distinctive colours, they would be piped in the same middle-green as the tunic; where a facing remained middle-green, as for example the cuffs of the 18th Dragoons, it would be piped in the regimental colour (in this case pink).

A total of thirty-three pewter buttons ornamented each habit. Embossed with the regimental number, the buttons came in two sizes: twenty-two small ones of which seven were placed on each lapel, one on each shoulder (to which the shoulder-strap or epaulette would attach) and three on each cuff-flap; and eleven large ones, of which three were at the top of the right hand skirt, two were in the small of the back and one was in each angle of the two trefoil pockets on the skirt.

From 1804 until 1812, the habit changed slightly in its cut, becoming 'sharper' under the influence of civilian dress as the years passed; however, the 1812 pattern was distinctly slimmer and shorter than the 1804 model. The appearance of the turnbacks was the most obvious alteration: at first genuinely folded back and secured by stitching to one another at their angle, they became false and stitched along their entire length. The illusion of a true turnback was at first maintained by the retention of the triangle of middle-green visible beneath their juncture, but towards 1810 this practice ceased, leaving the fake turnbacks flush with the bottom of the skirts.

A white waistcoat was worn beneath the habit and the cutaway front of the habit revealed its twin pockets at the waist, and single row of pewter buttons.

An alternative to the habit was the middle-green *surtout* worn in everyday wear, exercise and, despite the frowns of superior officers, frequently on campaign. Regulation until 1809, it was single-breasted with six to nine pewter buttons, and had no lapels, pockets, cuff-flaps or, often, shoulder-straps or epaulettes. Occasionally decorated with the regimental colour on the same facings as the habit, it was more often entirely middle-green. Its cut was slowly modified, as was that of the habit. It

63

was worn in conjunction with either the waistcoat described above or a similar but round-fronted, and occasionally double-breasted type.

Dated 8 February 1812, a regulation altering the dress of all line troops ordained the abolition of the old-fashioned habit and the introduction of the *habit-veste*. The habit-veste differed in that it fastened to the waist and had a considerably shorter skirt, but the basic colour and the regimental facing colours and their positions remained identical to those of the old issue. The regulation further specified that the old pointed waistcoat was to be replaced by a round-fronted model, invisible beneath the habit-veste. However, contemporary illustrations show many troops wearing the old habit after 1812 and, of those clad in the habit-veste, the points of the old waistcoat frequently protrude beneath the front of the tunic: the orders of the Ministry of War should therefore not be taken too literally.

Legwear

The calf-length, off-white, coarse hide riding breeches common to dragoons were as often as not replaced for all but parade dress by overalls of highly diverse cut, pattern and colour. Most frequently made of unbleached fabric with similarly coloured cloth-covered buttons along the length of the outside leg, overalls were also made of almost any combination of grey or middle-green cloth, with cloth-covered or white metal buttons and regimental coloured piping or lace. The inside leg and crotch were often reinforced with leather, cut straight, or into 'wolves' teeth', along the length of the leg and forming a cuff of varying height about the calf. The 1812 Regulations, for the first time officially recognizing the use of this garment, specified that they would henceforth be of unbleached (almost any tone of greyish-beige) cloth with cloth-covered buttons down the outer leg. There is no reason to suppose that this decree was regarded with any more reverence than any other.

Greatcoats and capes

The three-quarter length, sleeveless greatcoat-cum-cape worn until at least 1812 was often in an off-white fabric (white thread mixed sparingly with blue) though middle-green versions were not

unusual. A short, elbow-length cape was attached about the base of the collar to protect the webbing (worn over the coat) from the elements. The interior was lined on each side of the single back vent and the front opening with serge of the regimental colour. The 1812 Regulations introduced a more sophisticated model: sleeves were added, with large cuffs; the front was equipped with five buttons with which to fasten it, while the cape was given four for the same purpose; two hip-height pockets were put in and, finally, the coloured serge of the lining was removed.

Headgear

The distinctive headgear of dragoons was their

An officer and dragoon in walking-out dress, Consulate period. On the left, an elegant officer draws tight his kid-skin gloves in preparation for a night on the town. The dark waistcoat, black cashmere breeches and black woollen stockings are distinctive of winter wear; in the summer he would sport a white waistcoat, fine linen breeches and silk stockings. Otherwise the costume would remain the same from his silver-tasselled felt bicorn to his silver-buckled shoes. Note the straight épée in lieu of the cumbersome sabre.
On the right, a dragoon trooper makes off for his particular haunt. The uniform differs from parade dress only in the use of shoes and stockings in place of gaiters and knee-length boots. Of interest is the fuller mane of horsehair on these early helmets and the considerably baggier cut of the tunic in contrast to later patterns. (National Army Museum)

64

helmet: a copper* cap encircled by a fur turban, with a heavily embossed copper crest supporting a black horsehair mane, a peak, and chinstraps of either plain leather or copper scale, attached by a rosace. Many models existed, some of which are illustrated, and there were variations on each: copper-edged or plain peaks; copper-edged or plain, round or pointed turbans; and innumerable varieties of crest ornament.

For parade dress, a plume was inserted in the copper holder just forward of the left hand chinstrap rosace. The length, volume and colours of these plumes appear, like most details appertaining to uniforms, to vary endlessly not only from regiment to regiment, but from squadron to squadron and year to year. The table below, compiled from the contemporary evidence of Martinet and the information contained in the Alsation Collections for the year 1807, demonstrates but a fraction of the inconsistencies and contradictions available to anyone patient enough to tabulate the existing records:

Plume colours
White: 4th, 5th, 8th, 11th, 16th, 17th, 19th, 21st, 23rd, 24th, 28th and 29th.
Red: 1st, 2nd, 9th, 17th, 22nd and 30th.
Crimson: 10th.
Green base with top of regimental colour: 1st, 2nd, 6th, 19th, 20th and 25th.
Red and green: 7th, 8th, 12th and 13th

* Throughout this text the literal translation 'copper' for cuivre *is used, but note that this term refers in this context to a yellow alloy rather than a pure red copper.*

Red and white: 12th and 18th.
$\frac{2}{5}$ *red,* $\frac{2}{5}$ *white and* $\frac{1}{5}$ *red:* 3rd.
White and yellow: 20th, 22nd and 24th.
Base black with top of regimental colour: 7th and 23rd.
Green with a yellow top: 23rd.

Contemporary portraits confirm some, but produce still more possibilities for the above regiments, and the present writer does not feel he is shirking any responsibility by leaving it to the individual reader (or conglomerates for that matter) to complete the catalogue of possibilities at their leisure.

The 1812 Regulations, no doubt recognizing the difficulty, ordered plumes to be replaced by discs of the following colours for each company of each squadron: *first company:* red, sky-blue, orange or violet; *second company:* as the first but with a white centre. This rather thoughtfully narrows the odds, but, given that plumes were retained for some while by many regiments, only widens the range of potential combinations within any one regiment at any given date.

Replacing the helmet for fatigue dress was the *bonnet de police*, a middle-green cloth cap. It was composed of a 'turban' and 'flame': the uppermost edge of the turban was edged in white lace and piped in the regimental colour; the flame was piped in the regimental colour and ended in a white tassel. The front of the cap bore a white or regimental coloured grenade badge. The 1812 Regulations introduced an entirely new model of fatigue cap called the Pokalem.

The middle-green Pokalem cap consisted of a turban, a large, round, flat top and ear-flaps, all piped, laced and decorated, with either a grenade or the regimental number, in the appropriate colour.

Lancer Uniform

The organizational Decree of 15 July 1811 also specified the dress of the *chevau-légers lanciers*. As for dragoons, the regiments were distinguished by the colours of the facings of the tunic.

Tunics
The habit-veste of the lancers differed just a little from that adopted by the dragoons in 1812, the only

large difference consisting in the cuff being pointed rather than straight with a buttoned cuff-flap. The lapels were reversible—that is, they could be either buttoned back and joined by hooks and eyes down the front to reveal the facing colour fully; or buttoned across, to right or left, to cover all but a narrow strip of regimental colour. This middle-green tunic was lined in white and had collar, turnbacks, cuffs and lapels of the following distinguishing colours:

1st Regiment: scarlet.
2nd Regiment: orange.
3rd Regiment: pink.
4th Regiment: crimson.
5th Regiment: sky blue.
6th Regiment: madder red.

The turnbacks were supposed to be decorated with Imperial eagle patches but were frequently

Trumpeters of a regiment of dragoons of the *ancien régime*, c.1789. The livery seen here was abolished with the Revolution and the dress of trumpeters became, until the issue of the Imperial Livery in 1812, a matter left to the discretion of each regimental colonel. The result was colourful if not a little confusing since, as colonel replaced colonel, trumpeters tended to be dressed in whatever fabric was locally most plentiful and cheap, with complete disregard (for the most part) of any precedent, as long as the colour sufficiently distinguished the trumpeters from the men. (National Army Museum)

devoid of any ornamentation whatever. None of the facings were decorated with piping. All thirty-two buttons were of yellow metal.

A sleeveless white waistcoat, round-edged, was worn beneath the habit-veste and was fastened by a row of yellow metal buttons. A sleeved, plain middle-green shell-jacket was worn in stable and fatigue dress.

Legwear

The lancers' equivalent of the off-white breeches worn by the dragoons were middle-green Hungarian breeches. These were laced down the outer leg and the edges of the front flap in yellow. The ornament of the flaps consisted of a simple inverted arrowhead device for the 1st to 4th Regiments, while the 5th and 6th favoured a fairly complicated Hungarian knot.

Middle-green overalls, reinforced with black leather, with a strip of lace of the regimental colour and yellow metal buttons down the outer leg were the most common campaign dress in the period immediately following the creation of the lancer regiments. As the wars progressed, however, variations still more diverse than those of dragoons became apparent. Contemporary illustrations capture the men of the 2nd Regiment wearing, in 1814, grey overalls otherwise conforming to order; troops of the 4th clad in overalls of middle-green with leather reinforcements and two parallel strips of lace down outer seams devoid of buttons; and finally, men of the 6th sporting patterns made of madder red cloth, without piping or lace but complete with buttons. With this garment it was very much a case of 'anything goes' as but a cursory glance at the colour plates will reveal.

Greatcoats

The greatcoat common to all lancers was the model already described for dragoons after 1812; a sleeved and caped, white-threaded-with-blue, button-up overcoat over which the webbing would be worn.

Head-gear

The distinctive head-dress of lancers was no more than the dragoon model helmet with modified embellishment. Where the dragoons' copper crest bore a horsehair mane, the lancers' supported a

This trumpeter of the élite company of the 21st Dragoons, c.1810, is colourfully dressed in a yellow surtout with medium-green facings. The surtout tunic often replaced the habit on campaign, being more comfortable and less expensive. The bearskin has a scarlet plume, white cords and tassels and copper chinscales. An unusual feature is the use of white trefoil shoulder straps instead of the more usual red, fringed epaulettes distinctive of élite companies. The trumpet cord is here a mixture of white and green thread, where yellow and green would be more common. Note the knot in the horse's tail, a fairly widespread practice. (National Army Museum)

neo-Grecian horsehair crest; where the rear of the dragoons' copper cap was simply rounded, the lancers' received a second, rear peak to protect the back of the neck from cuts and rain.

These were the differences, but there is in their comparison one striking similarity: a great deal of perplexity concerning the plumes. Contemporary illustrations portray red and white ones entirely similar to those of dragoons soon after the creation of the regiments, but increasingly few helmets are represented with any plumes at all as the end of the Empire approached; indeed, many existing lancer helmets have no plume holders whatsoever. Do we

assume that, upon conversion to lancer regiments, the troopers retained their old dragoon unit plumes? A possibility, as long as the colour did not clash with the new regimental colours, which would account for the recording of so many red and white ones. But then what of the 1812 Regulations' order to replace plumes with company-coloured discs? The writer has yet to find a period drawing depicting a lancer's helmet with such a pompon. It is perhaps possible that with the order abolishing the plume, lancer regiments never received the disc pompons and were quite happy, if not relieved, to do without both them and their tall plumes.

The fatigue-cap was identical to that of the dragoons, with the exception of the grenade patch at the front. As of 1812, they too were issued the flat-topped Pokalem model with the substitution of crossed lances for the grenade badge.

Having now completed a superficial examination of the basic dress of both dragoons and lancers, it would be interesting to delve a little further into the more specific dress of the different ranks of both arms, but space requires this be left to the illustrations and captions. Instead, we shall turn our attention to the much-neglected subject of saddles and harness.

Horse Furniture

Dragoons

A Decree dated the 4th Brumaire An X prescribed the form of horse furniture of dragoons as comprising French saddle, complete with holster covers, horse-cloth and portemanteau; bridle; snaffle-bridle and parade halter; and stable halter and bridle.

The saddle, including the pistol holsters and seat, was of plain leather while the girth was of fabric; the stirrup leathers and the martingale were of white Hungarian leather; the stirrups were of blackened iron; the breastplate, securing straps and crupper were of black leather. The bridle and reins were also of black leather, as were the snaffle-bridle, the parade halter and their reins.

The pistol-holster covers and the horse-cloth were of middle-green fabric, edged with white lace 45mm wide. The middle-green portemanteau, strapped upon the saddle behind the rider, bore the

Attached to the élite company, this Chef de Sapeurs of the 30th Dragoons would command a force of eight sappers whose duties lay in clearing the way for the column and protecting the regimental standard. The rank and service stripes are silver, piped in red, and the cords and tassels adorning his bearskin are mixed silver and red thread, as are his epaulettes. He wears a long hide apron and crossed-axe patches, familiar symbols of his status. (National Army Museum)

holsters, but the greatcoat which was tied over the holsters, and the lower body of the rider.

Lancers

The saddle of lancers was of entirely different composition to that of dragoons. Beechwood, reinforced with metal bands, formed the base and, with the suspended seat, was covered in leather. All the reins and other accessories were of black leather, bar the straps for the greatcoat and the pistol, which were of white leather, and the musketoon securing strap, which was of yellow leather.

The bridle was of the Hungarian pattern as adopted by all light cavalry and made of black leather with copper ornaments throughout, except for the iron bit. The watering, snaffle-bridle was of white Hungarian leather.

Sapper of the 1st Dragoons, 1806–1811. This relaxed fellow wears the standard sappers' uniform, but for a couple of embellishments: his bearskin has been adorned with a copper grenade badge, a popular symbol among the élite dragoons, and his crossbelts have not only similar badges but also large copper buckles and accessories. His apron has been rolled up, no doubt to facilitate mounting and dismounting, and is held in place by his swordbelt. It should be remembered that only dragoon regiments were accorded the use of sappers out of respect for their traditional role as mounted infantry. (National Army Museum)

regimental number and lace 27mm wide on its rectangular ends.

The 1812 Regulations gave official sanction to the widespread practice of placing a white, sheepskin shabraque over the whole of the saddle. This shabraque would be edged in 'wolves' teeth' material of the regimental colour.

Officers' saddles were without cantle and covered in green fabric. Green leather holsters and bronzed stirrups differentiated them further from those of the troops. The horse-cloth was middle-green and edged with a single stripe of silver lace for subalterns; and two stripes (the inner being thinner than the outer) for more senior officers.

Like the men, officers employed sheepskin shabraques, but of only half-size and in black. It would seem that their use was never officially recognized but their popularity is well established, protecting, as they did, not only the pistols and

The portemanteau, middle-green and laced in yellow, was strapped behind the cantle while the greatcoat was tied over the pommel and holsters. The whole was covered by a white sheepskin shabraque (frequently black for trumpeters), edged in 'wolves' teeth' of regimental colour.

The officers' saddle was essentially the same, though the cantle was covered in green Morocco leather and finished in copper. All the leathers were black, excepting the stirrup leathers in yellow, and all buckles and other diverse metal ornaments were gilded, save the bronzed stirrups. The officers used a cloth shabraque of middle-green embellished with regimental colour piping and golden lace. The portemanteau was of the same colour, piping and lacing.

Both the portemanteaux and the horse-cloths of dragoons and lancers bore the regimental number in either white or yellow lace.

Having seen, however briefly, the horse furniture of dragoons and lancers, we shall now turn to the organization of the regiments.

Organisation

The conscripts would be organized into companies of two troops. By order of the Decree of the Ier Vendémiaire An XII (24 September 1803), the company was to total fifty-four mounted troops and, for lack of even remotely usable mounts, thirty-six dismounted troops. The balance of the company was composed of one trumpeter, for the mounted men, one drummer, for the dismounted, four *brigadiers* (corporals), one *brigadier-fourrier*, two *sous-lieutenants*, one lieutenant and a captain.

Two such companies formed a squadron: the smallest tactical unit of cavalry. The only addition to the ranks at this stage would be a *Chef d'Escadron*.

Four such squadrons made up a regiment. With each regiment was an *Etat Major* which comprised eight sappers (farriers for lancers), one *brigadier-sapeur*, one *maréchal des logis chef* or *maréchal des logis*, one *brigadier-trompette*, one *brigadier-tambour*, one *adjutant-sous-officier*, one *adjutant-major* and, finally, a colonel. Several amendments, both official and unofficial, were made to this unit structure over the years, including, inter alia: by the Decree of 26 February 1808, the *maréchal des logis/maréchal des logis*

chef were to be removed from the *Etat Major*; and, a regimental inventory dated 15 May 1811 mentions the acquisition of a trumpet-major and the retention of the *maréchal des logis chef* (the regimental sergeant major) by many dragoon regiments.

But the above relates only to an ideal situation; very few regiments were, other than on paper, of full trooper strength and as for the officer and *Etat Major* complement, let us let the following extracts from the '*Historique du 7eme Dragons*' speak for themselves of the fluctuations:

Situation d'avril 1809

Etat nominatif des officiers:
Etat Major: —Colonel.—2 × Chefs d'Escadron.
　　　　　　　—Major.—1 × Quartier-Maître trésorier.

1er Escadron:
1ere Cie: 　1 × Capitaine, 1 × Lieutenant, 2 × Sous-Lieutenants.
5eme Cie: 　1 × Capitaine, 1 × Lieutenant, 2 × Sous-Lieutenants.

2eme Escadron:
2eme Cie: 　1 × Capitaine, 1 × Lieutenant, 1 × Sous-Lieutenant.
6eme Cie: 　1 × Capitaine, 1 × Lieutenant, 2 × Sous-Lieutenants.

3eme Escadron:
3eme Cie: 　1 × Capitaine, 1 × Lieutenant, 1 × Sous-Lieutenant.
7eme Cie: 　1 × Capitaine, 1 × Lieutenant, 1 × Sous-Lieutenant.

4eme Escadron:
4eme Cie: 　1 × Capitaine, 1 × Lieutenant, 2 × Sous-Lieutenants.
8eme Cie: 　1 × Capitaine, 2 × Lieutenants, 1 × Sous-Lieutenant.

Situation du 1er juin 1812

Etat nominatif des officiers:
Etat Major: —1 × Colonel.
　　　　　　　—1 × Major.
　　　　　　　—2 × Chefs d'Escadron.
　　　　　　　—1 × Quartier-Maître.
　　　　　　　—2 × Adjutants-Major.
　　　　　　　—1 × Chirurgien-Major.
　　　　　　　—1 × Aide-Major.
　　　　　　　—1 × Sous-Aide-Major.

1er Escadron:
1ere Cie: 1 × *Capitaine,* 1 × *Lieutenant,* 2 × *Sous-Lieutenants.*

5eme Cie: 1 × *Capitaine,* 2 × *Sous-Lieutenants.*

2eme Escadron:
2eme Cie: 1 × *Capitaine,* 2 × *Sous-Lieutenants.*

6eme Cie: 1 × *Capitaine,* 1 × *Lieutenant,* 1 × *Sous-Lieutenant.*

3eme Escadron:
3eme Cie: 1 × *Capitaine,* 1 × *Lieutenant,* 1 × *Sous-Lieutenant.*

7eme Cie: 1 × *Lieutenant,* 2 × *Sous-Lieutenant.*

4eme Escadron:
4eme Cie: 1 × *Capitaine.*

8eme Cie: 1 × *Capitaine,* 1 × *Lieutenant,* 2 × *Sous-Lieutenant.*

5eme Escadron:
9eme Cie: 1 × *Capitaine,* 1 × *Lieutenant,* 2 × *Sous-Lieutenants.*

10eme Cie: 1 × *Capitaine,* 1 × *Lieutenant,* 2 × *Sous-Lieutenants.*

Etat des officiers aux escadrons de guerre le 1er juillet 1813

Etat Major: —1 × *Colonel.*
            —2 × *Chefs d'Escadron.*
            —1 × *Adjutant-Major.*

1er Escadron:
1ere Cie: 1 × *Capitaine,* 1 × *Lieutenant,* 1 × *Sous-Lieutenant.*

6eme Cie: 1 × *Capitaine,* 1 × *Lieutenant,* 2 × *Sous-Lieutenants.*

2eme Escadron:
2eme Cie: 1 × *Capitaine,* 1 × *Lieutenant,* 2 × *Sous-Lieutenants.*

7eme Cie: 1 × *Capitaine,* 1 × *Lieutenant,* 1 × *Sous-Lieutenant.*

Officiers dont les compagnies ne sont pas encore a l'armée:

An élite company of dragoons crushing a Russian infantry square, 1814. The tremendous loss in horses during the Russian campaign of 1812 irreparably damaged the Grande Armée's cavalry units with the result that however successfully an action might be fought, it could never be followed up with the decisive destruction of the retreating foe. Thus, despite the brilliant engagements executed by Napoleon's troops, the results of the German and French campaigns of 1813 and 1814 respectively were a foregone conclusion, given a co-ordinated allied command. (National Army Museum)

Two troopers of the 23rd Dragoons act as escort to visiting top brass. About them are troopers and a trumpeter of the Chasseurs à Cheval of the Imperial Guard, the crack light cavalry regiment of Napoleon's personal guard. (National Army Museum)

3eme Cie: 1 × *Capitaine,*   1 × *Lieutenant.*
8eme Cie: 1 × *Capitaine.*

It is clear then that regiments, whether dragoon or lancer, were only very exceptionally fully officered, let alone manned, and the duties of the vacant post would fall on the man of next highest rank.

As previously mentioned, thirty-six men were without mounts within the early dragoon regiments and these were formed into separate and distinct divisions of foot dragoons.

The Foot Dragoons

There were four different instances when necessity forced the formation of foot dragoon divisions: at the camp of Boulogne in 1803; on the Rhine in 1805; in Italy in 1805, and lastly in Germany in 1806.

Boulogne, 1803

Further to the directives of Generals Baraguey d'Hilliers and Klein, two divisions of foot dragoons were established of the following composition:

Klein's Division:
—Millet's Brigade (2nd, 4th and 10th Dragoons).
—Millet's Brigade (11th, 13th and 19th Dragoons).
—Ferrol's Brigade (1st, 14th and 20th Dragoons).

Baraguey d'Hilliers' Division:
—Louis Bonaparte's Brigade (5th, 9th, 12th and 21st Dragoons).
—Bonnard's Brigade (3rd, 6th and 8th Dragoons).
(Letter of Ministry of War dated 24 October 1803)

Each regiment provided two squadrons of two companies and, where necessary, any mounts were returned to the regimental depots.

Each foot dragoon was supplied with a pair of shoes, a pair of long black gaiters, a greatcoat and a haversack (to which his riding boots were tied).

71

A centre company of the 16th Dragoons is devastated by fire from Prussian infantry. On this occasion, 28 October 1806, the Prussian Grenadier Battalion 'Prinz August' defended itself against no less than three cavalry regiments. Of interest is the manner in which the dragoons' musketoons are slung over their shoulders rather than inserted in the boot slung below the saddle and attached to the pommel of the saddle by a leather strap.

The long, heavy cavalry cloaks and any saddles and harness were packed into baggage wagons and despatched to Boulogne for the prospective crossing. Only colonels and majors were permitted to retain their mounts which were to be allowed to embark.

As it was, however, hostilities with Austria precluded the sea-borne invasion and the regiments regained their respective depots as of August 1805 to prepare for the Bavarian campaign.

The Rhine, 1805

An order issuing from the Ministry of War and dated 25 August 1805 established a single division of four regiments of foot dragoons at Strasbourg. The twenty-four regiments of Baraguey d'Hilliers' corps of four divisions each supplied one squadron of two companies. The six companies normally forming a brigade now became a battalion and the two battalions of a division now equalled one regiment. The four regiments produced in this manner created an infantry division of 7,200 men equipped with ten cannon and organized as follows:

Colonel Privé's 1st Regiment:
1st Battalion: —One squadron of the 1st, 2nd and 20th Dragoon regiments.
　　　　　　　—Guidon: that of the 1st Dragoons.
2nd Battalion: —One squadron of the 4th, 16th and 26th Dragoons.
　　　　　　　—Guidon: that of the 4th Dragoons.

Colonel Le Baron's 2nd Regiment:
1st Battalion: —One squadron of the 10th, 13th and 22nd Dragoons.
　　　　　　　—Guidon: that of the 10th Dragoons.
2nd Battalion: —One squadron of the 3rd, 6th and 11th Dragoons.

An élite trooper of the 15th Dragoons. Elite companies were created following the Decree of 18 Vendemiaire An X (10 October 1801) which stipulated, *inter alia*, 'The first company of the first squadron of every cavalry regiment shall take the name of élite company. That company will be formed of men chosen from throughout the regiment who conform to the instructions of the Ministry of War.' Their élite status was to be indicated by the wearing of tall bearskins basically no different from their counterparts in the infantry; but the men soon began to sport red epaulettes and even aiguillettes to further distinguish themselves, to which officialdom turned a blind eye. (The Jean de Gerlache de Gomery Collection)

—Guidon: that of the 3rd Dragoons.

Colonel Beckler's 3rd Regiment:
1st Battalion: —One squadron of the 5th, 8th and 12th Dragoons.
—Guidon: that of the 5th Dragoons.
2nd Battalion:—One squadron of the 9th, 6th and 21st Dragoons.
—Guidon: that of the 8th Dragoons.

Colonel Barthélemy's 4th Regiment:
1st Battalion: —One squadron of the 15th, 17th and 25th Dragoons.
—Guidon: that of the 15th Dragoons.

2nd Battalion:—One squadron of the 18th, 19th and 27th Dragoons.
—Guidon: that of the 27th Dragoons.
(Amended from a slightly erroneous list of General Baraguey d'Hilliers, dated 9 Fructidor An XIII)

The above division was only provisional and contingent on the arrival of sufficient horses to mount all the troops (the colonels were never replaced in their old regiments). By the end of September the first two regiments were partly remounted and, on 20 October, the remaining two were issued captured Austrian hussar and lancer horses.

Though the ranks were soon refilled, these units were never intended to be other than temporary.

A trooper of the élite company of the 12th Dragoons dismounted to fire his piece. The tying of the greatcoat about the body was a common practice to protect the breast from sabre slashes and, to a lesser degree, musket balls. While on campaign, the hide breeches would be replaced by button-up overalls of almost every description and the plume of the bearskin would be packed in the saddle's portemanteau, to preserve it for the victory parades which would, hopefully, follow. (The Jean de Gerlache de Gomery Collection)

73

A trumpeter of the élite company of the 16th Dragoons in campaign dress, 1806. He wears a pink surtout tunic and a splendid white bearskin. An interesting point is that the tassels and cords have been left on the head-gear, as has the plume, though the latter has been carefully wrapped in waterproof fabric to protect it from the elements. He rides a grey as did all trumpeters. (The Jean de Gerlache de Gomery Collection)

The morale of the troops was low and they consequently shaped-up rather badly, marching abominably and executing poorly the everyday functions of infantry from lack of both practice and good will. The sole benefit derived from the foot regiments was the fact that the enemy eventually paid for their mounts and, with the end of the campaign, the regiments were disbanded and the individual squadrons sent to rejoin their respective mounted regiments.

Italy, 1805

In Vendémiaire of An XVI, Marshal Masséna organized a battalion of foot dragoons drawn from the 23rd, 24th, 28th, 29th and 30th Dragoons and attached them to General Verdier's 2nd Division. Their number never exceeded 333 troopers (as recorded the 1st Brumaire) and the battalion was dissolved in January of 1806.

Germany, 1806

In order to take advantage of the wasted manpower present at every regiment's depot, Napoleon ordered the formation of a foot corps of two regiments of foot dragoons (12 September 1806). In an attempt to obtain better results from the ill-humoured men than hitherto experienced, the regiments were to be attached to the Imperial Guard.

General Dorsenne created the 1st Regiment at Mayence with companies of the 2nd, 14th, 20th and 26th Dragoons forming the 1st Battalion and companies of the 6th, 11th, 13th and 22nd the second. His regiment was duly appended to the Grenadiers à Pied of the Imperial Guard.

Major Fredericks organized the 2nd Regiment at Strasbourg with companies of the 8th, 12th, 16th and 21st forming the 3rd Battalion and companies of the 17th, 18th, 25th and 27th Dragoons the 4th. This regiment was assigned to the Chasseurs à Pied of the Imperial Guard.

The foot-slogging proved mercifully brief, for the troops were soon mounted on captured Prussian and Saxon horses in October and November of the same year. The squadrons were promptly despatched to their parent regiments.

This last action marked the final official attempt to employ dragoons as infantrymen for however short a period, since even the honour of being attached to the Guard did little to improve the quality of their performance and turnout. Popular references to officially organized units of foot dragoons existing as late as 1808 are based on originally faulty sources.

* * *

Before turning to the histories and war records of the individual regiments, a brief word on the creation of the lancers from dragoon regiments would not be out of place.

The effect of the lance used by foreign cavalry regiments on Napoleon's troops was far from desirable and, in an effort to reassure the men of French supremacy in all arms, the Emperor duly issued the Decree of 18 June 1811, ordering the establishment of nine line lancer regiments. The last three were created from two Polish cavalry regiments and a French regiment, the 30eme Chasseurs à Cheval, while the first six were formed of the 1st, 3rd, 8th, 9th, 10th and 29th Dragoons.

The lancers only came into existence by the end of 1811 and the élite lancers, at length, by the summer of 1812. The regiments took part in the Russian campaign, often ill-equipped and mounted, protecting the flanks of the long columns as well as screening their movements. These light horse proved invaluable, the lance being a weapon of pronounced effect on the morale of both enemy cavalry and infantry, and it is strange that their creation was so tardy given their long use in other continental armies.

War Service of Individual Regiments

The war records of the individual regiments on the following pages should be considered in the particular light of Napoleonic warfare or, more correctly, of the type of war Napoleon waged.

A trooper of the 12th Dragoons wrapped in the large cavalry cloak issued until 1812. As of that date a slimmer, sleeved version was issued. The plume of the helmet has been wrapped in waxed cloth as protection from the rain and wind. (The Jean de Gerlache de Gomery Collection)

A trooper of a centre company of the 2nd Lancers, 1814. He wears one of the many types of overalls used to cover or replace the tight Hungarian breeches on campaign. The points of his waistcoat are clearly visible beneath the front edge of his tunic; given that the dress specifications for lancers indicated that a round-fronted waistcoat was to be issued, this is further evidence that the official decrees relating to dress should never be taken too literally. (The Jean de Gerlache de Gomery Collection)

'. . . if such great objects may be obtained as the destruction of a whole hostile army, the State can afford to lose a few hundred horses from exhaustion,' the Emperor wrote, revealing in a couple of lines his whole philosophy towards losses in the cavalry. The incredible march to Ulm and Austerlitz in 1805 set the pace for the lightning offensives that were his hallmark, a method of warfare singularly unsuited to a non-mechanical army. That his troops fared so well on hopeless roads and empty stomachs is astonishing.

Though a daily ration of thirty grammes of bread, 250 of meat and a half-litre of wine was theoretically issued, officially sanctioned foraging was the main source of nourishment. In columns of four, or two where poor roads demanded, the cavalry would spearhead the advance of the army, leaving increasingly far behind them the wagonloads of grain intended for their use. As they rode deeper into generally hostile territory, so feeding both men and mounts became a greater problem until direct purchase and fair exchange gave way to theft and robbery. A trooper's salary, if and when he received it, was a bare 0.30F a day; and it is easy to see why pillaging prevailed when one compares this figure to the price of foodstuffs: a pound of sugar, 6F; a pound of rice or butter, 2.40F, and a pound of bread, 1.35F. These prices were recorded in Poland in 1806 at the very beginning of hostilities; is it any wonder that as costs rose so the number of incidents of indiscipline increased in proportion? Matters were worse still for the horses.

With the approach of the corps of the Grande Armée, the fleeing rural population of the invaded countryside would frequently burn their crops, leaving little or nothing in the way of cereals with which to nourish the cavalry mounts. It was common practice for regiments to arm special detachments of men with scythes, and despatch them as much as 50km from base to scour the land for fodder. The Russian campaign provides a ghastly example of the waste of horseflesh through lack of provision.

In June of 1812 80,000 cavalry mounts were taken on campaign; in no more than eight days 8,000 had died through lack of care and, in less than a month, Murat's 22,000 mounted men were reduced to 12,000. The troopers were remounted on frequently unsuitable captured horses, but the terrible toll only increased. With the coming of the snow during the retreat, 30,000 died within five days; by the time Murat's cavalry reached Smolensk, they numbered a pitiful 1,200 mounted men. Thereafter, the remaining horses served as food for the now starving men. Since there was only one veterinary surgeon for every 500 head of mounts, malnutrition over even a comparatively short length of time tended to be fatal.

It is with this in mind, therefore, that the war records should be considered, and due respect given a cavalry capable of achieving so much on so little.

The 1st Regiment of Dragoons

Created in Germany in 1656 following a treaty concluded between General Montecuculli and the King of France. Named that same year as the

Trooper of the 2nd Lancers, 1814. The dress specifications were a little vague as to the exact ornament of the skirts of the lancers' tunics and it would appear that the matter was left in the hands of the colonels of each regiment; some opting for pocket-less versions with piping about the back buttons, others preferring this example. In this case blank, the turnbacks of some lancer tunics were decorated with dark green eagle patches. Worthy of note is the fact that this individual has been issued with dragoon-style boots rather than the Hungarian pattern distinctive of lancers. (The Jean de Gerlache de Gomery Collection)

Dragons Etrangers du Roi and renamed the Royal-Dragons in 1668, it finally became the 1er Régiment de Dragons in 1791. Transformed into the *1er Chevau-Légers Lanciers* in 1811. With the return of the Bourbons in 1814, the regiment was renamed the Régiment de Lanciers du Roi only to take up its previous title with the reinstatement of Napoleon in 1815. After the '100 Days' the regiment was entirely disbanded at Agen in 1815.

War record:

1805: Part of the cavalry reserve of the Grande Armée. Actions of Wertingen, Ulm and Austerlitz. 1806–1807: With the Grande Armée at Jena, Golymin, Heilsberg and Friedland (at which the regiment so distinguished itself that the Emperor sent his personal felicitations to its Colonel, Dermoncourt, in the heat of the battle).

1807–1811: Attached to both the Army of Spain and that of Portugal. At Uclés, 1809, Maréchal des Logis Priant and Brigadier-Fourrier Gallet achieved the distinction of seizing an enemy standard apiece. At Chiclana, 1811, the now Sous-Lieutenant Priant captured no less than 400 prisoners with his single troop.

1812: With the Grande Armée at Smolensk and Borodino.

1813: Present at the battles of Dresden, Leipzig and Hanau.

1814: Reims and Paris.

1815: With the Armée du Nord at Waterloo.

The 2nd Regiment of Dragoons

Created in 1635 and given the title of Enghien-Cavalerie. In 1646, the name was changed to the Condé-Cavalerie and remained so until 1776 when the regiment formally became dragoons as the Condé-Dragons. Entitled the 2eme Régiment de Dragons in 1791. Renamed the Régiment de Dragons du Roi (No. 1) in 1814 and, after a brief return to its 1791 title in 1815, was finally dissolved at Besançon on 4 December 1815.

War record:

1805: As part of the Cavalry Reserve of the Grande Armée fought at Wertingen, Albeck (where Brigadier Gigot was cited for having single-handedly made prisoner an enemy colonel from the midst of a battalion of the foe) and Austerlitz.

1806–1807: With the Cavalry Reserve at Jena (where the regiment captured an entire battalion, fifteen cannon and two flags), Eylau, Heilsberg and Friedland.

1808–1813: Attached successively to the armies of Spain and Portugal and engaged at Uclés, Medellin, Talavera-de-la-Reina, Chiclana and Vitoria.

1809: A contingent was present at the battle of Wagram as part of the Army of Germany.

1813: With the Grande Armée at Danzig, Leipzig and Hanau.

1814: Part of the 2nd Corps of the Grande Armée at the actions of Rambervilliers, Saint-Dizier and Brienne.

1815: Attached to the 3rd Corps of the Armée du Nord at Waterloo.

The 3rd Regiment of Dragoons

Levied for the Duke of Enghien in 1649 and named Enghien until 1686 when it was retitled Bourbon. Became a dragoon regiment in 1776 and entitled Bourbon-Dragons. Renamed the 3eme Régiment de Dragons in 1791 and so remained until its transformation into the *2eme Chevau-Légers Lanciers* in 1811.

War record:

1805: With the Grande Armée at Austerlitz.

1806–1807: Remained with the Grande Armée and was present at Jena, Prentzlow, Karnichen (where Fourrier Jeuffroy captured a standard), Eylau and Friedland (where Commandant Barbut seized two guns and a howitzer while Capitaine Delesalle and his company made off with an entire Russian battery).

1808–1811: Attached to the Army of Spain and engaged at Alba de Tormes.

A trumpeter of a centre company of the 12th Dragoons, 1804. Dressed for parade, this trumpeter wears the common surtout of reversed colours with lacing about the breast buttons, a tall plume and hide breeches. Note that trumpeters' helmets had a white rather than black horsehair mane. (The Jean de Gerlache de Gomery Collection)

A sapper of the 12th Dragoons in parade dress, 1809. On this figure we can discern that the body of his epaulettes have been covered with copper scales to protect the wearer's shoulders from sabre blows. The large axe and long apron were trademarks of the sapper's profession, distinctions dating back to when dragoons were purely mounted infantrymen. (The Jean de Gerlache de Gomery Collection)

The 4th Regiment of Dragoons

Levied in July of 1667 and named the Chartres-Cavalerie in 1684. Renamed as Clermont in 1724 and again, in 1771, as La Marche. Became a regiment of dragoons in 1776 with the title Conti-Dragoons. In 1791 the regiment was restyled as the 4eme Régiment de Dragons—the name to which it returned in 1815 with the return of the Eagle, after a short period under the Monarchy of 1814 with the title of the Régiment de Dragons de la Reine (No. 2). Disbanded in July of 1815 at Moulins.

War record:

1805–1807: Part of Klein's Division of the Grande Armée at the crossing of the Lech, Wertingen, Dierenstein, Golymin, Deppen, Hoff, Eylau, Heilsberg and Friedland.

1807–1813: Attached to the 1st Corps of the Army of Spain and fought at Talavera-de-la-Reina, Ocaña, Albufera and Vitoria. Note however that in 1807 the 4th Provisional Regiment of Dragoons was with the Army of Portugal, engaged at Vimiero and surrendered at Cintra; this unit was dissolved in 1810.

1813: With the Grande Armée at Leipzig.

1814: Part of Treilhard's Division at the battles of Bar-sur-Aube, Sézanne and La Fère-Champenoise.

1815: Took part in the battle of Ligny.

The 5th Regiment of Dragoons

Created out of the division of the Dragons Etrangers du Roi into two and named, that year of 1668, Colonel-Général and Royal-Dragons. Renamed the 5eme Régiment de Dragons with the re-organization of 1791. Retitled the Régiment de Dragons du Dauphin after the abdication of Napoleon, it reclaimed its previous title for the '100 Days' campaign only to be disbanded later that year.

War record:

1805: With the Grande Armée at Wertingen and Austerlitz (at which Trooper Barbet captured a Russian adjutant-general).

1806–1807: Part of the Grande Armée for the actions of Nasielk, Eylau and Friedland.

1809–1813: Service in Spain where, 6 January 1809, Colonel de Sparre led twenty troopers, swimming, across a freezing affluent of the Douro to execute a spectacular charge ending with the seizure of two enemy cannon. The regiment fought at Almonacid, Ocaña and Vitoria.

1814: Engaged at the battles of Craonne, La Fère-Champenoise and Paris.

1815: With the Armée du Nord at Ligny and Waterloo.

The 6th Regiment of Dragoons

Formed in 1673, it was designated the La Reine-Dragons in 1675. Became the 6eme Régiment de Dragons in 1791. Renamed the Régiment de Dragons de Monsieur (No. 4) in 1814, but regained its numerical title with the return of Napoleon. The regiment was disbanded at Nimes in August of 1815.

1805: With the Grande Armée at Ulm, Ebensberg and Austerlitz.

1806: On the fields of Schleitz, Zehdenick and Prentzlov (at which both Lieutenant Jobert and Trooper Fabre captured enemy standards). December 23rd, on the battlefield of Biezun, Trooper Plet seized yet another standard while Maréchal des Logis Lecuyer, accompanied by four troopers, carried away no less than two guns, a howitzer and two ammunition caissons.

1807: Part of the Grande Armée at the actions of Bergfried, Hoff (where Colonel Lebaron lost his life), Eylau and Friedland.

1809–1813: Attached to the Army of Spain and engaged at Alba-de-Tormes, Ciudad-Rodrigo, Fuentes d'Onoro, Torres Vedras, Los Arapilos (Salamanca) and Vitoria.

1813: Fought with the Grande Armée at Leipzig.

1814: Present on the fields of Brienne, La Rothière, Mormant and Saint-Dizier.

1815: Attached to the Army of the Moselle and engaged at Ligny and Rocquencourt.

The 7th Regiment of Dragoons

Raised by the Marquis of Sauvebœuf at Tournai in 1673. Named the Dauphin-Dragons in 1675. Became the 7eme Régiment de Dragons in 1791 but retitled the Régiment de Dragons d'Angoulême (No. 5) under the First Restoration in 1814. Returned to their 1791 title in 1815 under the renewed Empire, but was dissolved on 16 July 1815.

War record:

1805–1809: Attached to the Army of Italy and engaged at Caldiero, the crossing of the Tagliamento and throughout the Calabrian campaign. In April 1809, at the crossing of the Piave, Lieutenant Blassel successfully led an under-manned foot detachment to the rescue of General Baraguey d'Hilliers and his staff, momentarily isolated and in imminent danger of capture. This same year, at the battle of Wagram, Chef d'Escadron Deberme, acting regimental commander in lieu of Colonel de Seron who lay wounded, executed a superb charge against two enemy cavalry regiments and siezed some 300 prisoners.

1812: With the Grande Armée at Borodino.

1813: Fought with the Grande Armée at Dresden.

1814: Present at the battle of La Fère-Champenoise.

1815: Engaged on the field of Waterloo.

Drummer of an élite company of foot dragoons. Like the grenadiers of infantry, élite foot dragoons boasted tall black bearskins and red epaulettes. With the turning of mount-less dragoons into infantry units, so trumpeters were replaced by drummers equipped with instruments of the same pattern as the infantry. Their equipment remained the same except for the wearing of gaiters and shoes instead of riding boots, and the carrying of an infantry-style pack.

The 8th Regiment of Dragoons

Created 1 March 1674 by the Marquis d'Heudicourt and named Toulouse in 1693. Renamed Penthièvre in 1737. Finally titled as Penthièvre-Dragons in 1776. Became the 8eme Régiment de Dragons in 1791 and so remained until 1811 when the regiment was restyled as the *3eme Chevau-Légers Lanciers*. In 1814 this last became the Régiment de Lanciers du Dauphin but resumed its former title for the Belgian campaign of 1815. The regiment was disbanded in 1815.

A foot dragoon, c.1806, equipped essentially in the same manner as if he were mounted. The sabre was retained and slung on the hook of the swordbelt. Here wrapped about his body in the cavalrymen's fashion, the greatcoat could more easily be strapped atop the pack as the infantry were wont to do.

War record:

1805–1806: Part of the Grande Armée at Wertingen, Ulm, Lambach, Austerlitz, Jena, Zehdenik, Prentzlov and Nasielk (where Colonel Beckler was struck dead).

1807: With the Grande Armée at Eylau, Heilsberg and Friedland.

1808–1811: Service in Spain. Present at Burgos, Tudela, Monterey, Braga, Oporto, Valladolid, Guarda, Santarem and Sabugal.

1812: Attached to the Grande Armée and on the fields of Polotsk (where Colonel Lebrun lost his life) and Berezina.

1813: Still with the Grande Armée at the battles of Bautzen, Reichenbach, Dresden, Leipzig and Hanau.

1815: Took part in the Belgian campaign and fought at both Ligny and Waterloo.

The 9th Regiment of Dragoons

Raised in the Franche-Comté by the Marquis of Listenois in 1673. Originally given the title of Lorraine in 1773. Became the 9eme Régiment de Dragons in 1791 and consequently retitled the *4eme Régiment de Chevau-Légers Lanciers* in 1811. With the return of the monarchy the regiment was renamed the Régiment de Lanciers de Monsieur; after reviving its former title for the 1815 campaign, the regiment was dissolved later the same year.

War record:

1805–1807: With the Grande Armée at the following actions: Wertingen (where Colonel Maupetit died leading a charge), Austerlitz (where Lieutenant-Colonel Delort received two lance wounds and the Adjutant-Major, Strolz, thirteen), Jena, Zehdenick, Jonkovo, Hoff, Eylau, Friedland, Willemsdorf and Königsberg.

1808–1810: Service in the Peninsula and presence at Burgos, Talavera-de-la-Reina, Ocaña, Cadiz and Busaco.

1812: Fought with the Grande Armée at Borodino, Mojaïsk, and Winkovo.

1813: On the fields of Leipzig and Hanau.

1814: Engaged in the battles of Champaubert and Vauchamps.

1815: Present at Waterloo.

1 Brigadier of the élite company of the 22nd Dragoons, 1810
2 Brigadier of the 12th Dragoons in 'petite tenue'
3 Trooper of the 4th Dragoons in campaign dress

ANGUS McBRIDE

81

A

1 Musician of the 16th Dragoons in parade dress, 1810
2 Maréchal des Logis Chef of the 12th Dragoons, 1813
3 Trumpeter of a centre company of the 1st Dragoons
  in campaign dress, 1810

B

ANGUS McBRIDE

1 Trumpet-Major of the 13th Dragoons in campaign dress, 1808–13
2 Chef de Sapeurs of the 19th Dragoons, c. 1810
3 Trumpeter of the élite company of the 25th Dragoons in parade dress, 1813

C

1 Sous-Lieutenant of the 9th Dragoons in walking-out dress, 1805
2 Superior officer of the 20th Dragoons, campaign dress, 1806
3 Colonel of the 12th Dragoons in campaign dress, 1814

1 Trooper of the élite company of the 2nd Lancers in parade dress, 1811–14
2 Maréchal-Ferrant in stable dress, 1811–14
3 Trooper carabinier of the 5th Lancers, early 1812

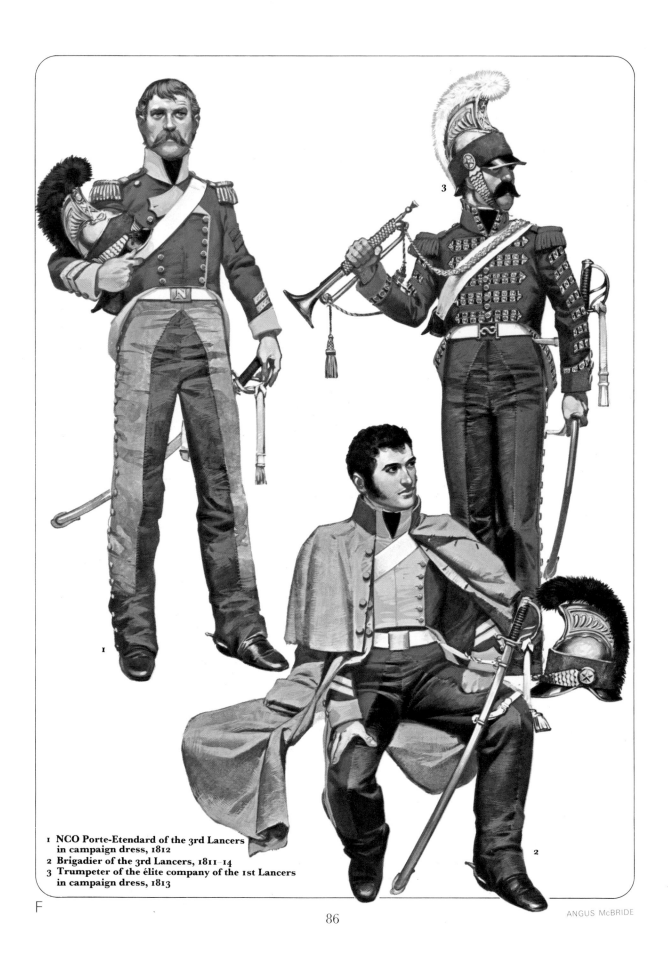

1 NCO Porte-Etendard of the 3rd Lancers
  in campaign dress, 1812
2 Brigadier of the 3rd Lancers, 1811–14
3 Trumpeter of the élite company of the 1st Lancers
  in campaign dress, 1813

F

ANGUS McBRIDE

1 Trumpeter, élite company, 1st Lancers,
  parade dress, 1815
2 Trumpeter, centre company, 3rd Lancers,
  campaign dress, 1812
3 Trumpeter, élite company, 5th Lancers,
  campaign dress, 1812

G

1 Major of the 6th Lancers in parade dress, 1811–14
2 Sous-Lieutenant of the 5th Lancers in campaign dress, 1813
3 Sous-Lieutenant of the 2nd Lancers in campaign dress, 1811–14

The 10th Regiment of Dragoons

Created in 1674 and named Mestre-de-Camp-Général in 1685. Renamed the 10eme Régiment de Dragons in 1791, it was subsequently transformed into the *5eme Régiment de Chevau-Légers Lanciers* in 1811. Newly entitled the Régiment de Lanciers d'Angoulême in 1814, it reverted to its numerical title for the '100 Days' and was finally dissolved after the campaign.

War record:

1803–1804: Stationed at the Camp de Boulogne for the proposed invasion of Great Britain.

1805: With the Grande Armée at Ulm and Austerlitz.

1806–1807: Took part in the battles of Eylau and Friedland attached to the Grande Armée.

1809–1811: Peninsula service: fought at Alba-de-Tormes, Ciudad Rodrigo and Fuentes d'Onoro (where Lieutenant Vesuty, leading the regiment's élite company, repulsed some 400 British hussars, taking many prisoners, and severely mauled a battalion of British infantry).

1812: Rejoined the Grande Armée for the battles of Borodino and Winkovo.

1813: Remained with the Grande Armée and fought at Wachau and Hanau.

1814: Engaged in the battle of Montmirail.

1815: On the fields of both Ligny and Waterloo.

The 11th Regiment of Dragoons

Formed by Royal commission at Tournai in 1674. In 1788 the regiment was presented to the Duke of Angoulême and received his name. In 1791 the regiment was retitled as the 11eme Régiment de Dragons. Following the restoration of the House of Bourbon, it was renamed the Régiment de Dragons de Berry (No. 6). After taking part in the 1815 campaign under its numerical title, the regiment was dissolved.

War record:

1805: Part of the Grande Armée at the battles of Landsberg, Ulm, Amstetten, Hollabrünn, Rausnitz and Austerlitz (where Colonel Bourdon was fatally wounded).

1806–1808: Remained with the Grande Armée and was present at Zehdenick, Prentzlov, Eylau and Friedland.

Left: an officer of an élite company wears the popular officers' overcoat; knee-length and double-breasted, it was entirely middle-green and decorated with silver buttons and the same epaulettes as would be worn on the tunic.
Right: an officer of a centre company in a cape of middle-green embellished with silver lace. While the overcoat was suitable for everyday wear, the cape was eminently more practical when mounted.

1809–1813: Took part in the following actions in the Peninsula: Alba-de-Tormes, Busaco, Redinha, Fuentes d'Onoro, Ciudad Rodrigo, Los Arapilos (Salamanca) and Vitoria.

1813: Attached to the 5th Corps of Cavalry of the Grande Armée at Leipzig and Hanau.

1814: Present at the battles of Saint-Dizier, Brienne, La Rothière and Montmirail.

1815: Stationed in Strasbourg, attached to the 6th Corps of Cavalry.

The 12th Regiment of Dragoons

Formed at Maestricht in 1675 in conjunction with some companies from Liège. Presented to the Count of Artois in 1774 and given his name. Became the 12eme Régiment de Dragons in 1791 but was renamed in 1814 the Régiment de Dragons d'Orléans (No. 7) with the restoration of Louis XVIII to the throne. Allotted the 1791 title once again in 1815 with the re-establishment of the Empire, the regiment was finally disbanded at Tours later that same year.

War record:

1805: Attached to the 5th Corps of the Reserve Cavalry and saw action at Wertingen, Ulm and Austerlitz.

1806: Part of the 3rd Division of Dragoons of the Grande Armée at Jena, Prentzlov and Nasielk.

1807: Present at Eylau, Heilsberg and Friedland.

1808–1813: Service in the Peninsula and presence at Burgos, Madrid, Medellin, Talavera, Almonacid, Ocaña, the Andalusian expedition, Alca-la-Real, Grenada, Venta-del-Baul, Huescar and Vitoria.

1813: With the Grande Armée at Danzig.

1814: Fought at the battle for Paris.

1815: Served with the Armée du Nord at Ligny and Namur.

1st Squadron	ΔΔΔΔΔΔΔΔΔΔΔΔΔΔΔΔΔΔΔΔΔΔΔΔΔ	1st Company
	ΔΔΔΔΔΔΔΔΔΔΔΔΔΔΔΔΔΔΔΔΔΔΔΔΔ	
	ΔΔΔΔΔΔΔΔΔΔΔΔΔΔΔΔΔΔΔΔΔΔΔΔΔ	
	ΔΔΔΔΔΔΔΔΔΔΔΔΔΔΔΔΔΔΔΔΔΔΔΔΔ	
	ΔΔΔΔΔΔΔΔΔΔΔΔΔΔΔΔΔΔΔΔΔΔΔΔΔ	5th Company
	ΔΔΔΔΔΔΔΔΔΔΔΔΔΔΔΔΔΔΔΔΔΔΔΔΔ	
	ΔΔΔΔΔΔΔΔΔΔΔΔΔΔΔΔΔΔΔΔΔΔΔΔΔ	
	ΔΔΔΔΔΔΔΔΔΔΔΔΔΔΔΔΔΔΔΔΔΔΔΔΔ	
2nd Squadron	ΔΔΔΔΔΔΔΔΔΔΔΔΔΔΔΔΔΔΔΔΔΔΔΔΔ	2nd Company
	ΔΔΔΔΔΔΔΔΔΔΔΔΔΔΔΔΔΔΔΔΔΔΔΔΔ	
	ΔΔΔΔΔΔΔΔΔΔΔΔΔΔΔΔΔΔΔΔΔΔΔΔΔ	
	ΔΔΔΔΔΔΔΔΔΔΔΔΔΔΔΔΔΔΔΔΔΔΔΔΔ	
	ΔΔΔΔΔΔΔΔΔΔΔΔΔΔΔΔΔΔΔΔΔΔΔΔΔ	6th Company
	ΔΔΔΔΔΔΔΔΔΔΔΔΔΔΔΔΔΔΔΔΔΔΔΔΔ	
	ΔΔΔΔΔΔΔΔΔΔΔΔΔΔΔΔΔΔΔΔΔΔΔΔΔ	
	ΔΔΔΔΔΔΔΔΔΔΔΔΔΔΔΔΔΔΔΔΔΔΔΔΔ	
3rd Squadron	ΔΔΔΔΔΔΔΔΔΔΔΔΔΔΔΔΔΔΔΔΔΔΔΔΔ	3rd Company
	ΔΔΔΔΔΔΔΔΔΔΔΔΔΔΔΔΔΔΔΔΔΔΔΔΔ	
	ΔΔΔΔΔΔΔΔΔΔΔΔΔΔΔΔΔΔΔΔΔΔΔΔΔ	
	ΔΔΔΔΔΔΔΔΔΔΔΔΔΔΔΔΔΔΔΔΔΔΔΔΔ	
	ΔΔΔΔΔΔΔΔΔΔΔΔΔΔΔΔΔΔΔΔΔΔΔΔΔ	7th Company
	ΔΔΔΔΔΔΔΔΔΔΔΔΔΔΔΔΔΔΔΔΔΔΔΔΔ	
	ΔΔΔΔΔΔΔΔΔΔΔΔΔΔΔΔΔΔΔΔΔΔΔΔΔ	
	ΔΔΔΔΔΔΔΔΔΔΔΔΔΔΔΔΔΔΔΔΔΔΔΔΔ	
4th Squadron	ΔΔΔΔΔΔΔΔΔΔΔΔΔΔΔΔΔΔΔΔΔΔΔΔΔ	4th Company
	ΔΔΔΔΔΔΔΔΔΔΔΔΔΔΔΔΔΔΔΔΔΔΔΔΔ	
	ΔΔΔΔΔΔΔΔΔΔΔΔΔΔΔΔΔΔΔΔΔΔΔΔΔ	
	ΔΔΔΔΔΔΔΔΔΔΔΔΔΔΔΔΔΔΔΔΔΔΔΔΔ	
	ΔΔΔΔΔΔΔΔΔΔΔΔΔΔΔΔΔΔΔΔΔΔΔΔΔ	8th Company
	ΔΔΔΔΔΔΔΔΔΔΔΔΔΔΔΔΔΔΔΔΔΔΔΔΔ	
	ΔΔΔΔΔΔΔΔΔΔΔΔΔΔΔΔΔΔΔΔΔΔΔΔΔ	
	ΔΔΔΔΔΔΔΔΔΔΔΔΔΔΔΔΔΔΔΔΔΔΔΔΔ	

A REGIMENT OF FOUR SQUADRONS DEPLOYED IN COLUMN

A regiment deployed in column, an ideal formation where impact was essential or when the field of battle was obstructed. Note the arrangement of the companies within each squadron. Each squadron comprised two companies of two troops who rode on a front of twenty-five with a depth of two.

The 13th Regiment of Dragoons

Formed in the Languedoc in 1676 and named the Condé-Dragons in 1724. Renamed the Comte-de-Province in 1774, then yet again as the Monsieur the same year. Retitled the 13eme Régiment de Dragons in 1791. Changed to the 8eme Régiment de Dragons (de Condé) in 1814, but resumed its former title for the 1815 campaign. The regiment was finally dissolved the 6th of December 1815.

War record:

1805–1806: Attached to the Grande Armée and engaged at the crossing of the Rhine at Kehl, the crossing of the Danube at Elchingen, Hollabrünn, Austerlitz, Nasielk and Pultusk.

1809–1812: Saw action in the Peninsula at Corunna, Oporto, the crossing of the Tagus at Arzobispo and the battle of Las Rosas.

1813: With the Grande Armée at Leipzig.

1814: Fought at Mormant and Saint-Dizier.

1815: On the battlefields of Wavre and Rocquencourt.

The 14th Regiment of Dragoons

Created 3 March 1672 by the Marquis of Seyssac. Named Chartres in 1758 and became a dragoon regiment in 1776 under the title of the Chartres-Dragons. Became the 14eme Régiment de Dragons in 1791, but were renamed the 9eme Régiment de Dragons under the Restoration. Having briefly returned to its 1791 title in 1815 under the Empire, the regiment was disbanded in December of the same year.

War record:

1805: With the Grande Armée at Wertingen and Austerlitz.

```
ΔΔΔΔΔΔΔΔΔΔΔΔΔΔΔΔΔΔΔΔΔΔΔΔ                          ΔΔΔΔΔΔΔΔΔΔΔΔΔΔΔΔΔΔΔΔΔΔΔΔ
ΔΔΔΔΔΔΔΔΔΔΔΔΔΔΔΔΔΔΔΔΔΔΔΔ                          ΔΔΔΔΔΔΔΔΔΔΔΔΔΔΔΔΔΔΔΔΔΔΔΔ
ΔΔΔΔΔΔΔΔΔΔΔΔΔΔΔΔΔΔΔΔΔΔΔΔ                          ΔΔΔΔΔΔΔΔΔΔΔΔΔΔΔΔΔΔΔΔΔΔΔΔ
ΔΔΔΔΔΔΔΔΔΔΔΔΔΔΔΔΔΔΔΔΔΔΔΔ                          ΔΔΔΔΔΔΔΔΔΔΔΔΔΔΔΔΔΔΔΔΔΔΔΔ
 ΔΔΔΔΔΔΔΔΔΔΔΔΔΔΔΔΔΔΔΔΔΔΔ                          ΔΔΔΔΔΔΔΔΔΔΔΔΔΔΔΔΔΔΔΔΔΔΔΔ
 ΔΔΔΔΔΔΔΔΔΔΔΔΔΔΔΔΔΔΔΔΔΔΔ                          ΔΔΔΔΔΔΔΔΔΔΔΔΔΔΔΔΔΔΔΔΔΔΔΔ
  ΔΔΔΔΔΔΔΔΔΔΔΔΔΔΔΔΔΔΔΔΔΔ                          ΔΔΔΔΔΔΔΔΔΔΔΔΔΔΔΔΔΔΔΔΔΔΔΔ
  ΔΔΔΔΔΔΔΔΔΔΔΔΔΔΔΔΔΔΔΔΔΔ   ΔΔΔΔΔΔΔΔΔΔΔΔΔΔΔΔΔΔΔΔΔΔΔΔ  ΔΔΔΔΔΔΔΔΔΔΔΔΔΔΔΔΔΔΔΔΔΔΔ   ΔΔΔΔΔΔΔΔΔΔΔΔΔΔΔΔΔΔΔΔΔΔΔΔ
                         ΔΔΔΔΔΔΔΔΔΔΔΔΔΔΔΔΔΔΔΔΔΔΔΔ                          ΔΔΔΔΔΔΔΔΔΔΔΔΔΔΔΔΔΔΔΔΔΔΔΔ
                         ΔΔΔΔΔΔΔΔΔΔΔΔΔΔΔΔΔΔΔΔΔΔΔΔ                          ΔΔΔΔΔΔΔΔΔΔΔΔΔΔΔΔΔΔΔΔΔΔΔΔ
                         ΔΔΔΔΔΔΔΔΔΔΔΔΔΔΔΔΔΔΔΔΔΔΔΔ                          ΔΔΔΔΔΔΔΔΔΔΔΔΔΔΔΔΔΔΔΔΔΔΔΔ
                         ΔΔΔΔΔΔΔΔΔΔΔΔΔΔΔΔΔΔΔΔΔΔΔΔ                          ΔΔΔΔΔΔΔΔΔΔΔΔΔΔΔΔΔΔΔΔΔΔΔΔ
                         ΔΔΔΔΔΔΔΔΔΔΔΔΔΔΔΔΔΔΔΔΔΔΔΔ                          ΔΔΔΔΔΔΔΔΔΔΔΔΔΔΔΔΔΔΔΔΔΔΔΔ
                         ΔΔΔΔΔΔΔΔΔΔΔΔΔΔΔΔΔΔΔΔΔΔΔΔ                          ΔΔΔΔΔΔΔΔΔΔΔΔΔΔΔΔΔΔΔΔΔΔΔΔ
                         ΔΔΔΔΔΔΔΔΔΔΔΔΔΔΔΔΔΔΔΔΔΔΔΔ                          ΔΔΔΔΔΔΔΔΔΔΔΔΔΔΔΔΔΔΔΔΔΔΔΔ
```

A REGIMENT OF FOUR SQUADRONS DEPLOYED IN ECHELON

This echelon formation was frequently adopted where the terrain permitted; it enabled cavalry to attack in devastating waves, the front squadrons drawing enemy fire in precisely the wrong direction from the imminent attack.

1806–1807: Still linked to the Grande Armée, saw action at Jena, Golymin, Watersdorf, Eylau, Heilsberg and Friedland.

1808–1811: Service in the Peninsula, engaged at Madrid, Medellin, Talavera, Ocaña, the siege of Cadiz, Alcanizas, La Gebora, Sabugal and Albufera.

1813: With the Grande Armée at the battles of Leipzig, Dennewitz and Danzig.

1814: Took part at the following actions during the French campaign: Montereau, Bar-sur-Aube and Arcis-sur-Aube.

1815: Fought at Charleroi, Ligny and Rocquencourt.

The 15th Regiment of Dragoons

Originally created as of 20 December 1688 by the Duke of Noailles, the regiment was formally listed as a dragoon unit in 1776. In 1791 the regiment was named the 15eme Régiment de Dragons. The return of the Bourbons in 1814 necessitated its renaming as the 10eme Régiment de Dragons. Assuming its old number for the 1815 campaign ensured the regiment's dissolution on 16 November 1815 at La Rochelle.

War record:

1805–1807: Attached to the Grande Armée at the battles of Ulm, Nordlingen, Austerlitz, Lübeck, Pultusk and Ostrolenka.

1808–1813: With both the armies of Spain and Portugal during the Peninsula campaign, attached to the reserve cavalry, and present at Ciudad Rodrigo, Busaco, Pombal, Redinha, Fuentes d'Onoro and Vitoria.

1813: Part of the 5th Corps of Cavalry on the fields of Leipzig and Hanau.

1814: Remained with the 5th Corps for the battles of Brienne, La Rothière, Nogent-sur-Seine and Mormant.

1815: Attached to the 5th Division of the Reserve Cavalry at Ligny and Rocquencourt.

The 16th Regiment of Dragoons

Formed of free corps and re-organized regiments' companies for the Duke of Orléans and named after him. Renamed the 16eme Régiment de Dragons in 1791 and, yet again in 1814, as the 11eme Régiment de Dragons. Returned briefly to its previous number on Napoleon's return and was consequently disbanded later the same year.

War record:

1805: With the Grande Armée at Austerlitz.

1806–1807: Remained with the Grande Armée and fought at Jena, Prentzlov, Bergfried, Eylau and Friedland.

1808–1813: Saw service in the Peninsula and engaged at Arzobispo, Talavera, Ocaña, Alca-Real, Malaga, Moralez and Vitoria. At Talavera, Lieutenant d'Ussel and his troop captured three standards.

1814: Saw action at Mormant, Valjouan, Bar-sur-Aube and Arcis-sur-Aube.

1815: Took part in the battle of Ligny.

The 17th Regiment of Dragoons

Created by the Comte de Saxe in 1743, with German, Polish and Rumanian volunteers, as a mixed regiment comprising three brigades of lancers and three of dragoons. Originally named the Volontaires de Saxe, the regiment was transformed into an entirely dragoon unit in 1762 and dubbed the Schönberg-Dragons. Retitled the 17eme Régiment de Dragons in 1791, it was again renumbered in 1814 as the 12eme Régiment de Dragons and yet again, in 1815, as the 18eme Régiment. The regiment was finally disbanded in 1815.

War record:

1805: Fought with the Grande Armée at Albeck and Austerlitz.

1806–1807: Remained with the Grande Armée and was present at the actions of Eylau, Mansfeld, Königsberg, Spanden and Friedland.

1808–1813: With the Army of Spain: Madrid, Benavente, Corunna, Braga, Amarante and Arzobispo; in Estramadura in 1810 and subsequently on the fields of Albufera, Villagarcia, Valencia, Torre and Vitoria.

1813: Part of the 10th Corps of the Grande Armée during the defence of Magdeburg.

1814: Part of the 6th Corps of Cavalry at Fontvannes, Troyes, Saint-Parre (where Colonel Lepic captured an enemy standard), Arcis-sur-Aube and Paris.

1815: Attached to the 6th Division of Reserve Cavalry during the Belgian campaign and fought at Ligny and Namur.

The 18th Regiment of Dragoons

Formed at Metz in 1744 with the sixteenth companies of the fifteen regiments of dragoons then existing, and named Le Roi. Renamed the 18eme Régiment de Dragons in 1791. In 1814 the regiment was renumbered as the 13eme Régiment de Dragons only to finally return, in 1815, to the title of 18eme. Disbanded shortly thereafter at Lunel.

War record:

1805: Part of the 4th Division of Dragoons of the Reserve Cavalry of the Grande Armée and present at Elchingen and Austerlitz.

1806–1807: Remained attached to the Reserve Cavalry and took part at Nordhausen, Sandow, Lübeck, Graudenz, Mohrüngen, Spandau and Friedland.

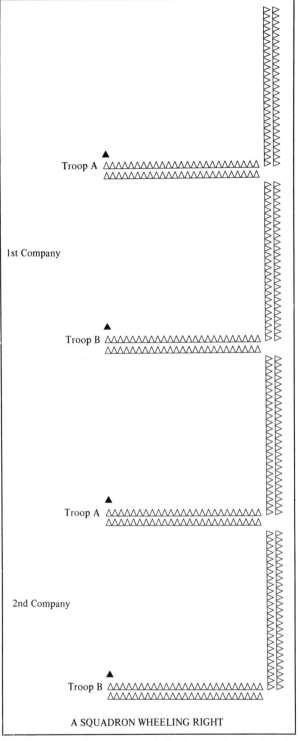

A SQUADRON WHEELING RIGHT

Squadrons marched at around 6-7 km an hour with the companies either close behind one another or, as in this case, at frontal length distance. This enabled the companies to wheel right or left into an assault line, ready within seconds to be launched into action. As illustrated, the troops would pivot on the end man, performing an arc to dress the line.

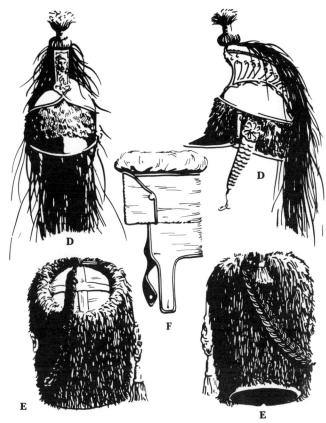

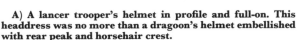

A) A lancer trooper's helmet in profile and full-on. This headdress was no more than a dragoon's helmet embellished with rear peak and horsehair crest.

B) The slightly modified version issued to NCO's; it differed only in its more elegant line. Both helmets were entirely copper with a brown fur turban.

C) The middle-green fatigue cap issued to dragoons and lancers prior to the adoption of the Pokalem model (F) in 1812. The lace was white, as was the tassel in most cases, and the piping was of the regimental colour. The regimental number was frequently added to the front.

D) The dragoon helmet in profile and full-on. The horsehair

mane became increasingly thin as the years wore on, but the shape of the helmet altered but little. The head-dress was entirely copper with a brown turban of fur. Note the plume holder just in front of the left side chinscale rosace.

E) The bearskin of élite troopers. The rear patch is red with a white cross of lace upon it; the cords and tassels are also red, the former passing on the left side beneath a tricolour cockade. This head-gear was often fitted with chinscales identical to the helmet.

F) The Pokalem model fatigue cap. The ear-flaps folded up and were buttoned to a single cloth-covered button on each side when not in use.

1808–1813: With the 4th Division of Dragoons of the Army of Spain at Somo-Sierra, Madrid, Corunna, the invasion of Portugal, Oporto, Arzobispo and Las Rosas.

1813: Attached to the Grande Armée and fought at Dresden, Leipzig and Hanau.

1814: Engaged at Saint-Dizier, Brienne and La Rothière.

The 19th Regiment of Dragoons

Created by the Decree of 27 February 1793 of the Volontaires d'Angers and named the 19eme Régiment de Dragons. Renumbered as the 14eme Régiment in 1814 only to be retitled the 19eme shortly before its dissolution at Moulins in September of 1815.

War record:

1805: Part of the 4th Division of Dragoons of the Grande Armée and engaged at Elchingen and Austerlitz.

1806–1807: Remained with the Grande Armée for the actions of Jena, Lübeck, Mohrüngen and Friedland.

1808–1813: Attached to the 4th Division of Dragoons with both the armies of Spain and Portugal; fought at Corunna, Morentase, Braga, Oporto, Arzobispo, Las Rosas, Medina Cœli and Vitoria.

1813–1814: With the 5th Corps of Cavalry of the Grande Armée at Dresden (where Captain Ponsonnet with only ten dragoons broke through an infantry square and made off with no less than three cannon), Flemingen, Wachau, Leipzig, Danzig, Saint-Dizier, Brienne, La Rothière, Mormant, Les Trois-Maisons and the second action at Saint-Dizier. Having played a vital role in covering the retreat of the Grande Armée, Commandant Cosnard and Lieutenant Mollard of the 19eme received a citation and the Cross of the Legion of Honour respectively.

1815: Attached to the Armée du Rhin and engaged at the minor actions of Ober-Hausbergen and Mittel-Hausbergen.

The 20th Regiment of Dragoons

Created in July of 1793 of the Régiment de Dragons de Hainault et Jemappes and named the 20eme Régiment de Dragons. Renumbered the 15eme

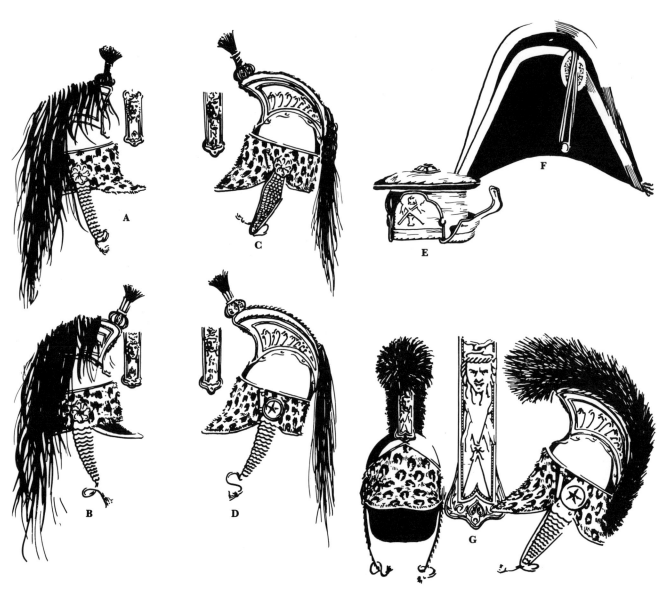

Figures A through D demonstrate the changing shape of dragoon officers' head-gear through the years: A) 1804–07; B) 1806–10; C) 1808–12 and D) 1810–14. The helmets were of copper with leopard skin turbans.

E) The officers' model of the Pokalem fatigue cap. Prior to its introduction in 1812, a pattern identical to that of the troops was worn, but laced in silver rather than in white. This particular one is that of an officer of lancers, as evinced by the crossed-lance patch on the front, but a dragoon's would differ only in the use of a silver grenade patch in its stead. It is

middle-green and laced and piped in the regimental colour.

F) An officer's bicorn, 1810. Earlier models of this head-dress were less tall and the folded-up brim was generally of equal length all the way round. But, as civilian couture demanded, the bicorns of later years tend to be increasingly high, stiff and with brims of unequal width.

G) A lancer officer's helmet. As that of dragoons, officers of lancers had more elegant helmets with turbans of leopard skin. The front plate of the copper crest differed in that it had the familiar crossed-lance device embellished upon it.

Régiment de Dragons in 1814. With the return of Napoleon, the regiment was retitled the 20eme. Dissolved in July of 1815.

War record:
1805: With the 1st Division of Dragoons of the Grande Armée at Wertingen, Memmingen, Neresheim (where Brigadier Blondel seized an enemy standard for which he was subsequently presented with the Cross of the Legion of Honour), Ulm and Austerlitz.
1806–1807: Remained with the Grande Armée and engaged at Jena, Pultusk, Eylau, Heilsberg and Friedland.
1808–1812: Took part in the following actions in Spain: Andujar, Tudela, Ucles, Ciudad-Real, Almonacid, Ocaña, Los Arapilos (Salamanca), Pampeluna and Tamames.
1813–1814: Part of the 5th Corps of Cavalry of the Grande Armée and fought at Leipzig, Dresden and Hanau.
1814: On the fields of Saint-Dizier, Brienne, La Rothière, Mormant, Montereau and Troyes during the campaign of France.
1815: Attached to the 2nd Corps of Cavalry of the Armée du Nord and engaged at Ligny, Waterloo and Rocquencourt.

The 21st Regiment of Dragoons
Originally created in April of 1796 with the Cavalerie de Légion de la Police and named the 21eme Régiment de Dragons. Disbanded in April of 1797. Recreated in 1801 from the Piedmontese 1st Regiment of Dragoons (Piedmont having been annexed to France that year) and again numbered the 21eme Régiment de Dragons. The regiment was finally disbanded in August of 1814.

War record:
1805: With the Grande Armée at Ulm and Austerlitz.
1806–1807: Remained with the Grande Armée and present at Prentzlow, Eylau and Königsberg.
1808–1812: Engaged at Almonacid in the Peninsula Campaign as well as the following small actions: Massaruleque, Martos, Fuengirola, Estepona and Osuna.
1813: With the Grande Armée at Jüterbock and Leipzig. Attached to the Army of Spain and fought

at Miranda and Vitoria.
1814: With the Grande Armée at Fontvannes, Troyes and Montmirail.

The 22nd Regiment of Dragoons
Raised in Piedmont in 1635 and named Orléans. In 1647, Anne of Austria purchased the regiment for her son the Duke of Anjou and renamed it the Régiment d'Anjou. Resumed its title of the Régiment d'Orléans in 1660 only to be disbanded the following year. The regiment was eventually recreated in 1665. Renamed the 13eme Régiment de Cavalerie in 1791 and yet again, in 1803, as the 22eme Régiment de Dragons. The unit was finally disbanded in May 1814.

War record:
1805: With the Grande Armée at both Ulm and Austerlitz.
1806–1807: Remained with the Grande Armée for the actions of Jena, Eylau, Ostrolenka and Friedland.
1808–1813: Took part in the following actions in the Peninsula: Baylen (where Lieutenant Ancelin captured an enemy standard), Mora, Braga, Barcellos, Oporto, Valverde, Alicante, Elche, Almanza and Las Rosas.
1813: Engaged at Strehla, Naumburg, Flemingen and Leipzig during the Saxon Campaign.
1814: The 3rd and 4th squadrons fought at Saint-Dizier during the Campaign of France.

The 23rd Regiment of Dragoons
Raised in Turin by the Duke of Savoy in 1670 as the Royal-Piémont. It was ceded to France the following year and renamed the Prince-de-Piémont. In 1690 it returned to its previous title. Retitled the 14eme Régiment de Cavalerie in 1791, and again, in 1803, as the 23eme Régiment de Dragons. The regiment was dissolved in 1814.

War record:
1804–1806: Attached to the Army of Italy and engaged at Verona and the crossing of the Tagliamento.
1806: Briefly transferred to the Army of Naples.
1809: Again with the Army of Italy, at Sacile, Piave, San-Daniel and Wagram.
1812: With the Grande Armée at Borodino (La

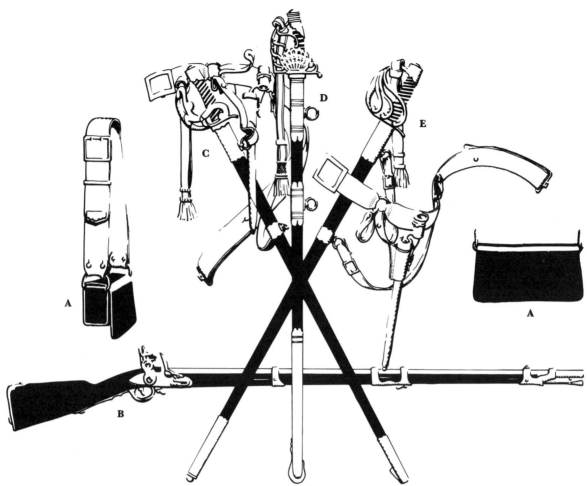

Dragoons' equipment.

A) Troopers' pattern cartridge-pouch. Suspended on a blancoed crossbelt passed over the left shoulder, the black leather cartridge-pouch contained the powder-and-ball cartridges for the musketoon. The model illustrated, the 1801 pattern, was in use throughout the wars.

B) The An IX pattern musketoon. This replaced the infantry muskets issued to dragoons under the Consulate for lack of supply, and was later in turn replaced by the An XI model which differed but little. Dragoons were also issued pistols; the brass-mounted 1763 pattern and the steel-furnished Republican model both saw continuous use throughout the Empire period.

C) The An IV model sabre and 1801 pattern swordbelt. The sabre has iron fittings though a similar type of sabre with copper guard is also in use until the eventual introduction of the An IX, XI or XII patterns. Note the strap attached to the swordbelt's first copper ring designed to hold the bayonet socket in place. The knot on the guard of the sabre was white.

D) The officers' sabre was fitted in gilt and came in two slightly different types, the one entirely straight and the other lightly curved. This sabre was only worn on service and was replaced by a straight épée for everyday wear.

E) The copper guard distinguishes this An XII model troopers' sabre from its predecessor. The copper-fitted swordbelt is the 1812 pattern.

Moskowa), Mojaïsk and Berezina.

1813: Remained attached to the Grande Armée and engaged at Dresden (where Captain Gegout captured two cannon and General Szecsen; Adjutant Agoustène seized an enemy standard; and Maréchal des Logis Brouvères captured a Russian general) and Leipzig.

1814: Fought at Vertus and Paris during the Campaign of France.

The 24th Regiment of Dragoons

Raised in 1761 and named the Royal-Lorraine.

Renamed the 16eme Regiment de Cavalerie in 1791 and again, in 1792, as the 15eme Régiment de Cavalerie (following the defection of the 15th Regiment, ex-Royal-Allemand). Became the 24eme Régiment de Dragons in 1803. Disbanded in June 1814.

War record:

1805: With the Army of Italy at Tagliamento and Caldiero.

1806: Attached to the Army of Naples.

1808–1813: Fought in the following actions in the

Peninsula: Rosas, Cardedeu, Molins-del-Rey, Wals, San-Columa, Tarragona, Villa-Real, Sagonte (where Captain Devons seized a Spanish standard), Castalla and the Ordal Pass.

1813: With the Grande Armée at Jüterbock.

1814: An unspecified detachment took part in the Campaign of France.

The 25th Regiment of Dragoons

Created in 1665 and named the Bourgogne in 1685, after the Duke of Bourgogne. Renamed Bretagne in 1711 after the Duke of Bourgogne's son. In 1751, resumed its previous title. Retitled Royal-Bourgogne in 1788. Became the 17eme Régiment de Cavalerie in 1791 but renumbered the 16eme the following year. Retitled the 25eme Régiment

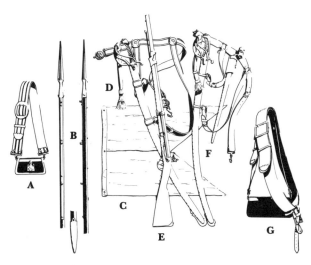

Lancers' equipment.

A) **Officers' pattern cartridge-pouch. This is one of many varieties employed by lancer officers, others include those of black leather, edged in gold lace and those, like this one, of scarlet but with five stripes of gold lace down the body instead of three. The gold Imperial eagle device on the pouch flap was often replaced by a crowned N.**

B) **The tip of the lance. The lance was a total length of 2.75m, ending in the iron foot illustrated. Note the 'buttons' to which the pennant (C) attached.**

D) **The officers' pattern sabre. It differs very little from the troopers' model but has a gilt guard. The swordbelt is one of many adopted by the officers and is scarlet edged in gold lace with gilt fittings.**

E) **The An IX pattern musketoon. This was at first only issued to lanciers-carabiniers but towards the end of 1811, all lancers already equipped with lances received one complete with crossbelt and sling. It is likely that troopers only retained either the lance or the musketoon, discarding the other as a useless burden.**

F) **The An IX model light cavalry sabre, as used by troopers. The swordbelt is narrower than that issued to dragoons and has a serpent-S buckle; but patterns with solid or frame buckles were not uncommon, and where the solid square buckle was used, it was frequently decorated with either a crowned N or an Imperial eagle.**

G) **The troopers' cartridge-pouch and the musketoon sling and crossbelt.**

de Dragons in 1803 and finally disbanded in 1814.

War record:

1805: With the Grande Armée at Elchingen and Austerlitz.

1806–1807: Remained with the Grande Armée throughout the Prussian campaign and engaged at Halberstadt and Ostrolenka.

1808–1813: Took part in the following actions in Spain: Baylen, Lugo, Alba-de-Tormes. Subsequently attached to the Army of Portugal and engaged at Almeida, Torres-Vedras, Fuentes d'Onoro, Los Arapilos (Salamanca) and Vitoria.

1813: With the Grande Armée at Dresden and Leipzig (where Colonel Montigny was mortally wounded).

1814: Fought at Saint-Dizier, Brienne, La Rothière, Mormant, La Fère-Champenoise and Paris during the Campaign of France.

The 26th Regiment of Dragoons

Created in and named after the province of Roussillon in 1673. Renamed Berry in 1690 after the Duke of Berry. Became the 18eme Régiment de Cavalerie in 1791 but renumbered the 17eme the following year. Renamed the 26eme Régiment de Dragons in 1803 and disbanded at Nantes in 1814.

War record:

1805: Attached to the Reserve Cavalry of the Grande Armée and engaged at Wertingen, Albeck, Neresheim and Austerlitz.

1806–1807: Fought at Jena, Waltersdorf, Hoff, Eylau, Heilsberg and Friedland.

1808–1813: Engaged in the following actions in the Peninsula: Tudela, Uclés, Medellin, Talavera-de-la-Reina, Ocaña, Olivenza, Badajoz, Gebora, Albuquerque, Campo-Major, Puente-del-Mæstro and Vitoria.

1814: Part of the 6th Corps of Cavalry during the Campaign of France and present at Craonne, Sens, Laon, La Fère-Champenoise and Paris.

The 27th Regiment of Dragoons

Created in 1674 by Count Victor-Maurice de Broglie. Named the Royal-Normandie in 1762. Became the 19eme Régiment de Cavalerie in 1791 to be renumbered the following year as the 18eme. Retitled the 27eme Régiment de Dragons in 1803 and disbanded in August 1814.

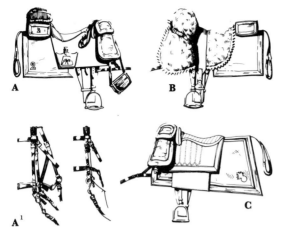

Dragoons' saddlery and harness.
A) Saddle and accessories of troopers, 1801 pattern. Note the patch attached to the skirt for a spare horseshoe and the 'boot' for the butt of the musketoon slung beneath the covered pistol holster.
A¹) The headstall and reins of troopers' horses, 1801 model.
B) Saddle and accessories of troopers, 1812 pattern. The bridle and reins remained the same as the 1801 pattern.
C) Saddle and accessories of officers for parade. A popular practice was to cover the front of the saddle with a black shabraque.

War record:
1805: Attached to the 4th Division of Dragoons of the Cavalry Reserve of the Grande Armée and engaged at Elchingen, Ulm and Austerlitz.
1806–1807: Remained with the same unit and fought at Biezun, Spanden and Friedland.
1808–1811: Part of the 4th Division of Dragoons of the 2nd Corps of the Army of Spain. Took part in the invasion of Portugal and was present at Corunna, the Ave passage, Oporto, Arzobispo, Albufera, Elvas and Las Vertientes.
1812–1813: With both the armies of Spain and the Midi and engaged at Villagarcia, Valencia de las Torres and Santa-Martha.
1813: Part of the 3rd Corps of Cavalry of the Grande Armée and fought at Neuss.
1814: Attached to the 6th Corps of Cavalry during the Campaign of France and engaged at Bar-sur-Aube and Arcis-sur-Aube.

The 28th Regiment of Dragoons
Raised at Saint-Germain in 1792 and named the 1er Corps des Hussards de la Liberté. Renamed the 7eme Régiment de Hussards (bis) in 1794. Became the 28eme Régiment de Dragons in 1803 and was dissolved in 1814.

War record:
1805–1811: Attached to the armies of Italy and

Naples and present at Gaëte, La Piave and Wagram.
1812: With the Grande Armée at Smolensk, Borodino (La Moskowa) and Berezina.
1813: Fought with the Grande Armée at Dresden, Leipzig and Hanau.
1814: With the 1st Corps of Cavalry during the Campaign of France and engaged at Vauchamps and La Fère-Champenoise.

The 29th Regiment of Dragoons
Raised in Turin from the 11th Hussars in 1803 and named the 29eme Régiment de Dragons. Became the *6eme Régiment de Chevau-Légers Lanciers* in 1811. Renamed the Régiment de Lanciers de Berry in 1814 but returned to its previous title for the '100 Days' campaign. Disbanded at Carcassonne in December 1815.

War record:
1805: With the Army of Italy at Caldiero, the crossing of the Brenta, Vicence and San-Pietro.
1806–1808: Attached to the Army of Naples and engaged at Lauria and the Abruzzes campaign.
1809: Returned to the Army of Italy, fought at La Piave, Laybach, Raab and Wagram.
1812: Part of the 9th Brigade of Light Cavalry attached to the 3rd Corps of the Grande Armée at Krasnoe, Smolensk, Valoutina, Borodino, Viasma and Berezina.
1813–1814: With the 4th Division of Light cavalry of the 2nd Corps of Cavalry of the Grande Armée at Jauer, Leipzig and Hanau.
1814: Engaged at Champaubert, Montmirail, Vauchamps, Arcis-sur-Aube and Saint-Dizier during the Campaign of France.
1815: Part of the 6th Corps of Cavalry, then the 2nd Division of Light Cavalry attached to the 2nd Corps of the Armée du Nord, at the actions of Fleurus and Waterloo.

The 30th Regiment of Dragoons
Created at Moulins from the 12th Hussars in 1803 and named the 30eme Régiment de Dragons. The regiment was dissolved in October 1815.

War record:
1805: With the Army of Italy at Verona, Caldiero, Olmo, Citadella, Lestizza, Morsana, Villach,

Klagenfurth and Gaëte.

1809: Remained with the Army of Italy and engaged at the Tagliamento crossing, Udine, Gratz, Stein-am-Anger, the Danube crossing, Wagram, Nikolsburg and the Westernitz bridge action.

1812: With the Grande Armée at Bautzen, Dresden, Leipzig and the Rhine crossing.

1814: Fought at Brienne, La Rothière, Champaubert, Montmirail, Montereau, Arcis-sur-Aube, La Fère-Champenoise and Paris during the Campaign of France.

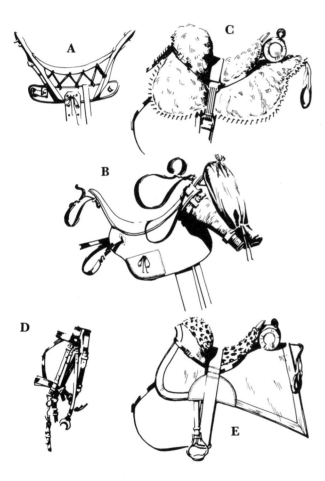

Lancers' saddlery and harness.
  A) The basic tree of the Hungarian-style light cavalry saddle employed by lancers.
  B) The tree covered in leather, here we see the pistol holsters, the rolled greatcoat and the spare horseshoe pocket.
  C) The saddle covered in the characteristic shabraque. The 'wolves' teeth' edging would be of the regimental colour. The middle-green portemanteau strapped behind the cantle was edged in yellow lace.
  D) Troopers' bridle and reins as specified by the 1812 Regulations.
  E) The officers' saddle complete with middle-green cloth shabraque, edged in gold lace, and leopard skin-covered pommel and seat.

The Plates

The Dragoons

A1: Brigadier of the élite company of the 22nd Dragoons, 1810.

The fur bearskin and epaulettes of this NCO reveal his status as an élite cavalryman. Here scarlet, the ornaments adorning the head-dress of élite troopers of other regiments were frequently either white or red; another regimental variation was the wearing of aiguillettes about the left shoulder. Company, if not individual, differences include the addition of a copper grenade badge to the cartridge-pouch and the adoption of a solid belt buckle bearing the same grenade symbol.

Troopers would be dressed more or less identically, save for the rank stripes on the forearm, as would the officers, except for silver cords and tassels on the bearskin and silver epaulettes. Trumpeters were at this period (1810) dressed in reverse colours—lemon yellow tunic with middle-green facings—and sported a white plume with lemon yellow tip, for centre companies, or scarlet if élite; the facings were laced in white and white epaulettes or trefoils were worn. The regiment was at this time in the Peninsula.

(Illustration after Cmndt. Bucquoy)

A2: Brigadier of the 12th Dragoons in 'petite tenue'.

He wears the pre-1812 fatigue-cap, the popular surtout and overalls. This figure is unusual in several respects. The surtout tunic, most frequently plain, has here the collar of regimental colour, the rank insignia and the shoulder-straps of the habit (as worn by *A1*). The overalls are devoid of the leather-reinforced inside leg and cuffs, and buttons the length of the outer seams, but supplemented by twin flap pockets.

As of 1812, dragoons were issued with fatigue-caps of the Pokalem variety, as that of *E2*, but with a grenade or regimental number patch on the front. At this period, troopers would wear a similar surtout, but from 1809 it was no longer issued to any bar NCO's and officers.

(Illustration after Benigni)

99

Eagle and guidon of the 23rd Dragoons. The total height of the eagle was 2.10 metres and the guidon measured 70 × 60 centimetres. Many eagles and guidons were lost during the wars at the following engagements:
1805 campaign: **Battle of Haslach:**
—That of the 2nd Squadron of the 15th Dragoons.
—That of a squadron of the 17th Dragoons.
1812 campaign:
—At Viasma: that of the 28th Dragoons.
—At Berezina: that of the 3rd Lancers.
Peninsula campaign:
—At the capitulation of the Madrid arsenal: that of the 13th Dragoons.

A3: Trooper of the 4th Dragoons in campaign dress.

This trooper on campaign in the Peninsula wears the familiar dragoon helmet and tunic. The tunic or habit was secured by a series of hooks and eyes down the breast; the skirts were folded back into turnbacks, stitched together and adorned with the grenade symbol common to heavy troops. He carries the familiar An XIII pattern sabre.

Of considerable interest are his baggy saroual-style trousers. Frequently obliged to replace their breeches and overalls as best they could on campaign, many French troops are represented in the Peninsula as having trousers made of brown fabric filched from stocks destined for the fabrication of monks' habits; this rough and ready material was very hard-wearing. Short ankle gaiters gather the trousers at the lower calf, a practical measure in a world without bicycle clips. The red stripes on the figure's left upper arm indicate that the wearer has seen between sixteen and twenty years service.
(Illustration after Fort)

B1: Musician of the 16th Dragoons in parade dress, 1810.

Musicians were attached to all regiments of this period, either on a permanent basis or hired as occasion demanded. The distinctive dress of musicians as often as not consisted of the simple replacement of the epaulettes by trefoil shoulder-straps on a trumpeter's habit. In this case, however, he wears white-fringed epaulettes on a tunic identical to that of the troops except for the lace on the facings. This was no doubt a move towards economy, since trumpeters of this regiment wore habits of pink cloth faced in middle-green with white lace. Musicians were issued bicorns instead of helmets. These black felt head-dresses were permeable and were therefore covered in a protective waterproof cloth on campaign. The tall plume inserted behind the cockade was worn solely in parade dress and was otherwise packed in the portemanteau of the saddle.
(Illustration after Fort)

B2: Maréchal des Logis Chef of the 12th Dragoons, 1813.

This senior NCO of the élite company demonstrates the changes in dress of dragoons post-1812. Although the 1812 Regulations prescribed that thereafter élite troops were to adopt the helmet common to all dragoons with the sole distinction of a red plume, the *Masses d'Habillement* edited by Magimel in 1812 relates the retention of the bearskin for dragoons, chasseurs and hussars. This contradiction left the matter to the personal decision of the colonel of each regiment.

The figure wears the new habit-veste; fastening to the waist (again by hooks and eyes) and with considerably shorter skirts, this garment was issued to all line regiments. The facing colours remained identical to those of the old habit. As rank distinctions, we note the silver lace on both forearms and the silver crescents on the red epaulettes, distinctive of élite companies. Also of note is the 'wolves' teeth' cut of the leather reinforcements of his overalls—a popular cut throughout the Empire period.
(Illustration after Benigni)

B3: Trumpeter of a centre company of the 1st Dragoons in campaign dress, 1810.

This fellow illustrates a fairly frequent departure from the normal practice of dressing trumpeters in the reverse colours of those of the troops. The tunic

100

adopted is the ordinary surtout decorated on the collar and down the breast with orange lace. The lace is stitched around five of the nine buttons of this high-waisted garment. Normally devoid of colour on the turnbacks, this surtout has turnbacks of regimental colour and green grenade patches thereon. He wears the usual pattern of overalls save for the strip of regimental colour piping along the length of the outer leg. He holds the standard cavalry trumpet as drawn in the Bardin MS of 1812. The cord and tassels, most frequently of yellow and green mixed thread, are in this case red.

Numbering two per squadron, trumpeters rode greys instead of bays or chestnuts. Their riding with the squadron into action necessitated the numerous differences in dress and mount so that they might be readily found for the speedy transmission of orders.
(Illustration after the Marckolsheim MS)

C1 : Trumpet-Major of the 13th Dragoons in campaign dress, 1808–1813.

The pink surtout tunic with middle-green facings is typical of the reverse colour method of distinguishing trumpeters. The silver lace and rank insignia would also decorate his habit, as would the silver grenade devices on the turnbacks and the silver service stripes on his left arm. This figure also wears overalls of similar cut and pattern to breeches; note the gaiters worn over them (to which attach the boot straps). His waist-belt is secured by a solid buckle with the flaming grenade symbol embossed upon it, a popular deviation.

A trumpeter of the same regiment has been recorded by the pen of El Guil in the Peninsula. His dress is identical save for the rank stripes and the substitution of white for silver lace. His helmet has been covered by a green protective cloth and, more interestingly, his saddle-cloth too with black, waxed fabric.
(Illustration after Fort)

C2 : Chef de Sapeurs of the 19th Dragoons, c.1810.

His regular habit is garnished with silver rank distinctions, service stripes and the famous crossed-axe patches of sappers. We notice that the red epaulettes' fringes are of mixed ponceau and silver thread. His profession is indicated by the large and lethal axe he is engaged in sharpening, the long buff apron and the bearskin. Dragoons were the only type of cavalry to enjoy the privilege of sappers, a tradition descended from the times when dragoons were strictly mounted infantrymen. His bearskin is without its red plume and white cords; their removal was common practice while on active service lest they became unnecessarily worn or damaged.

Of interest is the copper Medusa's head badge on his axe-case crossbelt. Such ornament was not unusual on the crossbelts of both sappers and élite troopers, though it might equally take the form of a grenade device.
(Illustration after Valmont)

C3 : Trumpeter of the élite company of the 25th Dragoons in parade dress, 1813.

This figure demonstrates not only the change to Imperial Livery by most regiments after 1812, but also the distinguishing features of élite trumpeters. The helmet has the white crest accorded to trumpeters with the addition of a red plume distinctive of élite troops. The tunic is the type specified in the 1812 Regulations, for which a special lace was devised. The lace was an alternating design of capital N's (for Napoleon) and Imperial eagles, and came in two varieties, the one for horizontal and the other for vertical use. The front of the coat was fastened with nine buttons descending to the waist, of which five had horizontal lace embellishment not dissimilar to that on the tunic of illustration B3; the lace employed was, of course, the same as we see here decorating the rear of the habit. The epaulettes are further indication of this trumpeter's élite status.

In this case, the trumpet cords and tassels are the familiar mixed green and yellow variety. Trumpet banners, so frequent pre-1812 for parade dress, were by now discontinued owing to the imbalance between their cost and their utility.
(Illustration after Roux from 'La Giberne')

D1 : Sous-Lieutenant of the 9th Dragoons in walking-out dress, 1805.

This officer sports the popular surtout often worn in all but parade-dress. Peeping above the collar is the

starched collar of his chemise. This garment was worn beneath a waistcoat which is in this case round-bottomed and possibly double-breasted. His breeches are plain, but Hungarian breeches, with matching middle-green knots astride the front flap edges and lace down the outer seams, were not unusual. His boots are of the Hungarian pattern; similar ones with the addition of silver tassels in the V's of the front were not uncommon. The tall bicorn was worn in both walking-out and ball dress. Heavy silver tassels were frequently added to the corners to make for still grander appearance. The slim-bladed épée shown here was one of many patterns carried by officers in ball and walking-out dress; of note is the finer knot attached to it than that tied to the sabre. This particular model of épée was also issued to musicians.
(Illustration after Benigni)

D2: Superior officer of the 20th Dragoons, campaign dress, 1806.

This officer in pre-1812 uniform wears a helmet of slightly different pattern to that of *D3*. As the habits became of slimmer cut with the influence of civilian high-fashion, so the helmets became increasingly Grecian in aspect; this model has the distinctive rosaces and fur-less peak of the early varieties. The tunic is intrinsically no different from that of the rank and file, though made of finer fabric and equipped with silver buttons and grenade patches. His overalls are, unusually, buff with twin hip-height, flapped pockets secured by single, cloth-covered buttons.
(Reconstruction)

D3: Colonel of the 12th Dragoons in campaign dress, 1814.

This senior officer is wearing the new habit-veste of officer pattern. Essentially the same as that issued to the troops, it has longer tails, is made of superior cloth and has silver buttons and heavy bullion epaulettes. His helmet is of the more elegant and expensive kind habitually worn by officers. Of note are the fine plume and the knotted horsehair mane of this headgear which, with the leopard skin turban, speak of the rank of the owner. Worthy of attention are his black, cuffed leather gloves and black leather swordbelt, a departure from the norm

which was no doubt afforded by his position.
(Illustration after Benigni)

The Lancers

E1: Trooper of the élite company of the 2nd Lancers in parade dress, 1811–1814.

Here we see the standard uniform of troopers of Chevau-légers Lanciers for parade dress. The dragoon pattern helmet is embellished with a horsehair crest and back-peak. The red plume indicates his belonging to an élite company, as do the epaulettes, in lieu of shoulder-straps, on the habit. Unlike the similar habit-veste of dragoons, this tunic could not only be fastened by hooks and eyes, but also by crossing either of the lapels across the chest to button up on the opposite side—thereby obscuring the facing colour, as on *E3*. The Hungarian breeches are tucked into Hungarian boots piped and adorned with tassels on their upper edge. The lace on the breeches was standard for the 1st through 4th Regiments, but the 5th and 6th opted for Hungarian knots on either side of the front flap instead of the reversed 'arrow-head'. Of note is the copper grenade badge on the crossbelt, a common addition by troops of élite companies of both dragoons and lancers.
(Illustration after Rousselot)

E2: Maréchal-Ferrant in stable dress, 1811–1814.

His profession is indicated by the red horse-shoe patch on the right upper arm of his plain stable jacket. The tools of his trade are conveniently tucked into the folds of his hitched-up apron, ready at a moment's notice to enable him to reshoe a mount.

Carelessly slung on a branch behind his head is his fatigue-cap. Of the Pokalem model, this head-dress was common to both lancers and dragoons of this period, proving a more practical type than its predecessor. Its descending ear-flaps were a neat arrangement, buttoned under the jaw when in use, or to the copper buttons on each side of the cap with the ends slipped inside the turban, when not. The crossed lances on the front were sometimes replaced by the regimental number.
(Illustration based on Leliepvre)

E3: Trooper carabinier of the 5th Lancers, early 1812.

Originally, musketoons were reserved only for chevau-légers carabiniers, to whom a second crossbelt was issued to which it might be clipped. The figure is wearing just such a belt over his left shoulder, the musketoon clip resting against the cartridge-pouch. He carries his waistbelt in his hand and we can see the bayonet frog which was attached to the middle section of the sabre belt. We notice that, unlike the élite trooper next to him, he has simple shoulder straps instead of epaulettes on his tunic and that the lapels have been crossed over to reveal but a narrow strip of piping of the facing colour. The overalls are non-regulation in that they are grey instead of the prescribed medium green, and have no lace along the outer leg.
(Illustration based on Rousselot)

F1: NCO Porte-Etendard of the 3rd Lancers in campaign dress, 1812.

This Maréchal des Logis Chef standard bearer was accorded the honour of carrying the regimental standard owing to his being the eldest NCO of the élite company. The rank insignia on his forearms are gold, while his epaulettes are fringed with mixed gold and ponceau thread. On his left upper arm are two service stripes denoting between sixteen and twenty years service. His swordknot is worth noting in that the tassel is of the same mixture of threads as his epaulette fringing.

The standard, or Eagle as it was more correctly termed, was a total height of 2.10 metres; the flag proper was 55 × 55cm and edged with a golden fringe 2.5cm in width. For parades, a tricolour scarf was tied in a bow about the Eagle socket.
(Illustration after Rigondaud)

F2: Brigadier of the 3rd Lancers, 1811–1814.

Here we can clearly see the new model overcoat issued to lancers and dragoons as of 1812. It has four cloth-covered buttons on the cape and five on the body with which to fasten the whole. The crossbelts would be worn over the top of the coat proper, with the cape to protect them. His rank is denoted by the chevrons of lace on each forearm of the tunic and by the slightly modified shape of the

helmet. His overalls are the official pattern and colour; that is, concurring with the Decree of 15 July 1811 in being of the same middle-green as the tunic, having black leather inserts and bearing a broad stripe of lace in the regimental colour down the outer leg.
(Reconstruction)

F3: Trumpeter of the élite company of the 1st Lancers in campaign dress, 1813.

This figure portrays nicely the front of the Imperial Livery worn by trumpeters of lancers and dragoons after 1812. We note the button-hole lace about five of the nine breast buttons, and the seven chevrons of similar lace down both arms. This fellow has, of course, the red epaulettes distinctive of élite troops on his tunic, where a trumpeter of a centre company would have white. Of interest is the addition of copper buttons on the regimental lace down the outer seams of his overalls. Also, the trumpet cord has been plaited, a fairly common practice infrequently illustrated by modern artists. Instead of the familiar frame or solid buckles, this trumpeter's swordbelt is held together by a serpent-S clip more often seen on officers' belts than those of the troops.
(Illustration after Roux from 'La Giberne')

G1: Trumpeter of the élite company of the 1st Lancers in parade dress, 1815.

With the brief Restoration of 1814, trumpeters were issued tunics of Royal Livery—dark blue with white and crimson lace—to replace the Livery of Napoleon. With the return of the Emperor in 1815, there was no time to change the dress again and it was decided simply to substitute white lace, cheap and plentiful, for the Royal white and crimson. The result is the uniform of this trumpeter; the breeches, boots and headgear remain identical to those worn pre-Restoration but the white-laced, dark blue tunic reveals the hasty preparation of the unit for the '100 Days' campaign in Belgium.

The trumpet banner, no doubt rolled up and hidden away in the regimental stores during Louis XVIII's purge of all things Imperial, has been affixed to the trumpet, a rare sight in post-1812 cavalry regiments who could ill-afford this luxury.
(Illustration after the Boersch Collection)

103

G2: Trumpeter of a centre company of the 3rd Lancers in campaign dress, 1812.

This and the following figure illustrate the dress of trumpeters prior to the change to the Imperial Livery as worn by *F3*. His tunic is the reverse colour of that issued to the troops and the facings consequently take on the basic middle-green of lancer uniforms, edged in lace. We can see yellow eagle patches on the turnbacks which, unlike those of the preceding figure, are devoid of decorative lace. The lapels have been buttoned to the right, obscuring the laced facings, and we can discern a small copper button on the crossbelt indicative of the presence of the musketoon sling (the button held the cartridge-pouch and musketoon belts together).

He has wrapped a waterproof cloth about his helmet to protect the metal from the elements and it is clear that the large hair crest has been removed and placed in his portemanteau for safekeeping. Tied to the front is a second wrap-round which, when untied, would be lowered to protect the wearer's ears. The cuffs at the bottom of his overalls are considerably longer than those illustrated so far and are seemingly intended to give the false impression that he is wearing boots, a common stratagem on overalls later in the century but fairly rare in this period.
(Illustration based on Rousselot)

G3: Trumpeter of the élite company of the 5th Lancers in campaign dress, 1812.

He wears a single-breasted, short tunic of the same pattern as adopted by some officers for secondary dress. It is the colour of the regiment's facings but is without the expected middle-green collar and turnbacks. This garment was no doubt an updated surtout with short skirt, embellished only at the collar—with lace—and shoulders—with the familiar red epaulettes of élite troops. His swordbelt buckle is ornamented with an Imperial eagle rather than the grenade or capital N symbol so frequently seen on these solid buckles. His overalls are those prescribed by the Decree of 15 July 1811, with leather inserts and stripe of regimental-coloured lace down the outer seams to which copper buttons were sewn.
(Illustration after Marckolsheim MS)

H1: Major of the 6th Lancers in parade dress, 1811–1814.

This figure illustrates the rear of the officers' pattern habit-veste which is, again, no different from that of the rank and file other than the gilt buttons and eagle patches on the turnbacks. The individual's rank is indicated by the silver-bodied, heavy gold epaulettes and the four arrow-heads of lace (one of which is silver) on the front of the breeches. His swordbelt is identical to that of *H2*, as are his costly cartridge-pouch and crossbelt. Note that, in the same manner as dragoon officers, lancer officers' helmet turbans were of leopard skin.
(Illustration after Rousselot)

H2: Sous-Lieutenant of the 5th Lancers in campaign dress, 1813.

This colourfully-dressed fellow wears the standard officers' version of the lancers' habit-veste, differing from that of the troops solely in its finer quality and gilt buttons. His overalls follow the officers' frequent predilection for fabric of the regimental colour; they have scarlet lace, edged with gold piping, and gilt buttons. His equipment is of interest: the pouch-belt, identical to that of *H1*, has been covered in a crimson wrap to save it from the everyday wear and tear of active service; his swordbelt and slings are of black leather wired with gold, an expensive foible.
(Illustration after the Freyberg MS)

H3: Sous-Lieutenant of the 2nd Lancers in campaign dress, 1811–1814.

His single-breasted tunic, identical in ornament to the habit-veste, was a popular garment for officers, replacing the more expensive habit-veste on campaign. His cartridge-pouch crossbelt is of black leather and bears gilt badges of an Imperial crown and a shield; in parade dress a gilt chain would be added, linking the two. The swordbelt has the familiar serpent-S type buckle, in this case augmented by decorative plaques featuring the head of Hercules. The overalls are plain except for the single stripe of regimental coloured lace down the outer leg.
(Illustration after Leliepvre)

3

Line Chasseurs

*' Cuirassiers are required to be tall, but height is altogether
useless in hussars and chasseurs : on the contrary,
it is to their detriment. '*
(Napoleon to Lacuée, 15 March 1807)

*' A colonel of chasseurs or hussars who goes to sleep, instead
of spending the night in bivouac and remaining in constant
communication with his piquets, deserves to be shot. '*
(Napoleon to Berthier, 2 January 1812)

Organisation

By 1793 the number of light cavalry regiments of the French army had more than doubled their total of 1789, while the number of medium and heavy regiments had increased by a paltry four. The fact that the *chasseurs à cheval* regiments should now number twenty-six against a bare twelve, four years previously, is highly indicative of the state of the army as a whole; the role of light cavalry involved reconnaissance and the screening of the main army, leaving the body blows to the more professional heavy cavalry, and they were thus far more easily raised and trained. The chasseurs, being the indigenous French light horse, can perhaps therefore be equated best with the infantry *demi-brigades* of this period, a half-trained, unprofessional, make-shift collection, making up with zeal what they lacked in experience.

By the turn of the Empire, the chasseurs numbered twenty-four regiments, listed 1 through 26 with the 17th and 18th being vacant. Five further regiments were created during the course of the wars:

The 27th Chasseurs, formed 29 May 1808 from the Belgian *Chevau-Légers d'Arenberg*.
The 28th Chasseurs, created on the same date from Tuscan dragoons originally organised in January 1808.
The 29th Chasseurs formed late in 1810 from the *3eme Régiment Provisoire de Cavalerie Légère* raised in Spain in 1808.
The 30th Chasseurs, formed by an Imperial decree of 3 February 1811, were chasseurs on paper only, as they were promptly converted to *Chevau-Légers Lanciers*.
The 31st Chasseurs raised 7 September 1811 from the amalgamation of the *1er and 2eme Régiments Provisoires de Cavalerie Légère*.

Chasseurs regiments were composed of between four and six squadrons. A squadron comprised two companies of two troops and was commanded by an *adjutant*. Companies were commanded by *capitaines* and troops by *lieutenants* or *sous-lieutenants*. The regimental chain of command was identical to that of the heavy cavalry, and readers are referred to the author's introductory remarks in Chapter 1, *Cuirassiers and Carabiniers*.

Chef d'escadron in full dress, 1800. In near hussar dress, *mirliton* **cap, dolman, barrel-sash, Hungarian breeches and boots, this superior officer based on a painting by Hoffman serves to illustrate the origins of chasseur uniform against which hussar-based influence it continually strove throughout the Empire, terminating in an individual chasseur style all its own. (Huen. Courtesy National Army Museum)**

Officers, 1800. They wear the 1806-pattern shako, recognized officially at that date despite having been worn under the Consulate, and the 1791-model chasseur *caracot*, similar though longer than the hussar dolman, beneath which we can see the heavily braided, sleeveless waistcoat. Though both wear sabretaches, these became an increasingly rare sight during the Napoleonic Wars. The shako cords, soon to become obsolete, at this period served to secure the headgear when riding. (Benigni. Courtesy NAM)

Dress and Equipment

At the beginning of the Consulate, chasseurs' dress was essentially that prescribed by the decree of 1 April 1791. By 1795 the *mirliton* hussar-cap had universally replaced the fur-crested Tarleton-style helmet. The dolman tunic was still worn, though, as we shall see, it was soon to be replaced by the familiar *habit-long*; this in turn was to be superseded by a short-tailed, single-breasted 'Kinski' tunic, predecessor to the *habit-veste* of 1812 pattern. These four phases of dress overlapped one another considerably; as there were also four major changes of headgear, the details of the steadily developing uniform are best considered in an orderly sequence.

Tunics

Irrespective of the tunic worn, the chasseur regiments were distinguished from one another by a facing of regimental colour, distributed to the regiments in the following manner.

Colour	Collar and cuffs	Cuffs only	Collar only
Scarlet	1	2	3
Yellow	4	5	6
Pink	7	8	9
Crimson	10	11	12
Orange	13	14	15
Sky Blue	16	17	18
Aurore	19	20	21
Capucine	22	23	24
Madder red	25	26	27
Amaranth	28	29	30
Chamois	31		

The dolman: despite the fact that this garment was never manufactured under the Empire, the dolman tunic was worn at least for full dress by all regiments prior to 1805. Probably a modified version of the 1791 *caracot*, it resembled the hussar dolman and had three rows of pewter buttons and between thirteen and eighteen rows of braid. The waist, back-seams, front vent, collar and cuffs were all liberally decorated with white lace. The version worn by the 5th Chasseurs had the added embellishment of shoulder-straps.

After 1804 we have the following information: inspection reports indicate the dolman was still commonly worn by the 3rd, 12th, 15th and 19th Chasseurs in 1804, the 1st, 6th, 7th, 9th, 10th, 20th and 24th Chasseurs in 1805 and the 4th, 5th and 16th Chasseurs in 1806. An existing garment in the Musée de l'Armée, Paris, attributed to the 4th Chasseurs, has the year 1808 stamped on the lining. Contemporary illustrations confirm the dolman to have been worn by the 1st Chasseurs during 1806 and the 5th Chasseurs as late as 1811.

Chasseur in full dress, 1802. Armed with the brand new *An IX*-pattern musketoon (the old 1786 model was also used for a good many years to come), this chasseur also boasts the 1801-pattern shako, so named despite having been in service since 1798. It was roughly the same shape as the one made regulation in 1806, but had the added features of a detachable peak and wrap-round turban. Though here the cords are plaited and looped about hooks at the sides, they would normally be wrapped around the wearer's body and knotted to keep it in place. The hair, although queued and plaited, was no longer powdered; this style of dressing persisted in the 15th and 26th Chasseurs as late as 1813. (Huen. Courtesy NAM)

109

The dolmans of NCOs and officers were identical to those of the men except that those of the officers would bear five rows of buttons and all lace would be silver. Rank distinctions are illustrated in detail on page 142; note that officers' lace could measure 14mm or 23mm in width, depending on rank. Finally, it should be mentioned that officers would supplement the dolman with an hussar-style *pélisse* if it took their fancy; contemporary illustrations record officers so attired of the 3rd, 5th and 27th Chasseurs as late as 1808, 1807 and 1810 respectively.

The habit-long: prior to 1806, the *habit-long* had been reserved for everyday and campaign wear but thereafter it was increasingly worn for full dress. This long-tailed and lapelled tunic was of identical colouring to the dolman save in the following particulars: the tails of the skirt were turned back to reveal the facing colour and ornamented, generally, with a green bugle-horn device. The collar and cuffs were devoid of the white lace which festooned the dolman, and would be piped in the opposite colour (i.e. green piping on a scarlet collar and scarlet piping on a green collar). The lapels, shoulder-straps and imitation pockets on the skirt would be piped in the facing colour.

While NCO's rank distinctions remained much the same, officer's rank was now indicated by epaulettes as illustrated on page 142. From surviving illustrations and records, it would appear that officers took to wearing the *habit-long* for full dress some time before the men did, and, though otherwise of identical cut, the officers' tunics frequently had the tips of the lapels rounded-off – no doubt a fashionable whim.

The Kinski: as of 1808, the single-breasted, short-tailed Kinski began to make its appearance. Fastening down to the waist by means of nine pewter buttons, and piped the length of the breast in the regimental colour, the tunic bore the same ornaments as the *habit-long* for all ranks. Simple, comfortable and devoid of the encumbering tails of that garment, it gradually replaced the *habit-long* for most functions until the advent of the 1812 *habit-veste*. Certain examples boast the addition of collar tabs of the opposing colour, serving to distinguish still more clearly the wearer's regiment. Officers

Chasseur in campaign dress, 1800–2. In service dress, the chasseurs changed from the dolman or *caracot* to the more conventional *habit-long* in conjunction with a waistcoat and overalls. The waistcoat should officially have been single-breasted, plain and white in summer and green in winter but, staunch individualists that they were, the chasseurs adopted all manner of unofficial garments – in this case a plain red double-breasted type. (Similarly unofficial are his grey overalls which commonly replaced the tight Hungarian breeches, but which only became regulation in 1812.) (Benigni. Courtesy NAM)

Chasseurs of the élite company, 1805–6. Created by decree of the *18 Vendémiaire An X* (1 October 1801) the first company of the first squadron was to be an élite unit, in imitation of the grenadiers of the infantry. As symbols of the élite status, the men were accorded black bearskin colpacks in place of shakos; typically, each company so formed quickly took on the additional trappings of their infantry contemporaries, including red plumes, cords and tassels, fringed epaulettes and even the flaming grenade emblem (which was used to ornament the turnbacks, webbing, belt buckles and cartridge-pouches). The lace on the breeches differed from the Hungarian knot to the bastion-shaped loop. (Benigni. Courtesy NAM)

110

111

tended to conserve their *habits-long* for walking-out dress though the Kinski would be worn for all other occasions.

The habit-veste: the 1812 *habit-veste*, introduced in 1813, was basically identical to the Kinski except that it had lapels. All ornaments and rank insignia remained precisely the same as those worn on the *habit-long*.

Beneath all the above-mentioned tunics, chasseurs wore sleeveless waistcoats, officially single-breasted and cut of white cloth for summer and green for winter, but, especially before 1812, endless different varieties were worn: double-breasted of white or scarlet cloth, single-breasted of red, green or regimental colour, and some were liberally festooned with lace and braid in imitation of the dolman. Buttons would either be identical to those of the tunic, pewter or silver, or covered in the same colour cloth as the waistcoat itself.

Troopers and NCO's were further issued with single-breasted, waist-length, green stable-jackets with collar and cuffs matching those of the *habit* and two flapless pockets at the waist. Examples of similar, double-breasted, versions also exist. Officers were issued a *surtout* for undress wear, closely resembling the *habit* save that its skirt was devoid of turnbacks and its breast bare of lapels; fastening was generally be means of nine silver buttons.

Legwear

Throughout the Empire period, chasseurs most commonly wore green Hungarian breeches of hussar pattern; very close-fitting, they were decorated with piping 1 cm in width down the outer seams and with the same piping in the shape of either a Hungarian knot or a bastion loop about the twin vents on the front. They were further equipped with straps at the bottom of the leg to stop the breeches riding up inside the boots.

Chasseur in stable-dress, 1805. The stable-jacket was dark green with collar and cuffs identical to those of the *habit-long*, it could be single or double-breasted with eight or nine pewter buttons per row. As of 1813, the garment became entirely dark green and single-breasted, fastening by means of ten pewter buttons. The trousers, of rough undyed cloth, opened laterally by means of cloth-covered or bone buttons down the outer seams; as the inclination towards trousers progressed, so versions appeared with button-up vents from the knee down only, to facilitate their wearing over boots. (Huen. Courtesy NAM)

On campaign the breeches were either replaced with coarse hide riding-breeches – *pantalons de cheval* – or covered by overalls. These overalls were of diverse cut and varied from undyed cloth through grey and green. They opened laterally and the outer seams bore eighteen pewter or bone buttons and regimental-coloured lace trim. The inner leg and cuffs of the trouser legs were reinforced with leather. Three-pointed flaps equipped with one or three buttons sealed hip pockets which were frequently attached to the front of the garment. Long after the overalls ceased to open laterally, they still frequently bore buttons, in much the same way as contemporary men's jackets carry redundant buttons at the cuff.

The 1812 regulations altered the stable-jacket solely in making it entirely dark green, while for the overalls they specified piping in lieu of lace down the outer seams.

Chasseurs of an élite and centre company, 1805. These chasseurs in undress uniform wear *surtout* tunics, overalls and fatigue-caps. The fatigue-caps, or *bonnets de police*, consisted of dark green turban and *flamme*; piped in the regimental colour, ornamented with a white bugle-horn patch and finished with a white tassel, the headdress was to last until 1813 when the Pokalem version, as prescribed by the 1812 regulations, began to be issued. The scalloped cut of the leather inserts of the overalls is of particular interest. (Huen. Courtesy NAM)

113

114

Coats, capes and greatcoats

The chasseurs were first issued the tent-like green cavalry cape with hood. Thereafter followed the *manteau trois-quart* somewhat shorter, devoid of hood but with the addition of a short shoulder-cape stitched around the collar. In 1813 the *manteau-capote* was introduced; it was similar to the foregoing cape except for the addition of cuffed sleeves, and buttons down the front closure. The shoulder-cape was attached in such a way as to allow the wearer to wear the webbing outside the *manteau*, but underneath the cape. Officers wore similar capes save that in certain instances the shoulder-cape would be trimmed in silver lace. Officers also wore a full-length, double-breasted greatcoat—*redingote*—for foot duty; this was entirely green save for a collar of regimental colour.

Accessories

Chasseurs were generally shod in clogs for fatigues and riding-boots for all other duties. These boots were of Hungarian pattern, black leather and ornamented along the top with white lace and tassel. The 1812 regulations altered the decoration by specifying black leather trim and tassel. Spurs were originally of the detachable strapped variety, but they were later changed to the type that was screwed directly to the heel of the boot. Officers' service-dress boots were identical save for silver lace and tassel. For full dress, fancy goatskin boots, dyed red or green, were not uncommon. Officers' spurs were usually plated in silver or bronze.

For walking-out dress, shoes with large white metal buckles were worn with stockings. The stockings were white in summer and black or green in winter.

In full dress, cuffed gloves of white, or sometimes black for officers, were adopted in place of the wrist-length variety employed for most other duties.

Officer of an élite company, 1805–6. Although initially reserved for the élite companies, the colpack was swiftly adopted by officers, irrespective of company. Increasingly worn solely for full-dress occasions, the dolman he sports was arrayed with eighteen rows of braid and five rows of buttons as well as being liberally bedecked in silver lace. Less common, but certainly not unknown, was the wearing of a matching fur-trimmed *pélisse* in direct imitation of hussars. (Wilke. Courtesy NAM)

Officer of a centre company, 1805–6. This fellow wears the 1801-pattern turbanned shako, with the addition of a chinstrap which made the cords unneccessary and purely decorative; the cartridge-pouch crossbelt has been covered in a red Morocco leather protective case, fastened by means of silver studs. The barrel-sash has been dispensed with and, in lieu of the very common *sabre à la hussarde*, he is armed with the officers'-pattern *sabre à la chasseur* – the difference being that the latter had additional pommel guards. (Wilke. Courtesy NAM)

Headgear

The main varieties of chasseur headgear are shown on page 144; for further details, readers are referred to the colour plates and their commentaries. The complex question of plumes and pompons requires discussion, however.

The pompon, or lentil-shaped disc as decreed by the 1812 regulations, referred to the wearer's squadron and company. There were endless variations, however, and following is the official guide: a red aigrette for the first company of the first squadron and a sky-blue, aurore or violet pompon for the first companies of the succeeding squadrons. The second company of the first squadron had a red pompon and the second companies of the remaining squadrons wore one of the same colour as the first but with a white centre, frequently bearing an

116

embroidered squadron number. The first company of the first squadron would usually emphasize its élite status by wearing a red plume, their simple aigrette being regarded as insufficiently different from the pompon of the second company.

The plumes referred to the wearer's regiment or arm. In the latter case it would simply be green, a colour universally indicative of light troops. In the former case, however, an anarchic situation existed whereby each regiment's plumes could be of either the facing colour or green with tip or base of the facing colour. The proportion of the plume's length that this facing colour occupied varied from a fifth to a third.

In undress uniform a *bonnet de police* of green was worn by both troopers and officers. The cap itself of this headgear was laced in white and ornamented with a white cloth patch of the bugle-horn device; the *flamme* or bag, left trailing or folded and tucked into the cap, was piped in the regimental colour and tipped by a white tassel. Officers' patterns were in the main identical, save that silver replaced white, but versions with a *flamme* of regimental colour are not unknown.

Webbing

This term includes the cartridge-case and crossbelt, musketoon-sling and crossbelt and the sabre's waistbelt and slings. Once again the reader is referred to the line illustrations and captions for the precise specifications.

Chasseurs were at first issued with equipment of the 1801 pattern, which varied little from that issued in 1786. The white buff leather (yellow for the 5th and 27th Chasseurs) crossbelts were 80 mm wide and both passed over the left shoulder, bound to one another by means of a spherical copper stud visible on the breast of many of the figures illustrated. All metal ornaments were copper apart from the steel musketoon clip. The waistbelt and slings were manufactured from the same materials.

Chasseur of a centre company in marching order, 1805–6. Again recorded during the German campaign of 1806: the shako has given way to the more comfortable *bonnet de police* whilst on the march; the leather inserts in his overalls are of 'wolf's teeth' cut, and the service chevron on his left upper arm designates between eight and ten years service. (Wilke. Courtesy NAM)

Composed of three separate sections interlinked with copper rings, the waistbelt was adjustable by means of a buckle on the third section which permitted its length to be altered by folding the section back on itself. As of 1813, two amendments were made: the addition of a small copper hook to the first link-ring, from which the sabre would be hung by the first ring of its scabbard when the chasseur was on foot, and a bayonet frog immediately behind that ring.

Edged weapons

During the early Empire the *sabre à la hussarde* and *sabre à la chasseur* were simultaneously in use. The former varied considerably in the degree of curve to the edged blade, which was designed for both cut and thrust, and could have either an iron or a copper guard; its scabbard was of black leather with either iron or copper fittings. The latter

Chasseur of an élite company in campaign dress, 1805–6. Recorded in Germany, this individual's uniform has several points of interest: the scarlet plume has been wrapped round in oilskin to preserve it from the elements, an alternative to packing it away in the portmanteau of the saddle, and the otherwise typical overalls have the added distinction of hip pockets with button-down flaps. He wears cuffed gloves, more normally reserved for full dress, and carries the 1786-pattern hussar musketoon. (Wilke. Courtesy NAM)

Trumpeter in No. 2 dress, 1806. Before the advent of the single-breasted, short-tailed Kinski tunic in 1808, an alternative to the *habit-long* was an otherwise identical but lapelless *surtout* tunic. Cut in the cloth of the regimental colour with facings of dark green, a popular means of more readily distinguishing musicians on the battlefield. The garment is embellished with white lace as would be facings of the *habit-long*. His shako is the 1806 model, augmented with chinscales and shako plate. Most usually this lozenge shape, many regiments' plates differed in having an embossed eagle upon them surmounting the regimental number which would be cut out of the metal. He is armed with 1786-model hussar sabre. (Huen. Courtesy NAM)

pattern had an N-shaped copper guard and a relatively shallow arc of curve; its scabbard was of black leather with copper fittings. As the years passed, the *An XI*-model light cavalry sabre gradually came to replace both preceding models. Its copper guard was composed of three bars and its scabbard was iron. Sword-knots were of white buff leather for all save the 5th and 27th Chasseurs who had yellow ones. The steel bayonet was 487 mm long; the 400 mm blade was triangular in shape and guttered on all three sides, to facilitate its removal from the victim's body.

Officers' sword patterns varied from the forego-

ing in that iron was silver-plated and copper-gilded. Further, embellishments were often embossed on the guard, scabbard fittings and blued-steel blade. Their gold sword-knots came in two varieties, with either a flat lace or braid strap, and tassel composed either of slim filaments or chunky twisted coils.

Firearms

Originally, chasseurs carried the 1786-model hussar musketoon but this was slowly replaced by the updated *An IX* pattern, superseded in turn by the *An XIII* pattern. All were of varnished natural wood colour, had a steel barrel and were finished in copper throughout, save for the steel lock mechanism. Neither officers or trumpeters were armed with musketoons.

All ranks were supposedly issued with a brace of pistols apiece, but it is far likelier that only officers, trumpeters and, perhaps, NCO's were so armed. If troopers were issued pistols at all, they might well have a single weapon only, carried in the left saddle holster.

Saddles and Harness

The harnessing was of the Hungarian variety, the saddle covered in a white sheepskin schabraque edged in 'wolf's teeth' lace of the regimental colour. The portmanteau was green and its round ends were either laced or piped in white and ornamented with the regimental number in white. Bridles were also of Hungarian pattern. Trumpeters were supposed to have been issued black sheepskin schabraques to contrast with their grey mounts, but it is likely that as often as not they used the same type as the troopers.

The officers' harness comprised a Hungarian-pattern saddle, covered in leather and with cantle embellished in red or green Morocco leather, with red stirrup-leathers, and a green cloth schabraque, piped in the regimental colour and laced in silver. This silver lacing varied in a similar manner to the rank chevrons: 27 mm for *sous-lieutenants* and lieutenants, 40 mm for *capitaines* and one of 40 mm with one of 27 mm for all officers above that rank. The corner of the schabraque usually contained the regimental number embossed in silver, though officers of élite companies sometimes favoured a silver flaming grenade device. A more ornate leopard-skin schabraque was frequently employed by superior officers, though on campaign, they were replaced by simpler ones: plain green with a slim line of white piping about the edges or black bearskin decorated in the same manner as the troopers' sheepskin ones. Sometimes the schabraque was abandoned altogether, replaced by a black bearskin cover over the pistol holsters and a square green saddle cloth edged in silver lace beneath the saddle. All bridle strap buckles and ornaments were silver-plated.

War Records and Regimental Histories

The 1st Chasseurs à Cheval

Regimental history:
1651: Raised by Mis. d'Humières.
1733: Named the Conti Chasseurs.
1776: 25 March, became a regiment of dragoons.
1788: 17 March, renamed Régiment de Chasseurs d'Alsace.
1791: Became the 1er Régiment de Chasseurs.
1814: Renamed the Régiment de Chasseurs du Roi.
1815: Disbanded.

War record:
1805: Part of 1st Corps of the Grand Armée: Ulm, Amstetten, Mariazell and Austerlitz.
1806: Part of 3rd Corps of the Grand Armée: Auerstädt.
1808: Lowicz and Nasielsk.
1809: Part of the Armée d'Allemagne: Abensberg, Raab and Wagram.
1812: With the 1st Corps of the Grande Armée: Mohilev, Smolensk and Borodino.
1814: Took part in the defence of Maubeuge.
1815: Quatre-Bras and Rocquencourt.

The 2nd Chasseurs à Cheval

Regimental history:
1673: Raised 6 November by Le Chevalier de Fimarçon as a regiment of dragoons.

Colonel Baron Méda of the 1st Chasseurs, 1807. Resplendent in full dress uniform, this superior officer wears the 1806-pattern shako, richly ornamented with silver lace and equipped with a chinstrap of interlinking rings rather than the more familiar scaled versions; the *habit-long*, adopted by many officers long before the troopers, with twin fringed epaulettes as rank distinctions in place of the chevrons of the dolman, and lavishly ornate waistcoat and breeches. The boots are black although red or green pairs were not uncommon, and they bear matching lace to the shako. The heavily ornate belt buckle is embossed with bugle horn and laurel leaves; the sword-belt supports the 1803-model light cavalry sabre, normally reserved for chasseurs of the Imperial Guard. (Benigni. Courtesy NAM)

1788: Re-formed as chasseurs and named the Régiment de Chasseurs de Evêchés (No. 2).
1791: Renamed the 2eme Régiment de Chasseurs.
1814: Renamed the Régiment de Chasseurs de la Reine.
1815: Disbanded.

War record:
1805: With the Grande Armée: Dachau, Mariazell, Austerlitz, Auerstädt, Pultusk, Eylau, Mysziniec and Heilsberg.
1809: Part of the Armée d'Allemagne: Abensberg, Landshut, Eckmühl, Neumarkt, Ebensberg, Raab, Wagram and Znaïm.
1812–13: With the Grande Armée: Smolensk, Borodino, Mojaïsk, Wiasma, Bautzen, Wachau, Leipzig and Hanau.

1814: Paris and Champaubert.

1815: With the Armée du Rhin: action on the Suffel.

The 3rd Chasseurs à Cheval

Regimental history:

1675: Founded by Charles du Fay at Philippsburg as a regiment of dragoons.

1788: Became the Régiment de Chasseurs de Flandre (No. 3).

1791: Renamed the 3eme Régiment de Chasseurs.

1814: Renamed the Régiment de Chasseurs du Dauphin.

1815: Disbanded.

War record:

1805: With the Armée d'Italie: Caldiero.

1807: Part of the Réserve de Cavalerie de la Grande Armée: Passenwerder and Heilsberg.

1809: With the Armée d'Allemagne: Vilsbiburg, Essling and Wagram.

1812–13: With the Grande Armée: Krasnoe, Borodino, Dresden and Leipzig.

1814: Champaubert and Nangis.

1815: With the Armée du Nord: Quatre-Bras and Waterloo.

The 4th Chasseurs à Cheval

Regimental history:

1675: Raised 11 December by the Comte de Dreux-Nancré as a regiment of dragoons.

1788: Became the Régiment de Chasseurs de Franche-Comté (No. 4).

1791: Renamed the 4eme Régiment de Chasseurs.

1814: Renamed the Régiment de Chasseurs de Monsieur.

1815: Disbanded 16 July.

War record:

1805: Part of the Armée de Naples: Padua, Venice and Saint-Michel.

1806–12: Involved in pacifying Puglia and Calabria: Palmi.

1812–13: With the Grande Armée: Niemen, Vitebsk, Krasnoe, Smolensk, Valoutina, Borodino, Berezina, Katzbach, Wachau, Leipzig and Glogau.

Officers, 1807. The figure on the left is in morning dress with an officers'-pattern greatcoat, usually reserved for foot duty. Although here in felt bicorn, he might equally have worn the officers' version of the *bonnet de police,* **identical to the men's save for silver lace and bugle-horn device. He carries the** *An XI* **pattern** *sabre à la chasseur.* **On the right is an individual in campaign dress, not necessarily of the élite company, since colpacks were popular throughout the officer class. The simple double-breasted waistcoat fastens to the left and has two flapless pockets. His pipe, embedded in its embroidered tobacco pouch, is looped about the gilded pommel of his** *An XI* **sabre. (Benigni. Courtesy NAM)**

Chasseur in campaign dress, 1807. The *habit-long* **had by now replaced the dolman almost entirely in most regiments, although the 5th and 27th Chasseurs clung to it until as late as 1811; prior to the advent of the Kinski tunic, it became the first distinctive item of dress of chasseur uniform as opposed to the hussar/chasseur style of the early Empire. This chasseur is armed with the** *An XI* **chasseur sabre, although many still carried the** *sabres à la hussarde* **and** *à la chasseur An IX***-pattern. (Huen. Courtesy NAM)**

1814: Montmirail and Arcis-sur-Aube.

1815: With the Armée du Nord: Ligny and Waterloo.

The 5th Chasseurs à Cheval

Regimental history:

1675: Founded as a corps of dragoons.

1676: Became regular regiment of dragoons 13 March.

1788: Became Régiment de Chasseurs du Hainaut (No. 5).

1791: Renamed the 5eme Régiment de Chasseurs.

1814: Renamed the Régiment de Chasseurs d'Angoulême.

1815: Disbanded.

War record:

1805–7: With the Grande Armée: Munich, Wasserburg, Haag, Austerlitz, Schliez, Fürstenburg, Waren, Crewitz, Lübeck, Morhungen, Lobau, Krentzburg and Friedland.

121

Chasseur in campaign dress. 1809. He wears the single-breasted Kinski tunic introduced in 1808. Simple, short-skirted and comfortable, its use was widespread until the distribution of the 1812-pattern *habit-veste*. Ornaments remained the same as on the *habit-long*, shoulder straps for centre, and fringed epaulettes for élite, companies, as did the facing colour distribution. The twin chevrons of white lace indicate his rank to be that of *brigadier* (corporal). His shako has been covered in protective cloth, and his breeches with overalls strongly reminiscent of his fatigue-duty stable trousers. His firearm is the relatively new *An IX*-pattern musketoon. (Benigni. Courtesy NAM)

1808–13: Alcolea, Baylen, Burgos, Somosierra, Almaras, Medellin, Torrigos, Talavera, Cadiz, Bornos, Alhambra, El-Coral, Caracuel, Olmedo, Hillesca, Burgos and Vitoria.
1813: With the Grande Armée: Jüterbock, Dennewitz, Mockern, La Partha, Leipzig and Hanau.
1814: With the Armée d'Espagne: Orthez and Toulouse. Campaign of France: Remagen, La Chaussée, Châlons, Mormant, Troyes, Bar-sur-Aube, Arcis-sur-Aube, Sommepius and Saint-Dizier.

The 6th Chasseurs à Cheval

Regimental history:
1676: Created 4 October by the Etats du Languedoc as a regiment of dragoons and named the Languedoc-Dragons.
1788: Became Régiment de Chasseurs du Languedoc (No. 6).

1791: Renamed the 6eme Régiment de Chasseurs.
1814: Renamed the Régiment de Chasseurs de Berry.
1815: Disbanded 30 November.

War record:
1803–4: Part of the Armée d'Italie.
1805–8: With the Armée de Naples: Castel-Franco. Occupation of Calabria and the Abruzzo.
1809–11: Part of the Armée d'Italie: Sacile, La Piave, San-Michel and Wagram.
1812: With the 3rd Corps of Cavalry of the Grande Armée: Smolensk, Borodino and Malojaroslawetz.
1813: Part of the 1st Corps of Cavalry of the Grande Armée: Bautzen, Wachau and Leipzig.
1814: Remained with the 1st Corps: Champaubert and Vauchamps.
1815: With the Armée du Nord: Mont-Saint-Jean, Waterloo and Rocquencourt.

The 7th Chasseurs à Cheval

Regimental history:
1745: Created 15 August as a mixed corps of foot and horse light troops and named the Volontaires Royaux.
1747: Renamed the Légion Royale.
1776: 25 March, regiment disbanded and troops dispersed into existing infantry and dragoon regiments.
1779: 29 January, four squadrons of the old Légion Royale reformed as the 1er Régiment de Chasseurs à Cheval.
1784: 8 August, transformed again into a mixed corps and renamed the Régiment de Chasseurs des Alpes (No. 1).
1788: 17 March, infantry became chasseurs à pied and cavalry renamed the Régiment de Chasseurs de Picardie (No. 7).
1791: Became the 7eme Régiment de Chasseurs.
1814: Renamed the Régiment de Chasseurs d'Orlèans.
1815: Disbanded.

War record:
1805–7: Part of the 7th Corps of the Grande Armée: Embs, Jena, Wismar, Hameln, Eylau, Königsberg and Heilsberg.
1809: With the Armée d'Allemagne: Pfaffenhausen, Raab and Wagram.
1810–11: Fuentes d'Onoro.

Chasseur of an élite company, 1813. Newly accoutred for the most part in accordance with the 1812 regulations, this individual wears the lapelled *habit-veste*, otherwise identical to the Kinski; the grenadier-pattern 1812 shako, with red upper band and side chevrons, and the non-regulation pompon and plume of scarlet. He carries the *An XI* sabre, and his 1812-pattern belt has the recently introduced bayonet frog and a small hook to which the first ring of the steel scabbard would be attached so as to facilitate the sabre's wear when the chasseur was on foot. (Huen. Courtesy NAM)

1812–13: With the Grande Armée: Polotsk, Drissa, Berezina, Danzig, Bantzen, Liegnitz, Katzbach, Reichenbach and Leipzig.

1814: Bar-sur-Aube.

1815: With the Armée du Rhin: action on the Suffel.

The 8th Chasseurs à Cheval

Regimental history:

1749: A mixed corps formed of the Arquebusiers de Grassin, Fusiliers de la Morlière and Volontaires Bretons.

1757: Divided into the Volontaires de Flandre and the Volontaires du Hainaut.

1762: Became the Légion de Flandre.

1776: 25 March, disbanded in same manner as the Légion Royale.

1779: Re-formed from four squadrons of the old Légion de Flandre as the 2eme Régiment de Chasseurs à Cheval.

Officer in campaign dress, 1813. The 1812 regulations was not very different from the men's except of finer quality and with silver ornaments. The dark-green trousers, embellished with twin strips of regimental-coloured lace, have replaced the Hungarian breeches and the webbing is black leather edged in silver instead of plain white. (Huen. Courtesy NAM)

Officer in full dress, 1813. At this period, officers' dress make no mention of the bearskin colpack, but it is widely recorded that officers retained theirs for the duration of the wars. Beneath the Morocco-leather cover, this officer's crossbelt is probably prescribed by those same decrees: of dark-green leather with silver lace edging. The *redingote* coat, worn in place of cape, lacked the folded down collar of regimental colour that was typical of previous models but otherwise was the same. Some authorities maintain that, though normally dark green, the cuffs were sometimes also of regimental colour or piped therein. (Benigni. Courtesy NAM)

1784: Became a mixed corps again and renamed the Régiment de Chasseurs des Pyrénées (No. 2).

1788: Infantry companies severed and cavalry renamed the Régiment de Chasseurs de Guyenne (No. 8).

1791: Renamed the 8eme Régiment de Chasseurs.

1814: Renamed the Régiment de Chasseurs de Bourbon.

1815: Disbanded at Perpignan 3 December.

War record:

1805: Part of the 2nd Corps of the Grande Armée: Ulm, Gratz and Nordlingen.

1806–11: Part of the Armée d'Italie: Sacile, Montebello, La Piave, Saint-Michel, Raab and Wagram.

1810–11: Stationed in the Tyrol.

1812: With the Grande Armée: Dnieper, Ostrowno, Krasnoe, Smolensk, Borodino, Mojaïsk and Winkowo.

1813: Remained with the Grande Armée: Möckern, Bautzen, Dresden, Goldberg and Leipzig.

1814: Saint-Dizier, Champaubert, Berry-au-Bac, La Fère-Champenoise and Paris.

1815: The Sambre passage, Ligny, Villers-Cotterets and Versailles.

The 9th Chasseurs à Cheval

Regimental history:

1757: Created 1 April as a mixed corps by division of preceding regiment and named the Volontaires du Hainaut.

1762: Renamed the Légion de Hainaut.

1768: Renamed the Légion de Lorraine.

1776: Disbanded 25 March.

1779: Reformed as the 3eme Régiment de Chasseurs à Cheval.

1784: Became mixed corps and renamed the Régiment de Chasseurs des Vosges (No. 3).

1788: Renamed the Régiment de Chasseurs de Lorraine after infantry companies were axed.

1791: Renamed the 9eme Régiment de Chasseurs.

1814: Renamed the Régiment du Colonel-Général.

1815: Disbanded, 21 September.

War record:

1801: With the Armée de Naples: Saint-Euphémie, Monteleone.

1808: Reggio, Messina and Scilla.

P. Benigni

1809: With the Armée d'Italie: Brenta, Piave, Saint-Michel, Leoben, Raab and Wagram.

1810: Part of the Armée de Naples during the Calabrian campaign.

1812–13: With the Grande Armée: Borodino, Wiasma, Lützen, Bautzen, Dresden, Löwenberg, Goldberg, Leipzig and Hanau.

1814: Champaubert, Château-Thierry, Brienne, Montmirail, Sézanne, Reims, La Ferté, Montereau, Melun and Paris.

1815: Ligny and Waterloo.

The 10th Chasseurs à Cheval

Regimental history:

1758: Mixed corps created, 7 May, for the Comte de Clermont and named the Volontaires de Clermont-Prince.

1763: Renamed the Légion de Clermont-Prince.

1766: Renamed the Légion de Condé.

1776: Disbanded, 25 March

1779: Reformed of four squadrons of the Légion de Condé as the 4eme Régiment de Chasseurs à Cheval.

1784: Reformed as a mixed corps and named the Régiment de Chasseurs des Cévennes (No. 4).

1788: Became the Régiment de Chasseurs de Bretagne (No. 10) after infantry companies had been axed.

1791: Renamed the 10eme Régiment de Chasseurs.

1815: Disbanded 30 August.

War record:

1805–7: Part of the 6th Corps of the Grande Armée: Elchingen Jena, Hoff, Eylau, Deppen and Friedland.

1808–13: With the Armée d'Espagne: Medina-del-Rio-Seco, Medellin, Albacon, Talavera, Almonacid, Ocaña, Malaga, Baza and Vitoria.

1813: With the Grande Armée: Leipzig.

1814: With the Armée des Pyrénées: Orthez, Viella and Toulouse.

1814: Part of the 6th Corps of the Grande Armée: Montereau and Fontvannes.

The 11th Chasseurs à Cheval

Regimental history:

1762: Created 11 January as a mixed corps named the Volontaires Etrangers de Würmser.

1762: Renamed 21 December as the Volontaires de Soubise.

1766: Renamed the Légion de Soubise.

1776: Disbanded 25 March.

1779: Re-formed of four squadrons of the old Légion de Soubise as the 5eme Régiment de Chasseurs à Cheval.

1781: Became a mixed corps again and renamed the Régiment de Chasseurs du Géraudan (No. 5).

1788: Renamed the Régiment de Chasseurs de Normandie (No. 11) after the infantry companies were separated from the regiment.

1791: Renamed the 11eme Régiment de Chasseurs.

1815: Disbanded.

War record:

1805: Part of the 4th Corps of the Grande Armée: Ulm and Austerlitz.

1806–7: With the Grande Armée: Jena, Lübeck, Eylau, Danzig, Guttstadt, Heilsberg and Friedland.

1809: With the Armée d'Allemagne: Eckmühl, Ratisbonne and Znaïm.

1810–12: Part of the Armées d'Espagne et du Portugal: Fuentes d'Onoro.

1812: With the 2eme Corps de Réserve de Cavalerie of the Grand Armée: Borodino and Winkowo.

1813: With the Grande Armée: Lützen, Bautzen, Leipzig and Hanau.

1814: Vauchamps.

1815: Part of the 3rd Corps of the Armée du Nord: Waterloo.

The 12th Chasseurs à Cheval

Regimental history:

1769: Mixed corps created after the conquest of Corsica and named the Légion Corse.

1775: Renamed the Légion du Dauphiné. Disbanded 25 March.

1779: Re-formed of four squadrons of the old Légion Corse as the 6eme Régiment de Chasseurs à Cheval.

1784: Became a mixed corps once again and named the Régiment de Chasseurs des Ardennes (No. 6).

1788: Renamed the Régiment de Chasseurs de Champagne (No. 12) after infantry companies had been separated from the regiment.

1791: Renamed the 12eme Régiment de Chasseurs.

1815: Disbanded.

Chasseur of an élite company in campaign dress, 1813. Sketched during the 1813 campaign, this illustration after a contemporary artist is of interest on several counts. Though the overalls are as prescribed in the 1812 regulations, dark green, reinforced with black leather and opening laterally by means of pewter buttons, the vent ornamented with piping of the regimental colour, his accoutrements are far from regular. Firstly, a scarlet *aigrette* should have replaced the pompon and plume of the élite companies on the 1810 shako, and all the obsolete cords and tassels were strictly abolished; secondly, in place of the 1812-pattern waistbelt, he wears a pattern reminiscent of that of heavy cavalry and lancers, and in a most unorthodox way; over his tunic. Lastly, in place of the sheepskin schabraque issued to troopers, his saddle has the added feature of a dark-green saddle-cloth, edged in white, an item normally reserved for officers' horse furniture. **(Benigni. Courtesy NAM)**

War record:

1805–7: With the 3rd Corps of the Grande Armée: Auerstädt, Czentoschau, Golymin, Okunin, Czarnowo, Biezun, Heilsberg and Gross-Krug.

1808: With the Armée du Rhin: occupation of Silesia, Westphalia, Saxony and Franconia.

1809: With Montbrun's Division of the Armée d'Allemagne: Eckmühl, Ratisbonne and Wagram.

1812: Part of the Grande Armée: Wilia Pass, Rudnia, Krasnoe, Borodino and Winkowo.

1813: Könnern, Katzbach and Leipzig.

1814: Part of Saint-Germain's Division during campaign of France: Bar-sur-Aube.

1815: With the Armée du Nord: Ligny and Waterloo.

The 13th Chasseurs à Cheval

Regimental history:

1792: Created from squadrons of the Légion des Americains et du Midi and named 13eme Régiment de Chasseurs.

1794: 13eme (bis) Régiment de Chasseurs created from two squadrons of the Légion du Nord and the Volontaires.

1795: 13eme and 13eme (bis) Chasseurs amalgamated as 13eme Régiment de Chasseurs, 11 April.

1815: Disbanded at Niort and Belfort.

War record:

1805–7: With the Grande Armée: Ulm, Braunau, Halberstadt, Passewalk, Nasielk and Eylau.

1809: Part of the Armée d'Allemagne: Essling, Engereau, Wagram, Hollabrunn and Znaïm.

1810–13: Fuentes d'Onoro, Mondego, Los Arapilos, Villodrigo and Tordesillas.

1813: Four squadrons with the Grande Armée: Dennewitz.

1814: 4th, 5th and 6th squadrons took part in the campaign of France: Bar-sur-Aube and Montereau. 1st, 2nd and 3rd squadrons with the Armée des Pyrénées: Orthez and Toulouse.

1815: 1st, 2nd and 3rd squadrons: Belfort. Remainder with the Corps d'Observation du Jura.

The 14th Chasseurs à Cheval

Regimental history:

1793: Created from four squadrons of the Hussards des Alpes, one company of the Hussards de l'Egalité and a company of the Hussards de la Mort. Named the 14eme Régiment de Chasseurs.

1815: Disbanded.

War record:

1805: With the Armée d'Italie: Caldiero and Vicence.

1806: Part of the Armée de Naples: Gaëta.

1807: Part of the 8th Corps of the Grande Armée: Stralsund.

1809: With the Armée d'Allemagne: Ratisbonne, Eckmühl, Ebersberg, Essling and Wagram.

1812–13: Part of the Armée de Portugal: Nava-del-Rey, Los Arapilos, Monasterio, Villodrigo and Vitoria.

1813: With the Grande Armée: Dresden, Leipzig and Hanau.

1813–14: Siege of Belfort.

1814: Saint-Dizier, Brienne, Bar-sur-Seine, Champaubert and Montmirail.

The 15th Chasseurs à Cheval

Regimental history:

1793: Created from the Chasseurs de Beysser and several irregular companies of the Western départements. Named the 15eme Régiment de Chasseurs.

1815: Disbanded.

War record:

1805–6: Part of the Armée d'Italie: Caldiero and Tagliamento.

1807: With Colbert's Division of the Grande Armée: Lomitten.

1808–9: Part of the Armée d'Espagne: passage of the Guadarrama, of the Esla, Banos Pass and Alba-de-Tormes.

1810–11: With the Armée de Portugal: Torres Vedras.

1811–12: Some squadrons with the Armée d'Espagne: Sanguessa and Villodrigo. Remainder with the Armée du Nord and the Corps d'Observation de réserve.

1813–14: Pampeluna, Vitoria, Orthez and Toulouse. Remainder with the Grande Armée: Leipzig, Lützen, Weissenfels and Arcis-sur-Aube.

The 16th Chasseurs à Cheval

Regimental history:

1793: Created 7 March from the Chasseurs Normands de Labretèche and named the 16eme Régiment de Chasseurs.

1814: Disbanded 12 May.

1815: Re-formed 16 April from Belgian volunteers. Dissolved 1 July.

War record:

1805: With the Grande Armée: Amstetten, Posalitz, Vischau and Austerlitz.

1806–7: Part of the Grande Armée: Jena, Lübeck, Hoff, Eylau and Königsberg.

1809: With the Armée d'Allemagne: Landshut, Ebersberg, Essling, Raab and Wagram.

1812: With the Grande Armée: Vilna, Mohilew, Ostrowno, Vitepsk, Smolensk, Borodino and Krasnoe.

1 Trooper, 5th Chasseurs, campaign dress, 1806
2 Trumpeter, 1st Chasseurs, full dress, 1802
3 Colonel, 5th Chasseurs, full dress, 1804

A

1 Brigadier, 1st Chasseurs, campaign dress, 1804–05
2 Chef de Musique, 7th Chasseurs, full dress, 1805–06
3 Subaltern, 1st Chasseurs, service dress, 1806

ANGUS McBRIDE

1 Sous-Officier, 10th Chasseurs, full dress, 1809
2 Trumpeter, 6th Chasseurs, service full dress, 1809
3 Subaltern, 16th Chasseurs, full dress, 1809

1 Trooper, 13th Chasseurs, campaign dress, 1806
2 Trumpeter, 7th Chasseurs, service dress, 1810–12
3 Officer, 4th Chasseurs, campaign dress, 1809

D

ANGUS McBRIDE

1 Trooper, 26th Chasseurs, full dress, 1809–12
2 Trumpeter, 24th Chasseurs, campaign dress, 1809
3 Superior Officer, 20th Chasseurs, full dress, 1812

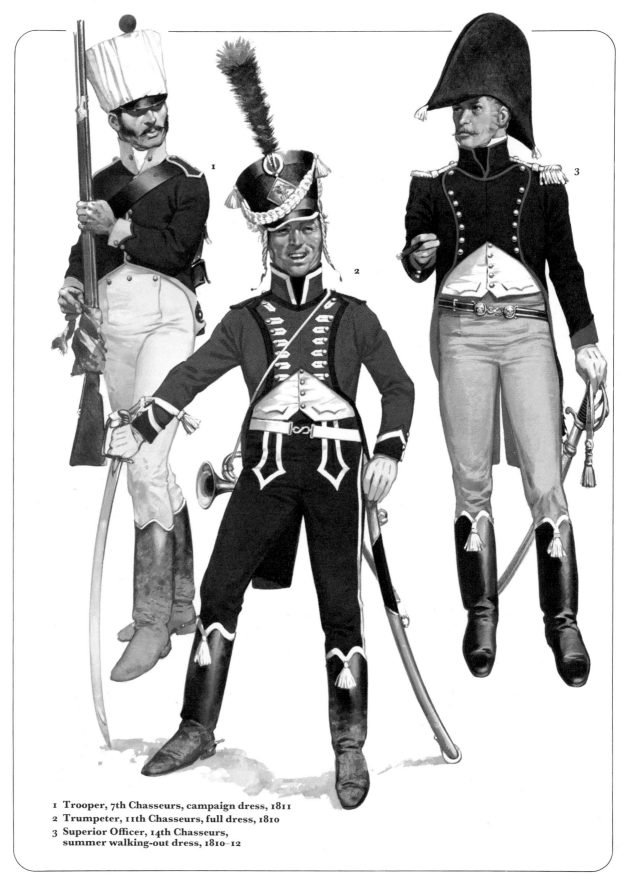

1 Trooper, 7th Chasseurs, campaign dress, 1811
2 Trumpeter, 11th Chasseurs, full dress, 1810
3 Superior Officer, 14th Chasseurs,
  summer walking-out dress, 1810–12

1 Trooper, 6th Chasseurs, service dress, 1813–14
2 Trumpeter, 12th Chasseurs, campaign dress, 1812
3 Subaltern, 8th Chasseurs, regulation full dress, 1813–14

1 Trooper, 2nd Chasseurs, campaign dress, 1813–14
2 Trumpeter, 27th Chasseurs, full dress, 1813–14
3 Subaltern, 19th Chasseurs, campaign dress, 1813–14

ANGUS McBRIDE

1813: Part of the Grande Armée: Lützen, Kulm and Leipzig.

1814: La Rothière, Champaubert, Vauchamps, La Fère-Champenoise and Paris.

The 17th Chasseurs à Cheval

Regimental history:

1793: Created from the Chevau-Légers de West-Flandre and named the 17eme Régiment de Chasseurs.

1794: Disbanded.

1815: Re-formed at Bordeaux on 16 August from the 15eme Régiment de Chasseurs and named the Régiment de Chasseùrs d'Angoulême.

The 18th Chasseurs à Cheval

Regimental history:

1793: Created 9 May from the 1er Régiment de Chevau-Légers Belges and the Compagnie de Dragons de Bruxelles. Named the 18eme Régiment de Chasseurs.

1794: Disbanded 18 July.

1815: Re-formed as the Régiment de Chasseurs de la Sarthe (No. 18).

The 19th Chasseurs à Cheval

Regimental history:

1793: Created from the Chasseurs de la Légion de Rosenthal and several irregular companies on 10 June. Named the 19eme Régiment de Chasseurs.

1814: Disbanded.

War record:

1804–6: With the Armée d'Italie: Caldiero, San-Pietro, Treviso and Tagliamento.

1806–7: With the Grande Armée: Marienwerder, Danzig and Stralsund.

1809: Part of the Armée d'Allemagne: Neumarkt, Ebersberg, Essling and Wagram.

1810–11: Part of the Armée d'Illyrie.

1812: With the Grande Armée: Ostrowno, Smolensk, Borodino.

1813: Malojaroslawetz, Wiasma, Krasnoe. Danzig, Torgau, Weissenfels, Bautzen, Dresden, Gorlitz, Borach and Leipzig.

1813–14: With the Armée d'Italie: Caldiero, Mincio and Taro.

The 20th Chasseurs à Cheval

Regimental history:

1793: Created from the Légion du Centre (or de Luckner) and named the 20eme Régiment de Chasseurs.

1814: Disbanded.

War record:

1806–7: Part of the 7th Corps of the Grande Armée: Jena, Eylau, Guttstadt and Heilsberg.

1809: With the 2nd Corps of the Armée d'Allemagne: Pfaffenhausen, Amstetten, Raab and Wagram.

1810–12: With the Armées d'Espagne et du Portugal: Fuentes d'Onoro and Altafulla.

1812–14: Part of the 2nd Corps of the Grande Armée: Polotsk, Borisow, Berezina, Katzbach, Leipzig, Hanau, Montmirail and Montereau.

The 21st Chasseurs à Cheval

Regimental history:

1793: Formed as the 21eme Régiment de Chasseurs from a corps of irregular hussars.

1814: Disbanded.

War record:

1805: Part of Lasalle's Brigade of the 5th Corps of the Grande Armée: Wertingen, Ulm and Austerlitz.

1806: With Treilhard's, then Lasalle's Brigade of the Grande Armée: Saalfeld, Jena, Spandau, Prentzlow and Pultusk.

1807: With the 5th Corps of the Grande Armée: Ostrolenka and Ostrowno.

1809–14: With the Armée d'Espagne: Arzobispo, Ocaña, the Andalusian expedition, siege of Badajoz, Gebora, Albufera, Los Arapilos, Vitoria, Orthez and Toulouse.

Detailed records of the histories of regiments numbered 22 to 26 inclusive are not given in the official French Ministry of War lists. Formed following the Directory re-organisations of 1791–92, these units, although formed as chasseurs, were assigned to *Guides* duties with the staffs of various army corps commanders.

The Plates

A1   Trooper of the 5th Chasseurs in campaign dress, 1806
Although chasseurs of this period are most commonly represented wearing an hussar-style dolman tunic, it was in fact the practice to resort to the *habit-long* as shown here for undress and campaign wear, the dolman being reserved for more formal occasions. Of interest is his curious headgear, the 1801-pattern shako (so named despite having been

officially recognised as early as 1798), with its distinctive detachable peak and wrap-round turban, strongly reminiscent of the hussars' *mirliton* cap. This regiment clung to several features of dress more readily associated with the hussars until well into the Empire: this pattern of shako until 1807, the dolman tunic as late as 1811 and, here in 1806, the 1786-pattern hussar sabre and musketoon. Further, the 5th Chasseurs, in common with the 27th, had the distinction of yellow webbing in place of the usual white. (Illustration after Benigni)

A2 Trumpeter of the 1st Chasseurs in full dress, 1802
Despite the fact that the dolman tunic was never manufactured during the course of the Empire, the chasseurs painstakingly conserved them for full-dress wear regardless of the fact that they dated back to 1791. Recorded in 1802, this uniform is known to have been worn throughout the 1805 campaign even though an inspection report dated 22 July 1805 assures us that all the dolmans of this regiment were worn-out and that none remained in the depot. This tunic becomes even more interesting when one notices that it bears five rows of buttons, in place of the normal three reserved for all ranks below officer class, and, although the familiar practice has been followed of making the tunic of the same colour cloth as the facings of the men, it has a scarlet collar instead of the more normal dark green one, an anomaly perpetuated until 1809 despite the advent of the Kinski tunic. He wears a cartridge-pouch and crossbelt, even though trumpeters were never equipped with musketoons, and also a sabretache, an uncommon accessory for chasseurs. (Illustration after Cmndt. Bucquoy)

A3 Colonel of the 5th Chasseurs in full dress, 1804
The 5th Chasseurs is credited with being the first regiment to adopt the colpack fur cap, which was to

prove enormously popular with officers, irrespective of company, and later as headdress for all troopers of the élite companies (in imitation of the tall bearskins sported by grenadiers in the infantry). The loose hanging bag, in this instance cut in the regimental colour, was also occasionally made of plain white cashmere. As the use of chinscales increased, the less practical cap lines or cords were retained solely for the sake of ornamentation.

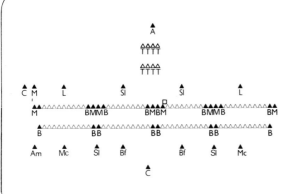

Squadron of chasseurs in battle order. This formation provided a squadron with its maximum frontage and minimal two-man depth. A regiment of four squadrons extended in this manner might be arranged in line or echelon, in which event the squadron numbers would read from one to four, right to left, or in column, in which case the squadrons would be in first, third, fourth and second order, reading from front to back.

Officers' dolman tunics were essentially the same as the troopers' save for five rows of buttons, supporting eighteen rows of braid, and, albeit infrequently, a silver lace *cadre* surrounding the whole. Interestingly, although both the 5th and 27th Chasseurs indulged in shoulder straps on their troopers' tunics, their officers did not follow suit, but adopted the more normal method of chevron rank distinctions on the sleeve with matching bastion-shaped lace on the breeches. In this case, we see that a colonel's rank was designated by alternating lace strips of 23 and 14 mm in width. He carries the officers'-pattern hussar sabre, dating well back to the Republic, rather than the more elaborate *sabre à l'allemande* with which many of his brother officers would be armed. Officers of the 5th are well documented as having worn a *pélisse* as late as 1807, which was more naturally associated with their hussar-style dress, but which was a rare accessory under the Empire. Officers' full-dress boots were frequently made of red or green goatskin, though here they are a conservative black. (Illustration after Benigni)

B1 Brigadier of the 1st Chasseurs in campaign dress, 1804–5

As mentioned above, the dolman was not manufactured during the Empire and those recorded must have been either the chasseurs' 1791-pattern *caracot*, with thirteen rows of braid, or hussar-pattern dolmans, boasting no less than eighteen loops of braid. On the NCO's dolman, which was identical to the troopers', rank was indicated by twin chevrons of white lace for *brigadiers* (corporals), single silver chevrons for *maréchaux-des-logis* (sergeants) and twin silver chevrons for *maréchaux-des-logis-chefs* (sergeant-majors). On campaign, the tight Hungarian breeches of the trumpeter in *A2*

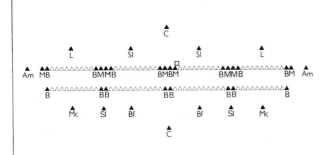

Lead squadron of chasseurs in *colonne serré* order. Drawn up for this column formation, the squadrons advanced on a fully extended front, one behind the other at a distance of sixteen metres, lead horse to lead horse. The depth of a two-rank line was six metres.

Master key:

B: *Brigadier* (**corporal**)
Bf: *Brigadier-fourrier* (**quarter-master corporal**)
M: *Maréchal-des-logis* (**sergeant**)
Mc: *Maréchal-des-logis-chef* (**sergeant-major**)
Am: *Adjutant-major* (**regimental sergeant major**)
Sl: *Sous-lieutenant* (**second lieutenant**)
L: *Lieutenant* (**first lieutenant**)
C: *Capitaine* (**captain**)
A: *Adjutant* (**adjutant**)
T: *Trompette* (**trumpeter**)

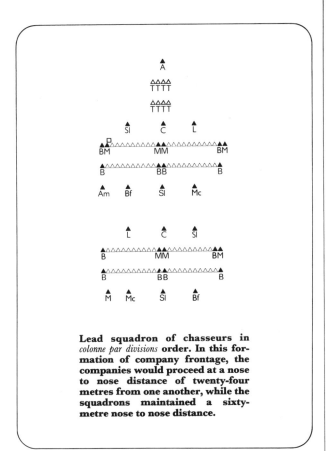

Lead squadron of chasseurs in *colonne par divisions* **order. In this formation of company frontage, the companies would proceed at a nose to nose distance of twenty-four metres from one another, while the squadrons maintained a sixty-metre nose to nose distance.**

Lead squadron of chasseurs in column by fours. In this close formation, troops and companies of a squadron would keep equal distance of twelve metres nose to nose from one another, while following squadrons maintained a gross, ie. lead horse to lead horse, distance of a hundred metres.

Lead squadron of chasseurs in *colonne par pelotons* **order. Of troop frontage, the individual troops and companies of a squadron would keep even distance of twelve metres, lead horse to lead horse, for this formation. Squadrons, measured in the same manner, would precede one another by fifty-nine metres.**

were replaced by hide riding breeches or covered by overalls. These last were of many varieties, but generally dark green or grey, reinforced with leather and laced the length of the outer seams in the regimental colour; they fastened laterally by means of eighteen bone, pewter or cloth-covered buttons. Clearly visible here is the strap which, passing beneath the foot, would attach to a calf button in order to stop the breeches riding up. The oilskin round both shako and plume is to preserve

141

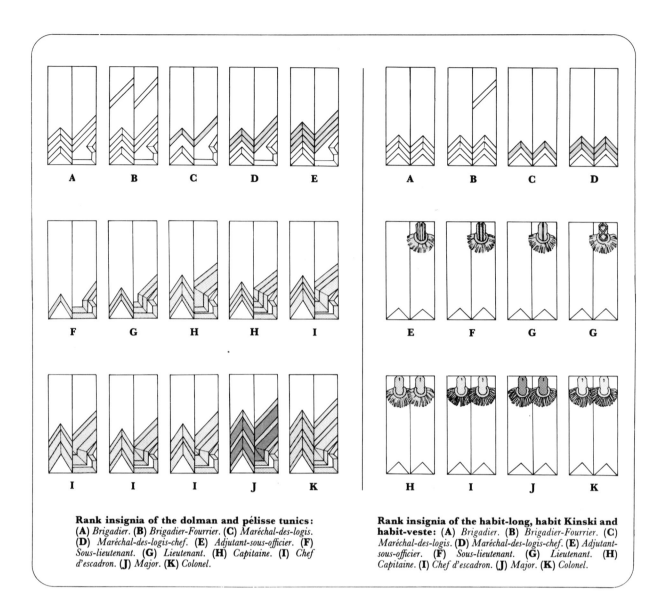

Rank insignia of the dolman and pélisse tunics:
(**A**) *Brigadier.* (**B**) *Brigadier-Fourrier.* (**C**) *Maréchal-des-logis.*
(**D**) *Maréchal-des-logis-chef.* (**E**) *Adjutant-sous-officier.* (**F**)
Sous-lieutenant. (**G**) *Lieutenant.* (**H**) *Capitaine.* (**I**) *Chef
d'escadron.* (**J**) *Major.* (**K**) *Colonel.*

**Rank insignia of the habit-long, habit Kinski and
habit-veste:** (**A**) *Brigadier.* (**B**) *Brigadier-Fourrier.* (**C**)
Maréchal-des-logis. (**D**) *Maréchal-des-logis-chef.* (**E**) *Adjutant-
sous-officier.* (**F**) *Sous-lieutenant.* (**G**) *Lieutenant.* (**H**)
Capitaine. (**I**) *Chef d'escadron.* (**J**) *Major.* (**K**) *Colonel.*

them from the elements. The musketoon, not yet replaced by the *An IX* pattern, is slung from the crossbelt so that it could be both fired and loaded without having to be unclipped. The hair queue, which was disappearing fast at the onset of the nineteenth century, remained popular with the more traditional regiments and was still fashionable as late as 1811 in the 20th, and 1813 in the 15th and 26th Chasseurs. (Illustration after Rousselot/Duboys de l'Estang)

B2 Chef de Musique of the 7th Chasseurs in full dress, 1805–6

The principal priority for musicians was, in theory, that they be readily distinguishable from the mass of troops, for which reason they were issued uniforms of identical cut but of contrasting colour to the men's, and rode greys (as did some officers). The basic rule was therefore to reverse the colours, the musicians wearing the facing colour where the troops wore dark green and vice versa – but nowhere was individuality, extravagance, dandyism and out-and-out foppery more tolerated than in the élitist light cavalry. What chance had the humble shako when colpacks or czapskas became available? The briefest glance at chasseur musicians leaves the observer with the impression that their uniforms must have been redesigned very frequently. Tunics, headgear, and ornamentation offer a bewildering spectacle to which no rhyme or reason can be attached. This figure is a perfect example; assuming that his old pink dolman with green facings has worn out, it seems likely that, pink cloth being a trifle scarce in the midst of a campaign, his coat was run up from the most easily obtainable, indigo-blue cloth. Yet a Negro *timbalier* has been recorded by Boeswilwald in the same year with full Eastern regalia in the correct colours; furthermore, if pink cloth was scarce, where did the trefoils and colpacks appear from? Musicians at this time wore uniforms like this one, but with white lace in lieu of silver, trumpeters almost the same but with lace only about the collar (those of the élite company added scarlet fringed epaulettes) and yet less than a year later we have evidence of pink tunics and even pink shakos.

The argument for expediency clearly only goes so far, but it is rather the self-indulgence of the regimental colonels, vying with one another for the most dashing heads of column that brought about the Emperor's decree in 1810 to the effect that henceforth a dark green Imperial Livery should be universal. (Illustration after Cmndt. Bucquoy/Carl/Boeswilwald)

B3 Subaltern of the 1st Chasseurs in service dress, 1806
Although German documents record that many of the 1st Chasseurs wore dolmans during the campaigns of 1805 and 1806, the garment was fast disappearing in favour of this *habit-long*, hitherto reserved for No. 2 dress. The officers' pattern was basically the same as the men's save for silver ornaments and buttons, and sometimes, as in this instance, the fashionable rounding-off of the tops of the lapels. Rank was now indicated by epaulettes, all ranks below *chef d'escadron* wore only one, on the left shoulder. At this period the felt shako originally issued under the Consulate became regulation and was termed 'the 1806 pattern'; it was devoid of turban, had a fixed peak, stood 160 mm tall and measured 230 mm in diameter at the top. Far too simple for contemporary tastes, it was often discarded for the colpack or was elaborately embroidered in silver. As the years passed, it became taller, embellished with black velvet and ornamented with a plate of white metal. Pompons of silver, surmounted by plumes of black or dark green tipped in the regimental colour, were promptly added – along with chinscales which the

original design omitted. In place of breeches, officers took to wearing trousers: at first steel grey and laced and buttoned down the outer seams, they soon lost their buttons but retained the lace in the form of twin strips down the outer leg. Gradually, the steel grey gave way to dark green as ground fabric, and so they remained throughout the Empire. But this is not to say that breeches were ever totally replaced; they remained in service for grand occasions. Sabres *à la hussarde* and *à l'allemande* had by this time given way to the officers' pattern *An XI* sabre *à la chasseur* with its gilded copper fittings. (Reconstruction)

C1 Sous-officier of the 10th Chasseurs in full dress, 1809
The rather old-fashioned and cumbersome *habit-long* began to decline in popularity with the introduction of the eminently practical Kinski tunic in 1808. Single-breasted and short-tailed, it was perhaps the most sensible garment yet devised for increasingly mobile warfare, and it was the forerunner of the 1812 *habit-veste* which was to transform the dress of the French Line army into a more appropriate one for the new century. However, old traditions die hard and the ornate, sleeveless waistcoat worn beneath the tunics remained a firm favourite: in theory single-breasted, plain-fronted, white in summer, dark green in winter, it was frequently personalised by being cut in the regimental colour, scarlet or dark green, and either emblazoned with braid and lace or, at the very least, cut double-breasted. Notice also, that all the ornamentation of the *habit-long* has been transferred to the new garment: the single silver chevron on his left upper-arm denotes between eight and ten years service; the cuff chevrons indicate his rank and the scarlet fringed epaulettes proclaim his élite company status. Further evidence of his belonging to the first company of the first squadron is his bearskin colpack and scarlet pompon and plume. These élite companies were created following the decree of 18 October 1801 (*18 Vendemiaire An X*) which accorded their members the bearskin cap as testimony of their distinction. Not to be outdone by the infantry grenadiers, the chasseurs promptly followed this with epaulettes, plumes, cords and colpack bags of scarlet; perhaps sensing they were on to a good thing, many companies even appended the flaming

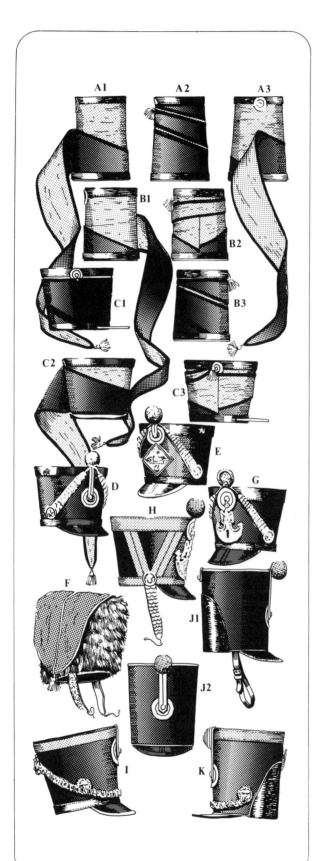

Chasseur headgear, 1790–1815. (A) The *mirliton* cap *c.* 1790 with *flamme* unravelled and viewed from the front (1); with *flamme* wrapped round to reveal the black protective side as worn in service dress, again from the front (2) and finally, again unravelled, but viewed from the right hand side (3). Height: 240 mm. (B) the *mirliton* cap *c.* 1795 with *flamme* unravelled viewed from the front (1); with *flamme* wound anticlockwise to reveal the facing colour, viewed from the left hand side (2) and lastly, with *flamme* wound clockwise, again viewed from left (3). Height: 220 mm. (C) The 1801-model shako with *flamme* wound clockwise (1); with *flamme* unravelled, viewed from front (2); finally, with *flamme* wound anti-clockwise (3). Height: 190 mm; width: 220 mm. (D) The 1806 model shako, 1805–07. Height: 160 mm; width 230 mm. (E) The 1806-model shako, 1807–12. (F) The bearskin colpack, 1805–14. (G) The 1810-model shako. Height: 220 mm; width: 270 mm. (H) The 1812-pattern élite company shako. Height: 190 mm; width: 245 mm. (I) Officers'-pattern 1810-model shako. (J) Troopers'-pattern 1812 cylindrical shako (1) and (2). (K) Officers'-pattern 1812 cylindrical shako.

grenade device to their turnbacks, cartridge-pouches and crossbelts. Perhaps the most extreme example was the company of chasseurs sketched by Suhr in Hamburg in 1812 who had gone so far as to attach a party of bearded sappers to their ranks, armed with lances flying scarlet pennants! (Illustration after Benigni)

C2 Trumpeter of the 6th Chasseurs in service full dress, 1809

In keeping with the beggar-my-neighbour policy of presenting increasingly exotic heads of column, the dress of this trumpeter leaves only the green plume to indicate to which branch of the army he belongs. Fantasy has clearly been allowed full rein in the choice of ground colour for the tunic in order to compete more flamboyantly with the no doubt equally pompous splendour of their neighbouring regiment. Although one must allow for the difficulty in purchasing bolts of cloth of the more obscure facing colours, such as aurore, amaranth or capucine, by the regiments in the field, it is hard to reconcile this with the fact that scarlet was at this period one of the most expensive colours available. (Illustration after Rousselot/Marckolsheim MS)

C3 Subaltern of the 16th Chasseurs in full dress, 1809

This full-dress figure illustrates a rather typical chasseur officer of the period: despite the introduction of the comfortable and simple Kinski tunic, most officers were loathe to part with their smarter *habit-long* which became reserved for full and walking-out dress. Although it might seem outdated when worn with braided waistcoat and Hungarian breeches, it should be borne in mind that though the garments remained the same, the cut changed considerably over the years, becoming 'snappier' and closer-fitting with the evolution of civilian fashions. Notice the webbing: there would seem to have been a great latitude in the choice of accoutrements, and webbing of black, green or red Morocco leather was quite acceptable. At first only edged in silver lace with silver studs along the body, the crossbelt and cartridge-pouch became increasingly ornate; silver devices of Imperial N's, eagles, shields embossed with the regimental number, and lions' heads began to abound to such an extent that the owners were obliged to protect their costly investment with red or crimson leather covers (see *B3*) when on campaign. He carries the officers' pattern *An XI* sabre, finished in silver rather than gilded. (Illustration after Rousselot)

D1 Trooper of the 13th Chasseurs in campaign dress, 1806

This trooper affords us a rearview of the *habit-long*. The rather sack-like early patterns were getting slimmer and the turnbacks of the skirt, which were originally literally pinned back and tended to appear baggy, were becoming increasingly narrow and were stitched along their entire length. Although originally functional, the pockets in the tails of the skirt were now obsolete, and piping in the distinctive *soubise* shape merely mimicked their presence. The buckle at the rear of his 1806-pattern shako allowed the headdress to be tailored to individual size. (Illustration after Rousselot)

D2 Trumpeter of the 7th Chasseurs in service dress, 1810–12

Of particular interest are the button loops on the collar and cuffs of his reversed-colour Kinski tunic. Authorities conflict on this detail: although Würtz and the Börsch Collection record similar loops about alternating breast buttons for the years 1808 and 1809, Vanson and Jolly both confirm their disappearance in 1810 and accord the tunic white lace about collar and cuffs only. The white chevrons on his left upper arm denote between sixteen and twenty years service. Finally, according to both Jolly and Vanson, a similar 1806-pattern shako, covered in pink cloth, bedecked with white

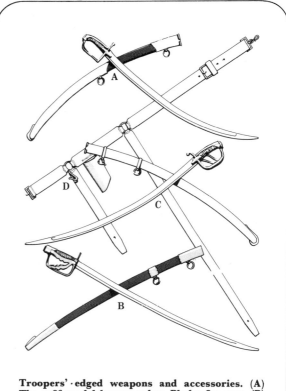

Troopers'·edged weapons and accessories. **(A)** The 1786-model hussar sabre. Blade: 800 mm. **(B)** The 1801-model chasseur sabre. Blade: 900 mm. **(C)** The *An XI* light cavalry sabre. Blade: 845 mm. **(D)** The 1812-pattern waistbelt and bayonet frog. Overall length: 107 cm. width: 40 mm; width of slings: 35 mm; length of first sling: 340 mm; length of second: 970 mm.

cords and tassels and surmounted by a white plume, would be utilised in full dress. (Illustration after the Marckolsheim MS).

D3 Officer of the 4th Chasseurs in campaign dress, 1809

In contrast to the subaltern in *C3*, this fellow illustrates the much simplified dress that officers would adopt when on active service. The bearskin colpack, now stripped of all ornament, reveals the manner in which the chinscales would be hung on a small hook at back of the headgear when not in use. A plain double-breasted waistcoat replaced the elaborately braided full-dress version, and steel grey trousers the Hungarian breeches. Trousers, increasingly in vogue, were rapidly becoming acceptable as full-dress items, in which event they would be identical to those shown here, but cut in dark green. (Illustration after Rousselot)

145

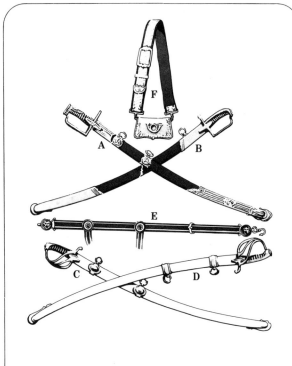

Officers' edged weapons and accessories. (A) *Sabre à l'Allemande.* (B) *Sabre à la hussarde.* (C) *An XI* **light cavalry sabre.** (D) *Sabre à la chasseur An XI.* (E) **The 1812-pattern officers' waistbelt.** (F) **Typical officers' cartridge-pouch and crossbelt. Width: 40 mm; diameter of roses: 50 mm; width of slings: 26 mm; length of buckles: 48 mm; width of piping: 6 mm.**

that can be specified with any certainty is that the pompons related to the companies and the plumes to the regiments. The preponderance of red-based regimental colours makes for difficulty in distinguishing one from the other: aurore from orange or capucine from scarlet or garance from crimson.

This regiment has opted for the Hungarian knot instead of the inverted bastion shape to ornament the breeches.* (Illustration after Rousselot/Martinet)

E2 Trumpeter of the 24th Chasseurs in campaign dress, 1809
With his reversed-colour Kinski, this trumpeter has the unusual distinction of wearing sky blue overalls in place of the more habitual dark green or grey patterns; though these lack the familiar leather insert on the inside leg, this individual has painstakingly appended leather cuffs to the trouser legs to save them from wear and tear. A further feature is that he still carries the old *sabre à la chasseur* instead of the new *An XI* model worn by the trooper in *E1*; the manufacture and distribution of new equipment was so haphazard and slow that enemy arms, looted from captured arsenals and supply trains, were frequently pressed into service.*
(Illustration after Suhr)

E3 Superior officer of the 20th Chasseurs in full dress, 1812
The officers, like the troopers, took readily to the Kinski tunic and, between 1808 and the advent of the 1812 *habit-veste*, it was the most widespread tunic in use. All ornaments and decoration were identical to those of the *habit-long* with the sole exception of the use of collar patches of regimental colour in place of piping (although this was not universal practice, it was certainly frequent and a more effective means of discerning the wearer's regiment). His white plume designates his rank as do the epaulettes, for only officers above the rank of *chef d'escadron* were permitted the *contre-épaulette* and white, instead of dark green or black, plume. In passing, note the cross and ribbon of the *Légion*

E1 Trooper of the 26th Chasseurs in full dress, 1809–12
From its inception, the 1806-pattern shako was disliked by the chasseurs and each regiment stretched the rules by having theirs constructed somewhat differently: with or without slim leather chevrons on the sides, with added chinscales, with the innovation of a folding neck-cover stitched to the interior headband, but all shakos had a tendency to be taller and broader than those prescribed by regulation. The most common shako plate was lozenge-shaped, embossed with an Imperial eagle and with the regimental number cut out of its white metal. However, rising-sun plates, such as the one illustrated have been recorded on shakos of the 25th, 26th and 27th Chasseurs; their origin was no doubt the same as the czapskas acquired for the bandsmen (see the trumpeter in *G2*). This individuality spread to the plumes and pompons and it is therefore nearly impossible to decode the meaning of the colour-combination. All

*Readers are referred to the note at the close of the section on regimental histories. Since these units served as *Guides*, a possible explanation of non-regulation uniform features may lie in the known tendency of senior commanders to indulge in a certain freedom of imagination when uniforming their *entourages*.

d'Honneur pinned to his breast. (Illustration after Rousselot)

F1 Trooper of the 7th Chasseurs, in campaign dress, 1811
Recorded in Spain, this uniform was probably the most frequently seen of the chasseurs' wardrobe during a campaign. Of primary interest are the protective cloths applied to the shako and musketoon lock, an extremely common practice to prevent damage from the elements but, in the case of the shako, quite possibly to conceal its foreign origin. Evidence in support of this possibility is his black leather crossbelt which is clearly not of French manufacture. No doubt assigned to foot duty, perhaps for lack of horses, he has discarded his sabre. The *An XI*-pattern light cavalry sabre's waistbelt had the innovation of a small hook attached to it precisely to facilitate its wear when on foot. His collar, though devoid of collar patch, bears buttons conceivably intended for fastening to the collar of the greatcoat. (Illustration after Feist/El Guil)

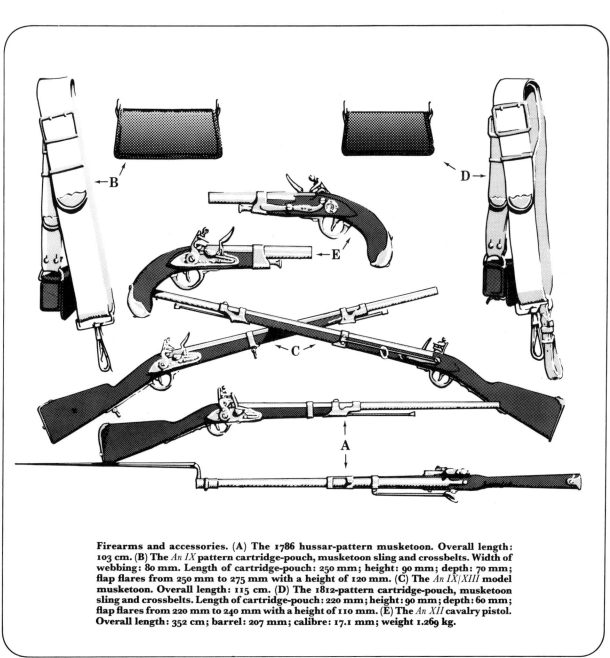

Firearms and accessories. (A) The 1786 hussar-pattern musketoon. Overall length: 103 cm. (B) The *An IX* **pattern cartridge-pouch, musketoon sling and crossbelts. Width of webbing: 80 mm. Length of cartridge-pouch: 250 mm; height: 90 mm; depth: 70 mm; flap flares from 250 mm to 275 mm with a height of 120 mm. (C) The** *An IX/XIII* **model musketoon. Overall length: 115 cm. (D) The 1812-pattern cartridge-pouch, musketoon sling and crossbelts. Length of cartridge-pouch: 220 mm; height: 90 mm; depth: 60 mm; flap flares from 220 mm to 240 mm with a height of 110 mm. (E) The** *An XII* **cavalry pistol. Overall length: 352 cm; barrel: 207 mm; calibre: 17.1 mm; weight 1.269 kg.**

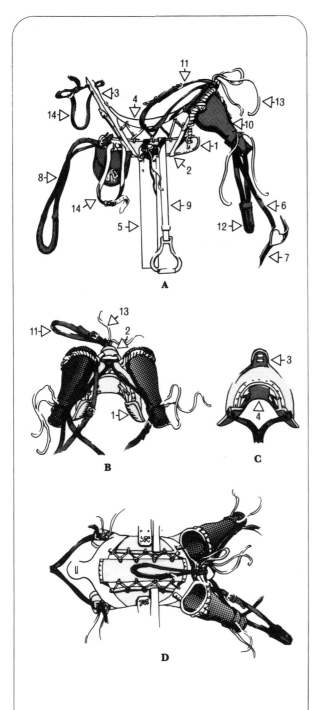

The tree and accessories of the Hungarian saddle. (A) Side view. (B) Full on. (C) Rear view. (D)
Top view. 1 Side panels. 2 Pommel. 3 Cantle. 4 Seat. 5
Girth. 6 Breastplate. 7 False-martingale. 8 Crupper.
9 Stirrup leathers. 10 Pistol holsters. 11 Musketoon
strap. 12 Musketoon boot. 13 Cape thongs. 14
Portemanteau thongs.

F2 Trumpeter of the 11th Chasseurs in full dress, 1810
Rare at this late date, he wears the *habit-long* in
place of the more comfortable Kinski tunic. That
this was the case for the troopers of this regiment as
well and not simply a full-dress fancy of the
musicians is borne out by a report dated 20
September 1809, which describes the *habits-long* of a
detachment arriving from France. Seemingly
further placing this figure at an earlier date than
that specified is the fact that he carries the 1786-
pattern *sabre à la hussarde* instead of the more
expected *sabre à la chasseur* or *An XI* pattern.
Further, though long obsolete, cords and tassels still
ornamented the shako for full dress occasions.
(Illustration after Marckolsheim MS)

*F3 Superior officer of the 14th Chasseurs in summer
walking-out dress, 1810–12*
As can be seen, off-duty wear differed little from
that normally worn save for the replacement of the
colpack or shako by a felt bicorn. It should be
added, however, that at this late date this was
probably the sole use to which the *habit-long* was
put, it being that much smarter than the Kinski
tunic most popularly adopted by officers. (Illustration after Rousselot)

*G1 Trooper of the 6th Chasseurs in service dress,
1813–14*
In 1810 a new pattern of shako was decreed, taller
and broader than ever: 220 by 270 mm. It is
considered likely, however, that the chasseurs used
the one prescribed for the infantry, a more stable
190 mm tall and 240 mm in diameter. In direct
accordance therefore with that issued to grenadiers,
chasseurs of élite companies were equipped with
models having red in lieu of black leather bands
and chevrons. This is not to say that colpacks were
abolished, indeed most élite companies retained
them throughout the Empire, but the new levies
were so equipped. This trooper wears the *habit-veste*,
as prescribed by the 1812 regulations, basically the
same as the Kinski, but fastening down the breast
by means of hooks and eyes; the lapels could be
buttoned back, as shown here, or buttoned across to
left or right. The red chevron on the left upper arm
designates eight to ten years' service. These same
regulations ordered the attachment of a bayonet
frog to the waistbelt. Of greatest interest are this

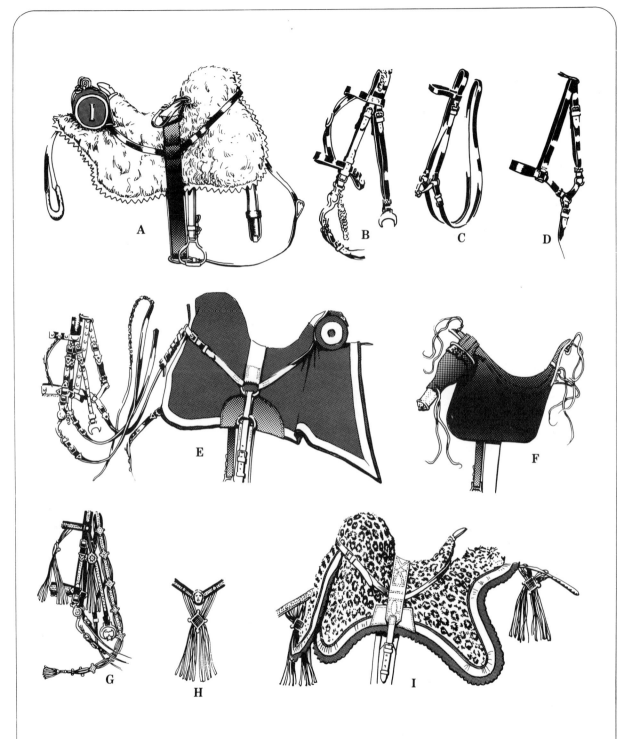

Saddles, harness and bridles. (A) Trooper's pattern Hungarian saddle and schabraque. (B) Troopers' Hungarian bridle. (C) Troopers' Snaffle bridle. (D) Parade halter of troopers' bridle. (E) Complete horse furniture of officers' mounts. (F) Officers' pattern Hungarian saddle in leather. (G) Bridle of superior officers' parade dress horse furniture. (H) Breastplate to G. (I) Superior officers' Hungarian saddle with leopard skin schabraque.

trooper's overalls: firstly, in place of the strip of regimental coloured lace, we see a band of white lace; secondly, the leather insert on the inside leg is gone, while the cuffs of the legs have been raised and ornamented with white piping describing the contour of the full dress Hungarian boot. All in all, the garment has come a long way from the laterally opening overalls we first saw, and now fairly successfully mimics breeches and boots. (Illustration after Benigni)

G2 Trumpeter of the 12th Chasseurs in campaign dress, 1812

The Marckolsheim MS records trumpeters of this regiment in the year 1810 in the reversed-colour habit of musicians, but 1812 found them again dressed in the sky-blue tunic and breeches they had sported in 1804. This is perhaps explained by the fact that the 10th and 11th Chasseurs also wore crimson tunics, and the need to distinguish between them, especially between the 12th and 10th, prompted the change. A further embellishment was the acquisition of czapskas for the musicians, seen here wrapped in oilskin against the elements; uncovered, it was crimson with a broad white strip of lace about the top edge. Most unusual was its copper plate which, in place of the familiar rising-sun pattern, described not an Imperial but a Polish eagle, so large that its wings spread across the width of the side panels. (Illustration after Rousselot)

G3 Subaltern of the 8th Chasseurs in regulation full dress, 1813–14

Though the officers clung jealously to their bearskin colpacks, the 1812 regulations prescribed a shako of identical pattern to that of the troopers. Subalterns were no longer to wear plumes, but rather pompons of company colour and, though cords and tassels would not be tolerated, the upper band of the shako could be ornamented with silver lace or embroidery. Despite this gracious generosity of the war department towards the vanity of their junior officers, most of them perversely opted for a conservative band of black velvet. All rank insignia and detail of the Kinski tunic were transferred to the new habit-veste. While the Hungarian breeches remained the only officially recognised form of legwear, dark-green trousers laced in the regimental colour were far more popular. Note that

the predilection of officers for personalised webbing has here reached its apogee, being entirely worked in silver with not a trace of leather remaining visible. (Illustration after Hilpert)

H1 Trooper of the 2nd Chasseurs in campaign dress, 1813–14

At the beginning of the Empire, chasseurs wore the dark-green cavalry cape with attached hood or the so-called three-quarter length cape, of considerably narrower cut than its predecessor, with a short shoulder-cape stitched about the collar but devoid of the hood. The 1812 regulations, applicable as of 1813, specified a new garment, more in the line of a greatcoat, called the manteau-capote. Unlike the previous version, this one had the luxury of cuffed sleeves and a button-up front. The shoulder cape described on the three-quarter length cape was carried over to this design, enabling the wearer to strap his webbing over the coat rather than beneath it, as had to be done with the hooded cape. Note the updated overalls; like those worn by the trooper in G1 they are devoid of leather insert but have cuffs of fawn leather on the legs. Both of the individuals should officially have been wearing overalls similar to those of the trooper in D1, but with piping in place of lace in accordance with the 1812 regulations. (Reconstruction)

H2 Trumpeter of the 27th Chasseurs in full dress, 1813–14

With a view to regularising the dress of musicians, an Imperial Livery was devised and ordered as of 1811. The Imperial lace was to be manufactured in two versions, the one for horizontal and the other for vertical use, and to be composed of alternating Imperial N's and eagles. These came in several varieties – green devices on yellow ground, vice-versa or alternating – but always separated by black thread and bordered in red. Such a costly garment smacking of a sovereign's royal livery did not please the individualist regimental colonels, who therefore tended to have tunics of correct cut manufactured, but in the same colours as the

Chef d'escadron of the 7eme Chasseurs à Cheval, 1805–1806. This officer is in full dress uniform. Note the splendid leopardskin schabraque over his Hungarian pattern light-cavalry saddle, the detail of which can be found in the previous illustration, on p.149 fig. I. (Benigni. Courtesy of the de Gerlache de Gomery Collection)

previous Kinski. The 27th Chasseurs, ex-*Chevau-légers d' Arenberg* and relative latecomers to the ranks of French chasseurs, were apparently never issued with the 1810-model shako and this fellow therefore wears the old 1806 pattern with the addition of

chinscales; though old, it none the less affords him the luxury of decorative cords and tassels and the now abolished pompon and plume. (Illustration after Benigni)

H3 Subaltern of the 19th Chasseurs in campaign dress, 1813–14
Clinging tenaciously to his bearskin colpack in the face of the austere regulation shako, this officer wears the new *habit-veste* identical to that of the rank and file save for the ornaments. Notice also his overalls of similar pattern to those of the trooper in *G1*, with cuffs giving the semblance of boots, except that the lace is silver in place of white. (Illustration after Rousselot)

Elite company of *chasseurs*, **1812. Drawn from Christian Suhr's** *Album du bourgeois de Hamburg*, **this illustration depicts the first** (*élite*) **squadron of a regiment of** *chasseurs*. **Of particular interest are the farriers of this regiment, their insignia being twin crossed axes on the right upper-arm, three of whom are armed with scarlet pennanted lances: although both rows of men are bearded, it is unlikely that the regiment boasted fourteen of these craftsmen; on the other hand, the lances are an equally unlikely form of armament. But in view of the fact that these illustrations were drawn from life, it would be undesirable to reject their evidence out of hand. Of further interest is the officer's colpack top, a detacheable leather lid which protected the** *flamme* **when folded within the headgear. (Author's Collection)**

4

Hussars

(General Sebastiani) must remind his hussars that a French soldier must be a cavalryman, infantryman and artilleryman; that he is required to lend his hand to everything and anything.

(Napoleon to Berthier, 22 September 1803)

Organisation

Doubtless the most distinctive of all forms of light horse, the hussars originated in eastern Europe and, by means of their dress, their roots can be traced all the way back to a cavalry corps of the mighty Ottoman Empire: the Gunalis, whose rather eccentric fur-covered, tall conical caps and fur-lined jackets, perilously draped over the left shoulder, were to set a military fashion from Turkey to Hungary and thence, by way of Germany and France, to the rest of the world.

In contrast to their fellow light cavalry, the numerous regiments of indigenous French *chasseurs à cheval*, the hussars consisted of only fourteen regiments during the Empire. Six of these existed well before the massive reorganisations of 1791 and the rest were raised over the following years: the 7th and 8th regiments in 1792; the 9th, 10th and 11th in 1793; the 12th in 1794; the 13th in 1795; and, finally, the 14th in 1814.

These regiments were composed of four squadrons, themselves comprising two companies each of which in turn consisted of two troops or *peletons*. See Chapter 1, *Cuirassiers and Carabiniers*, and Chapter 2, *Dragoons and Lancers* for the precise hierarchy of inter-regimental command, enumerating company and *état-major* NCOs and officers. In this title the role of light cavalry will be examined in the same manner in which we studied that of the heavy and medium.

Both the offensive and defensive roles of light cavalry consisted of reconnaissance on the one hand and advance, flank and/or rear and outpost protection of the main column on the other.

Although the hussars made their first real impact in 1806 with their astonishing pursuit of the Prussians over 1,160kms from the river Saale to the Oder in twenty-five days (capping this feat on arrival when, by dint of audacious demonstrations by the 500 men of the combined 5th and 7th

Hussars, the 6,000-strong Prussian garrison was bluffed into capitulating its fortress at Stettin along with 160 cannon), the large-scale use of flying

Colonel de Juniac of the 1st Hussars in full dress, 1807. This colonel's uniform provides us with a classic illustration of early officers' dress. His shako is basically the 1801 pattern but has variations which first appeared around 1802, such as a centrally placed cockade and loop; the headgear lacks both the detachable peak and the turban, which characterised the true 1801 model. The uniform is of note for its increasingly outdated cut and style: the dolman was to become sharper in cut, the pelisse less sack-like and considerably shorter, and the breeches were beginning to give way to trousers and overalls. (Huen. National Army Museum)

155

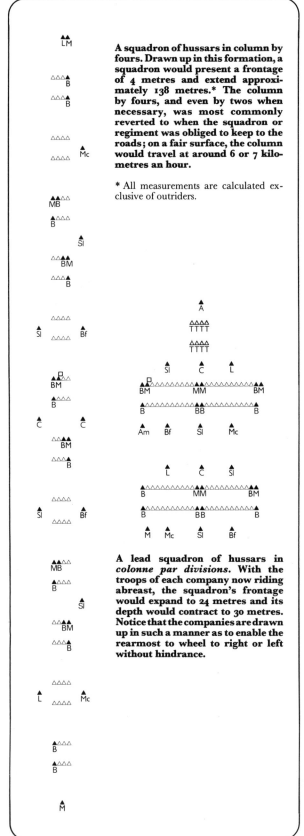

A squadron of hussars in column by fours. Drawn up in this formation, a squadron would present a frontage of 4 metres and extend approximately 138 metres.* The column by fours, and even by twos when necessary, was most commonly reverted to when the squadron or regiment was obliged to keep to the roads; on a fair surface, the column would travel at around 6 or 7 kilometres an hour.

* All measurements are calculated exclusive of outriders.

A lead squadron of hussars in *colonne par divisions*. With the troops of each company now riding abreast, the squadron's frontage would expand to 24 metres and its depth would contract to 30 metres. Notice that the companies are drawn up in such a manner as to enable the rearmost to wheel to right or left without hindrance.

Key to the figures on pp. 156 and 157:
A: *Adjutant* (adjutant)
AM: *Adjutant-major* (regimental-sergeant-major)
B: *Brigadier* (corporal)
Bf: *Brigadier-fourrier* (quarter-master corporal)
C: *Capitaine* (captain)
L: *Lieutenant* (lieutenant)
M: *Maréchal-des-logis* (sergeant)
Mc: *Maréchal-des-logis-chef* (sergeant-major)
Sl: *Sous-lieutenant* (second lieutenant)
T: *Trompette* (trumpeter)

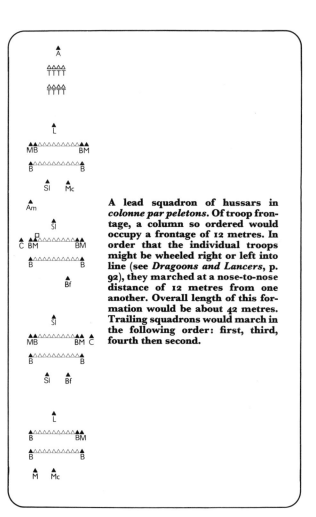

A lead squadron of hussars in *colonne par peletons*. Of troop frontage, a column so ordered would occupy a frontage of 12 metres. In order that the individual troops might be wheeled right or left into line (see *Dragoons and Lancers*, p. 92), they marched at a nose-to-nose distance of 12 metres from one another. Overall length of this formation would be about 42 metres. Trailing squadrons would march in the following order: first, third, fourth then second.

columns of *blitzkrieg*-style cavalry was never developed. Imaginative employment of highly mobile spearheads was confined to patrols of between twenty and a hundred men and consequently when, in October 1806, twenty hussars led by a *sous-lieutenant* walked unopposed into Leipzig, the bulk of the *Grande Armée* was bogged down 80kms away at Jena, incapable of exploiting the opportunity.

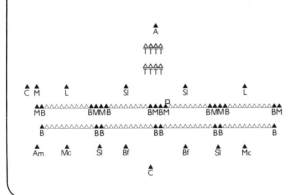

A lead squadron of hussars drawn up *en colonne serré*. In order to contract the depth of the column still further, squadrons would arrange their companies in this manner. The fully extended front would now measure some 48 metres, while the depth would shrink to a mere 6 metres. Following squadrons would probably not allow less than a troop's frontage to separate them from the squadron in front. In this way, a regiment in column might not exceed a depth of 54 metres (assuming a standard regiment of four squadrons).

Confined for the most part to scouring the countryside in the vicinity of the main columns, the hussar regiments would deploy their squadrons in battle order and sweep the surrounding landscape. Upon contact with the enemy, a troop of the leading squadron would disperse at the gallop to form a screen of sharpshooters about the regiment's front. If engaged, the hussar skirmishers would discharge their carbines at less than a hundred metres from a stationary position, their primary targets being enemy officers. Then, pistol in the right hand and drawn sabre hanging from the swordknot at the wrist, they would charge home, reserving the pistol ball to the last moment, then passing the handgun to their left hand and setting-to with cold steel.

Where such a charge required the back-up of the entire regiment, the squadrons would advance in extended waves staggered obliquely to either right or left, for maximum strike value.

Their defensive role might be described as the same as above but in reverse: maintaining surveillance of the enemy by forcing a contact, thereby eliminating any element of surprise, and masking the true movement of the main column by feints and general harassment.

This trouble-shooter role created a strong *esprit de corps* which resulted in the light cavalry believing itself to be rather more than just a cut above the rest. Indeed, such was the audacity of the hussars that their arrogant indiscipline brought a specific rebuke from the Emperor: 'These hussars must be made to remember that a French soldier must be a horseman, infantryman and artilleryman, and there is nothing he may turn his back on!'

Nowhere is evidence of their excesses, indulgences and pure egotism better illustrated than in their near-anarchic mode of dress.

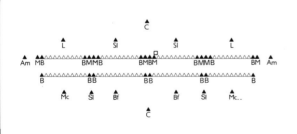

A squadron of hussars in battle order. In similar formation to the *colonne serré*, a squadron so ordered would find its regiment deployed alongside in either a straight line or in echelon, reading from right to left: first, second, third and finally fourth squadron. It should not be assumed, however, that formation of such a battle order was a prerequisite to combat; the precise manner in which a particular body of cavalry would enter the fray depended on its size and its preparedness—a regiment might, for instance, advance extended in echelon with its squadrons formed up in *colonne par pelotons* (i.e. troop frontage, see *Dragoons and Lancers*, p. 91).

Dress and Equipment

Hussar costume consisted principally of a short shell-jacket, the dolman; tight Hungarian riding breeches; calf-length Hungarian boots; and a second jacket slung on the left shoulder—the pelisse. Equipment comprised a shako, musketoon, curved sabre, sabretache, cartridge-pouch and attendant webbing. Accessories included short gloves, swordknot and barrel-sash. It is the enormous variety of these objects in their differing cuts, models and patterns that render hussar uniforms so complex; the following descriptions are therefore basic outlines, and readers are referred to the numerous black and white illustrations and their captions for further detail. This bewildering diversity of costumes represents just some of the costumes worn by just one regiment in the span of eleven years.

The hussar regiments were colourfully distinguished from one another by the different base cloths used in the manufacture of the dolmans, pelisses and breeches, and also by their facings and lace colours, as the chart below indicates.

Tunics

Unlike the pelisse, the dolman was fastened along its entire length by eighteen half-round buttons and their corresponding braid loops; in contrast, the pelisse loops were cut so that only the top five were long enough to be used. Both garments commonly had five rows of buttons except for those of the 2nd, 4th, 5th, 9th and 10th Hussars, which had only three rows. The pelisse was secured on the shoulder by a length of doubled-over cord which passed over the right shoulder and was then looped about a toggle sewn to the opposite side of the collar.

For other than full-dress occasions, hussars wore either the dolman or the pelisse beneath which they wore a sleeveless waistcoat. This garment was either single- or double-breasted and plain, or with miniature rows of buttons and braid identical to

Colonel Rouvillois of the 1st Hussars in full dress 1804–5. He wears an 1801-pattern shako, minus *flamme* but covered in scarlet cloth, with a centrally placed cockade and shako-plate; although this was increasingly the fashionable mode, it is interesting to note that his plume still reserves its old position on the right side of the headgear. The cords which loop about his left shoulder are just visible; their role was to become totally obsolete with the widespread introduction of chin-scales. His magnificent horse furniture is typical of that affected by superior officers, comprising metal-studded harness and leopard-skin schabraque liberally festooned with silver lace. (Benigni. Courtesy NAM)

Regt	Dolman	Collar	Cuffs	Pelisse	Breeches	Lace
1	Sky blue	Sky blue	Red	Sky blue	Sky blue	White/silver
2	Brown	Brown	Sky blue	Brown	Sky blue	White/silver
3	Silver grey	Silver grey	Red	Silver grey	Silver grey	Red/silver
4	Indigo	Indigo	Scarlet	Scarlet	Indigo	Yellow/gold
5	Sky blue	Sky blue	White	White	Sky blue	Yellow/gold
6	Scarlet	Scarlet	Scarlet	Indigo	Indigo	Yellow/gold
7	Dark green	Scarlet	Scarlet	Dark green	Scarlet	Yellow/gold
8	Dark green	Scarlet	Scarlet	Dark green	Scarlet	White/silver
9	Scarlet	Sky blue	Sky blue	Sky blue	Sky blue	Yellow/gold
10	Sky blue	Scarlet	Scarlet	Sky blue	Sky blue	White/silver
11	Indigo	Scarlet	Scarlet	Indigo	Indigo	Yellow/gold
12	Scarlet	Sky blue/scarlet	Scarlet/sky blue	Sky blue	Sky blue	White/silver
13	Brown	Sky blue	Sky blue	Brown	Sky blue	White/silver
14	Dark green	Scarlet	Scarlet	Dark green	Scarlet	White/silver

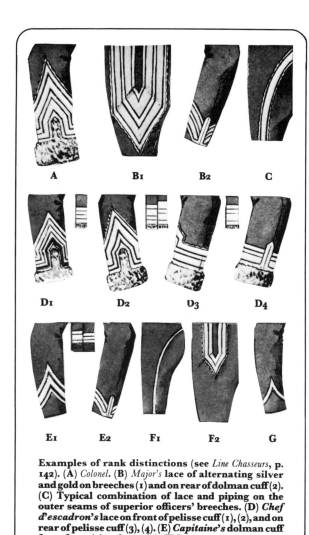

Examples of rank distinctions (see *Line Chasseurs*, p. 142). **(A)** *Colonel*. **(B)** *Major's* lace of alternating silver and gold on breeches (1) and on rear of dolman cuff (2). **(C)** Typical combination of lace and piping on the outer seams of superior officers' breeches. **(D)** *Chef d'escadron's* lace on front of pelisse cuff (1), (2), and on rear of pelisse cuff (3), (4). **(E)** *Capitaine's* dolman cuff from front (1) and rear (2). **(F)** Lace on outer seams of subaltern's breeches (1) and on front of lieutenant's (2). **(G)** *Sous-lieutenant's* dolman cuff.

Legwear

Riding breeches were of the tight-fitting Hungarian pattern with lace ornamenting the outer seams and the edges of the front flap which disguised the button-up fly, where it took the form of Hungarian knots, simple trefoils or bastion-loops. From Republican times, however, it was found more practical to envelop them in overalls in order to save wear and tear.

Overalls were cut of blue, grey, green and even red material. They opened down the side by means of eighteen bone or pewter buttons along the outer seams. The inside leg and cuffs were reinforced with leather to varying degrees. For fatigues, they would be replaced by overalls of rough, unbleached cloth.

The 1812 Regulations specified that the ornamentation of the front flap of the breeches should consist of the simple bastion-loop. They also officially recognised the overalls and required them to be cut of dark green cloth with eighteen blackened bone buttons and leather cuffs rising to a height of 11cm. By this date, however, overalls had developed as a garment and we might more readily identify them nowadays as trousers; they were equipped with a front fly concealed by a flap, but frequently still bore lace or piping and/or buttons the length of the outer seams. Some examples have buttons at the calf to facilitate their use over the high riding boots, others have the leather cuff extended to the height of the boots and the top scalloped in imitation of them.

Capes and greatcoats

Hussars were issued a cape with hood of immense proportions dating back to the Monarchy; re-

those on the dolman. For fatigue-duty, a dark green single- or double-breasted linen stable-jacket was worn, occasionally equipped with shoulder-straps.

The 1812 Regulations prescribed the following changes: a slim braid shoulder-strap was to be sewn to the left shoulder of the dolman and pelisse to secure the webbing; the waistcoat, or *gilet*, was henceforth to be plain and single-breasted, fastening by means of ten cloth-covered buttons; and the stable-jacket was to be knitted and single-breasted with ten uniform buttons.

Rank distinctions were indicated by chevrons of lace above the cuffs, as shown in the illustration on this page. Further reference is available in Chapter 3, *Line Chasseurs*, p. 142.

Maréchal-des-logis of a centre company and a trooper of an elite company. Recorded in Hamburg, 1806–7. The NCO, his status indicated by the single chevron of lace above each cuff, wears a shako typical of the period (160mm in height and 230mm in diameter) sufficiently evolved from the 1801 model to be dubbed the 1806 pattern. The distinctive feature is the chinscales, which were by this date almost universal; this together with the omission of the main characteristics of the earlier version, make this shako a headdress on its own, owing little to the past, with cords now redundant and simply decorative. The plain single-breasted waistcoat is non-regulation; the 'charivari' overalls, open at the side and have flapped hip-pockets. The NCO's companion wears the bearskin colpack accorded elite troops by the First Consul's decree of 18 *Vendémiaire An X* (10 October 1801). Although the elite companies were not, in effect, created until the beginning of the following year, some regiments were obliged to cover shakos with bearskin prior to acquiring patterns of this distinctive variety (see colour plate A2). He wears fatigue overalls of rough undyed cloth generally reserved for drill and stable duties. (Huen. Courtesy NAM)

Trooper and brigadier in drill uniform, 1807–10. These figures afford us a good look at the *bonnet de police* fatigue-cap common to all troops of the *Grande Armée*; although here smartly tucked within the turban of the cap, the long *flamme* was allowed to tumble elegantly about the shoulders when off-duty. Both figures also wear the woollen stable-jacket, with matching waist-pockets of which the left one was simulated for the sake of symmetry. the twin chevrons of lace on the brigadier's cuff proclaim his rank; for brigadiers or sergeants they would be of cloth of the same colour as the lace on the dolman, whereas for more exalted NCOs they would be the equivalent in either silver or gold. The chevron on his left upper-arm represents between eight and ten years' service in the army; his splendid moustache and elegantly fashioned hair attest that those years were certainly all with the light cavalry. It was the custom to intertwine a pistol ball in the ends of the side plaits in order that they might hang at a strict vertical. (Benigni. Courtesy NAM)

sembling a modern poncho, it would be wrapped about the wearer's body or, when on horseback, left to hang about wearer and mount. It was awkward and untidy, and was later replaced by the *manteau-capote*, a long greatcoat with a short shoulder-cape attached, which enabled the wearer to place his crossbelts on the outside of the garment. Both models were entirely dark green. Officers wore similar patterns of cape and greatcoat, but, in addition, generally sported a double-breasted overcoat, or *redingote*, for foot-duty.

Accessories

Boots were the classic Hungarian variety with superior edge bordered with piping of white lace and a tassel, although some varieties were similarly ornamented but in black leather. Troopers generally wore clogs in their place for all fatigue duties. Officers' patterns were identical save that the decorative piping and tassel were of silver; for full dress they sometimes indulged in goatskin versions of red, green or even yellow. Both officers and men used wrist-length white gloves when riding.

Headgear

The variety of hussar shakos is illustrated on p. 144, Chapter 3, *Line Chasseurs*. Around 1802 the 1801-model shako, 190mm tall by 220mm in diameter, lost its *flamme* and detachable peak, and the cockade and plume were removed to the front. Soon after that came the addition of a shako plate placed beneath the cockade; the 1st, 6th and 12th Hussars are recorded with a lozenge-shaped plate out of which the regimental number has been cut. At this period the headgear was maintained in place by a strap which passed beneath the wearer's queue, and a cord was attached to the uniform to prevent

Trooper in campaign dress, 1807. In keeping with the 1791 Regulations, this trooper's 1806 model shako boasts a black plume tipped in the regimental colour. In an equally outdated manner, his shoulderbelts, cartridge-pouch, swordbelt, sabretache, sabre and musketoon are all of 1786 pattern, little changed by the 1801 Regulations save that the swordknot is no longer of black leather. Surprising as it may seem, the webbing was supposed to last at least twenty years. (Bitry-Boëly. Courtesy NAM)

P. Benigni.

163

its loss should it be toppled. Around 1805 these were replaced by chinscales which were universally adopted by the close of 1806. By then the shako had become taller and more bell-shaped and, with the amendments mentioned above, is generally regarded as a model in its own right. Although redundant, shako cords were still employed in a decorative capacity.

A circular dated 9 November 1810 required the final abolition of the shako cords, along with the much-prized tall plumes which were replaced by a simple lentil-shaped pompon; unabashed, the commissary persisted in selling cords and tassels as late as December 1811 and we may be sure that their customers gladly parted with the price of one franc per set.

Further to the 1812 Regulations, an inventory dated 17 September 1812 indicates that shakos of centre companies were to be devoid of the neck-covers folded inside the crown common to models in use at this period. It further informs us that those of elite troops were to be identical to the shakos employed by the grenadiers in the infantry: 10mm taller and wider than that of ordinary troopers, with upper and lower bands and side chevrons of scarlet. Elite troops, however, persisted in wearing their bearskin colpacks till the end of the Empire if they had been previously issued them.

Despite the 1812 Regulations, a new shako made its debut in 1812, the *shako rouleau*. This pattern was somewhat taller than its predecessor; it exceeded 200mm and consisted of a reinforced black felt cylinder, often covered in coloured fabric of which the most popular was red, black leather peak and fold-down neck cover at the rear. The 6th and 8th Hussars are known to have worn it during the Russian campaign of 1812 and, by the end of the Empire, its popularity eclipsed that of the bell-topped shako, although it never made regulation issue.

Off-duty, hussars would sport the *bonnet de police* or, after 1812, the pokalem variety of fatigue-cap; the *bonnets de police*, consisting of a turban and long *flamme* with tassel, were of all combinations of the regimental colours.

Besides their own patterns of all the above headgear, officers also wore a bicorn hat in everyday wear and, particularly in the early years, even on the battlefield.

Brigadier-trompette and trumpeters in full dress, 1810. Trumpeters were expressly clothed and equipped in such a manner as to make them readily distinguishable from the rank and file. To this end their uniforms were most frequently of inverse colours to those of the men, their schabraques were of black in place of white sheepskin and they were mounted on greys. The NCO is identified by sky blue insignia on his scarlet pelisse. The centre trumpeter's black plume indicates that he belongs to a centre company; his companions' scarlet plumes show that they belong to an elite company. We can conclude that the distribution of the elite symbol, a bearskin colpack, to centre company musicians was an extravagance on the part of the regiment's undoubtedly vain and competitive colonel. (Malespina. Courtesy NAM)

Trooper in campaign dress, 1807–10. Uncompromisingly demonstrating the reality behind the tinsel of the hussar image, this trooper is entirely clad in uniform and equipment distributed to the hussars between 1806 and 1808. He wears the *Kinski* tunic, common to the *chasseurs à cheval*, as practical and comfortable as the pipe and tobacco hung on the pommel of his sabre is practical and comforting. The sabre is the light-cavalry pattern with copper guard and steel scabbard; it might be either the *An IX* or *An XI* model, both of which were issued as of 1807. His overalls open laterally by means of eighteen pewter buttons, which can only be seen because the sabretache is missing; it was common practice to leave them at the depot, but they were often lost in the field. (See colour figure B2.) (Benigni. Courtesy NAM)

Colonel in full dress, 1810. This superior officer wears the officers' pattern of the 1810-model shako, loftier and wider than any preceding example and possessing two further distinguishing features; unlike its predecessor, it reverted to the simple cockade and loop of the 1801 pattern, and, instead of chinscales which were by then universal, it boasted a chinstrap composed of interlocking rings upon a bed of leather. In this instance it is also extravagantly embroidered about the crown. The metal devices visible on his crossbelt were frequently so valuable that many officers were obliged to encase the entire belt and cartridge-pouch in a leather cover when on active service in order to protect their investment. (Rouffet. Courtesy NAM)

Webbing

Comprising swordbelt and slings, sabretache, and the musketoon and cartridge-pouch crossbelts, it conformed to the Decree of 4 *Brumaire An X* (27 October 1801) and was little different from that issued previously save that the swordknot previously of black leather was now of white buff. (See p. 117 of Chapter 3, *Line Chasseurs* for specifications, which were identical to those of the hussars.)

The sabretache also differed little from preceding models, the flap usually bearing the regimental number encircled by a wreath of laurel leaves although later models incorporated an Imperial eagle. The flap was covered in cloth of a diversity of colours and the elaborately embroidered motifs were such as to make them almost works of art. Indeed they were so valuable that a leather cover was generally slipped over the flap in order to protect it on the march and in action. Officers often possessed a second, plain, sabretache for wear with everything but parade dress; the embellishment on the flap was confined to either the regimental number alone or a combination of this and a shield or Imperial eagle device of metal. The 1812 Regulations simplified the sabretache to this minimum requirement, but the troops possessing the older versions guarded them jealously and they remained common throughout the Empire.

Edged weapons

Hussars were armed with either the 1786-pattern curved sabre, with copper guard and fittings on the black leather-covered scabbard, or the *An IV* model, with iron hilt and scabbard fittings, in the early years. Around 1807, however, the *An IX* and *An XI* models of light-cavalry sabre began to be distributed, with their distinctive N-shaped copper basket guard and iron scabbard. Officers' patterns were similar save that all copper fittings were gilded. (See Chapter 3, *Line Chasseurs* for further detail.)

Firearms

Discounting musketoons of foreign origin with which many hussars were doubtless armed, troopers carried both the 1766 and 1786 models at the dawn of the Empire, along with many others of rather doubtful Republican manufacture. The 1786 pattern is certainly the most frequently represented during the Empire period as a whole, but it gradually gave way to the *An IX* model. The 487mm bayonet which, in principle, accompanied them provides something of an enigma. The author has yet to see a contemporary illustration of a hussar with bayonet fixed or in the bayonet frog of the swordbelt. On reflection, it is perhaps rather difficult to imagine its use as, when it came to close action, the trooper was more likely to rely on his sabre, which was always looped by the swordknot to his right wrist even when he was firing. However, the Regulations of 1 *Vendémiaire An XII* specifically ordered their issue, and records exist from the 1st Hussars, dated January 1808, requesting them. That they were issued is in little doubt and yet no mention is made of them in the 1812 Regulations nor is there a reference to a bayonet-frog in the description of the hussar swordbelt. To confuse the issue, a general inventory of 17 September 1812 refers to '*ceinturons à porte-baïonette*' (swordbelts with bayonet frogs) as items of hussar paraphernalia. They were therefore an item of equipment with which the hussars were certainly supposed to be armed, but whether they actually used them or not and where they kept them is not known.

NCOs', trumpeters' and officers' armament did not include the musketoon, instead they were, in theory, equipped with pistols as firearms. Unfortunately, the holsters with which the Hungarian saddle was fitted were as often as not empty. All hussars were supposedly issued a brace of pistols apiece but even prior to the Empire these were in short supply: those issued included the 1763 model, various patterns 'bodged' together from bits and pieces during the Republic, and antiques dating back to the first half of the 18th century, newly dusted and polished. Excluding those acquired from captured arsenals after 1805, these types remained in service throughout the Empire along with the newer and very scarce *An XIII* model towards the end.

It should be concluded that firearms were seemingly considered a poor second to the sabre as far as the cavalry was concerned, despite their obviously crucial benefit in such instances as the classic impasse of cavalry versus infantry square or even versus fellow cavalry; consider the following revealing extract from an eyewitness' memoirs, referring to an incident at Eylau in 1807:

'Colonel Castex asked if the carbines were loaded ... he ordered "Present carbines!" ... and when the Russians [dragoons] were only six paces away the Colonel gave the order, rapidly, "Fire!". The order was executed by the regiment as if on an exercise. The effect of the discharge was terrible: nearly the whole of the first rank of the dragoons was put out of action ...' (*Souvenirs de Capitaine Parquin*, 1892.)

Admittedly the necessity for reserving fire until the last minute might have had less to do with *sang-froid* than the poor range of the weapon, but well-armed light cavalry were full of potential that had yet to be cultivated and developed. Instead, musketoons and carbines were more readily distributed to the infantry who, in the closing years of the Empire, were desperately short of firearms. Had the masses of cavalry, impotently facing the British squares at Waterloo, been deployed in skirmishing order with pouches full of cartridges and the newly developed rifled carbine, the outcome might have been quite different.

Chef d'escadron in full dress, 1810. Officers' dress reveals a seemingly inexhaustible appetite for lush extravagance. Although initially reserved solely for officers of elite companies, the bearskin colpack proved too delicious a morsel for the tastes of their brother officers to ignore and, by 1808, it was *de rigeur* for every light cavalryman of rank, irrespective of company. This superior officer's sabretache, constructed of scarlet Morocco leather and faced with richly embroidered fabric, has the added embellishment of coiled metal fringes about its perimeter. Such was the expense of these indulgences that most officers possessed two wardrobes, one for full-dress parades and the other for the more serious aspects of their profession. (M.O. Courtesy NAM)

Maréchaux-des-logis **of an elite and a centre company in full dress, c.1810. Except for their silver rank chevrons, these NCOs demonstrate full-dress attire for all ranks of hussar. The pelisses were originally to be lined with sheepskin but this proved too difficult and expensive, so it was reserved for the facings alone and the interior was instead lined in white flannel. Note that the toggle and loop affair by which means the pelisse was hung on the shoulder lacks the** *raquettes* **and tassels with which it is all too frequently illustrated. Although officers' pelisses sometimes bore them, they were bought at personal expense and were by no means an integral part of the garment. (Yvond d'Aubin. Courtesy NAM)**

Saddles and Harness

Because of the attractions of the men's costume, horse furniture is generally neglected in most publications and this in turn has led to neglect of the horses themselves and an underestimation of their importance. Indeed they were generally treated better than the men and were certainly more expensive and less easily obtained. Such was the devastating effect of the massive abuse of horseflesh during the Napoleonic Wars that European stocks suffer to this day.

Hussars were mounted on horses of all colours, with musicians having first claim to greys. At the beginning of the Republican Wars, the minimum height for a light cavalry horse was 147cm and, by *An XII*, it was 148cm; but, by their end, stocks were so short that in 1805 Napoleon had to drop the height requirement to 138em, and this still left the *Grande Armée* short of mounts. With the conquests of large chunks of Europe during the years 1807–13, the army was able to raise the standard to 140cm, but we may be sure that replacements were still a continuous headache considering the numbers of horses necessary to shift the enormous bulk of the *Grande Armée's* cavalry and goods. The proportion of men to horses in the *Grande Armée* of 1812 was 400,000 to 130,000, of which 80,000 were cavalry mounts and 50,000 were draught animals.

This campaign serves as a typical example of hideous wastage. Within the first eight days 8,000 of the beasts had died, and these were the best horses Europe had to offer. After twenty-four days, Murat's cavalry of 22,000 mounted troops was only able to mount 14,000. Such was the exhaustion of the ill-used animals (the French never walked beside their horses, but remained constantly in the saddle), that during the battle of Winkowo, a mere thirty days from the start of the campaign, a great many of the horsemen were obliged to dismount and drag their mounts by the bridle back to their rallying points. At Borodino the casualties numbered 6,000 and worse was to come. Despite six weeks' rest, the retreat from Moscow took a ghastly toll: the first 130km of the way to Smolensk produced the staggering figure of 30,000 losses, which works out at an average of around one

Brigadier **in full dress, c.1810. Although dated as late as 1810 by Martinet, this corporal neatly represents the classic hussar stereotype for most of the Empire period, from the top of his 1806-model shako to the tip of his 1786-pattern hussar sabre. He is undoubtedly further armed with a 1786 hussar-pattern musketoon and a brace of 1763-model pistols. In fact, hussars generally left on campaign with only the dolman and breeches or the pelisse and overalls. Frequently, whole detachments would own no more than a dolman and a pair of fatigue overalls apiece in the way of uniform. As to musketoons and pistols: the 1786-pattern musketoon was a highly valued rarity among the preponderance of foreign or Revolutionary-manufactured models (the latter being constructed from a variety of odds and ends). Pistols were in such short supply that were a trooper to receive even one of the pair, he would be lucky if it proved to be the 1763 model; other than that there were only those retrieved from the battlefield, those commandeered from the civilian population or the 'rejuvenated' models dating back to the first half of the 18th century with which the conscripts of 1813 and 1814 were equipped. (Benigni. Courtesy NAM)**

169

cadaver every four metres. Murat's cavalry was reduced to 1,200 horses; thereafter, it is sad to report that the survivors went into the cooking-pot for the most part.

The terrible conditions of the Russian campaign left 200,000 men with 15,000 horses for the campaign of 1813. None of these mounts was saddle-trained and, by the beginning of hostilities, it is estimated that only 3,000 were at all suitable as cavalry mounts. This shortage of cavalry undoubtedly cost France the Empire.

The horse furniture was of Hungarian pattern and has been extensively illustrated and documented in Chapter 3, *Line Chasseurs*. It consisted of a wooden tree with a suspended seat and a sheepskin schabraque trimmed in scalloped lace of the regimental colour. The wooden tree was naturally extremely hard, and many good animals' backs

Trumpeter in full dress, 1810. An interesting figure with light blue pelisse, breeches, facings, and *flamme* on his white colpack. His dolman is scarlet, as is his plume, designating his elite-company status. The horse furniture is unusual in that in place of the sheepskin schabraque one associates with other ranks, he possesses a scarlet cloth schabraque and matching woollen portmanteau, both edged in white lace. (Benigni. Courtesy NAM)

were permanently damaged by the negligent use of too thin a horse blanket. Although there was one veterinary surgeon per 500 head, the falling standard of trained riders in the later years, combined with the fact that the mounts were badly broken-in, resulted in the observation that a new detachment of cavalry was most immediately recognizable by the pungent odour of the horses' suppurating saddle sores. Attached to the tree were a pair of leather pistol-holsters, a leather case for pocketing spare shoes and natural-leather straps for securing the portmanteau, greatcoat and musketoon in position. The portmanteau was a cylindrical valise strapped behind the cantle, the round ends were edged in lace and often bore the regimental number. The Hungarian-style bridle was composed of black leather with white metal and copper fittings.

Officers' horse furniture was similar save that the tree boasted leather side-panels, pommel and cantle were covered in Morocco leather matching the schabraque, bronzed spurs and pistol-holsters were tipped in gold- or silver-plate. Although examples of schabraques with a false seat of black sheepskin are known, the most common were entirely of cloth, reinforced with leather at the girth. In everyday use, a plain schabraque with piping of coloured goats' hair was employed, but, for more formal occasions, superior officers would adopt the leopard-skin schabraque; while their subordinates utilised the standard cloth variety, trimmed with lace and ornamented with devices in the corners. The 1812 Regulations regularised the excesses thus: a 50mm-wide lace about the perimeter of the cloth for colonels and majors, with a concentric lace of 15mm-width within it, of identical colour for colonels but of opposite colour for majors; a single strip of 50mm-width for *chef d'escadrons*; a 45mm-strip for captains; and single strips of 40mm and 35mm for lieutenants and second-lieutenants respectively. The corners of the schabraque were to bear the regimental number inscribed in lace to a height of 80mm. The portmanteau came in for equally precise treatment with the decorative lace confined to a 35mm-width for superior officers, 20mm for all others, and the regimental number no taller than 35mm.

In closing the sections on dress, equipment and horse furniture it is important to stress that in the first instance hussars travelled without the encumbrance of their entire kit, leaving the depots on campaign in either dolman or pelisse and riding breeches or overalls. Secondly, it should not be assumed that the hussars were ever as fully equipped as official inventories of available stocks might suggest, the regiments did not dispose of unlimited funds and a fully equipped regiment was not only a rarity but probably a myth. Inspection reports for the year 1809 indicate arriving detachments joining the *Grande Armée* with combinations of the following dress: dolman and breeches; dolman and overalls; some in pelisses; others in fatigue overalls, and a very few with both breeches and overalls. The classic fully dressed and fully armed hussar of popular imagination, all too frequently repeated in print, is a figure, therefore, belonging more to the theatre than the battlefield.

War Records and Regimental Histories

The 1st Hussars

Regimental history:

1720: Raised by and named after Count Ladislas-Ignace de Bercheny in Turkey.

1791: Renamed the 1er Régiment de Hussards.

1814: Became the Régiment de Hussards du Roi.

1815: Renamed the 1er Régiment de Hussards and disbanded later that same year.

War record:

1805: With the Grande Armée at Ulm and Austerlitz.

1806–7: With the Grande Armée at Jena, Eylau, Friedland and Heilsberg.

1808–12: With the Armées d'Espagne and du Portugal at Braga, Santillo, Sabugal and Monasterio.

1813: The 1st Squadron served with the Grande Armée at Jüterbock, Leipzig and Hanau.

1814: Part of the Armée d'Italie: Mincio.

1815: Engaged at Namur.

The 2nd Hussars

Regimental history:

1735: Created partly of Hungarian volunteers in Strasbourg on 25 January, and named Chamborant.

Lieutenant of the elite company in full dress, 1810–12. This individual, though elegantly dressed, is considerably more soberly attired than most of the officers seen so far. Aside from his comparatively low rank, the reason could be that, having hit a peak of outlandish costume between 1809 and 1810, hussar officers were at last beginning to dress more modestly for both financial and practical reasons. Indeed, as early as 1810 an official circular was issued simplifying the headdress of officers of centre companies by prohibiting (albeit without any immediately noticeable effect) all cords, *raquettes*, tassels and plumes; further, Bardin's motive for the rationalisation of officers' and other ranks' dress in the 1812 Regulations was to curb the enormous expense inherent in a wardrobe so cluttered with unnecessary items of dress and equipment. Finally, five continuous years of warfare obliged even the officers to cut down on baggage, which doubtless accounts for this officer's simple scarlet schabraque devoid even of embroidered devices in the angles. (Vallet. Courtesy NAM)

1791: Renamed the 2eme Régiment de Hussards.

1814: Became the Régiment de Hussards de la Reine.

1815: Renamed the 2eme Régiment de Hussards and disbanded in September of that year.

War record:

1805–8: With the Grande Armée at Austerlitz, Halle, Crewitz, Mohrungen, Osterode and Friedland.

The two major points of interest in these figures are the shako of the NCO on the left and both their rank insignia. The centre company *brigadier* has acquired what has now been dubbed the 1810-model shako: officially described on 9 November of that year as a towering 220mm in height and 270mm in diameter; it is thought to have actually been somewhat smaller and narrower. It bore the distinctive Imperial eagle posed on a semi-circle as a cut-out plate. Turning to the rank insignia: despite the fact that the NCOs reviewed so far have had chevrons of the same colour as their uniform lace, both of these individuals' chevrons are scarlet. Although there are some other instances of this in other regiments, there is seemingly no explanation for it. (Boisselier. Courtesy NAM)

1808–13: Saw service in the Peninsula: Medellin, Alcabon, Ronda, Sierra de Cazala, Gebora, Los Santos, Albufera and Somanis.

1813: With the Grande Armée at Leipzig.

1814: Fought at Montereau.

1815: Attached to the Corps d'Observation du Jura: defence of Belfort.

The 3rd Hussars

Regimental history:

1764: Created by and named after Count Esterhazy, and formed from a squadron from each of the Bercheny, Chamborant and Nassau hussars.

1791: Renamed the 3eme Régiment de Hussards.

1814: Became the Régiment de Hussards du Dauphin.

1815: Renamed the 3eme Régiment de Hussards and disbanded later that same year.

War record:

1805–7: With the Grande Armée at Ulm, Jena, Magdebourg, Gollup, Bartenstein, Langenheim, Hoff and Guttstadt.

1808–13: Service in the Peninsula: Tudela, Astorga, Tanoris, Baños, Tamanies, Alba-de-Tormes, Ciudad-Rodrigo, Almeida, Leria, Alcoluto, Redinha, Fuentes d'Onoro, Los Arapilos and Vittoria.

1813: With the Grande Armée at Leipzig.

1814: Fought at Brienne, Montereau and Sézanne.

1815: Engaged at Belfort.

The 4th Hussars

Regimental history:

1783: Created by Royal Ordonnance of 31 July for the Duc de Chartres, for whom the title of Colonel-Général of Hussars was created in 1779. Formed from one squadron from each of the Bercheny, Chamborant, Conflans and Esterhazy hussars, and named Colonel-Général.

1791: Renamed the 5eme Régiment de Hussards.

1793: Became the 4eme Régiment de Hussards by Convention Decree of 4 June when the original 4eme Régiment (ex-Hussards de Saxe) emigrated.

1814: Renamed the Régiment de Hussards de Monsieur.

1815: Renamed the 4eme Régiment de Hussards and disbanded in September of that same year.

War record:

1805: With the Grande Armée at Austerlitz.

Brigadier-fourrier in full dress, 1811–12. Having noted his curious way of tucking his shako's chinscales out of the way, this quarter-master corporal is of interest for his rank insignia: typical *brigadier's* twin chevrons at the cuff, but a distinctive diagonal strip of lace where we might more readily expect service chevrons on his left upper-arm. (Huen. Courtesy NAM)

1806–7: Remained with the Grande Armée: Schleiz,
Jena, Lübeck, Liebstadt and Mohrungen.
1808–13: With the Armée d'Espagne at Alcanitz,
Belchite, Stella, Chiclana, Sagonte, Yecla and the
Ordal Pass.
1813: With the 3eme Corps de Cavalerie of the Grande
Armée at Gross-Beeren and Leipzig.
1814: Part of the 6eme Corps de Cavalerie of the Armée
de Lyon at Lons-le-Saulnier, Saint-Georges and
Lyon.
1815: Fought at Ligny and Waterloo.

The 5th Hussars

Regimental history:
1783: Created by Ordonnance of 14 September from the
cavalry of the Légion de Lauzun (formed in 1778 and
newly returned from the American War of Inde-
pendence) and named the Lauzun Hussars.
1791: Became the 6eme Régiment de Hussards.
1793: Renamed the 5eme Régiment de Hussards by
Decree of 4 June.
1814: Became the Régiment de Hussards d'Angoulême.
1815: Renamed the 5eme Régiment de Hussards and
disbanded on 1 November.

War record:
1805–7: With the Grande Armée at Austerlitz, Crewitz,
Golymin, Watterdorf, Stettin, Eylau, Heilsberg and
Königsberg.
1809: Part of the Armée d'Allemagne at Eckmühl and
Wagram.
1812: With the Grande Armée at Borodino, Winkowo
and the Berezina.
1813: With the Grande Armée at Bautzen, Leipzig and
Hanau.
1814: Fought at Arcis-sur-Aube.
1815: With the Armée du Nord at Ligny, Waterloo and
Versailles.

The 6th Hussars

Regimental history:
1792: Created as the 7eme Régiment de Hussards by
Convention Decree of 23 November from the Boyer
light horse (a freecorps alternatively known as the
Hussards Défenseurs de la Liberté et de l'Egalité
raised in September of 1792).

Maréchal-des-logis, sapper, 1810–12. Cavalry regiments generally numbered only farriers among their effectives—apart
from the dragoons whose sappers were a tradition carried over
from their mounted infantry origins—but hussar regiments
were recorded with sappers among the ranks in several
instances. The voluminous beard and crossed-axe devices on
their sleeves were hallmarks of their trade, along with the
flaming grenade symbol universal to elite troops. This
individual's rank is indicated by the chevrons above the cuffs
and the single chevron on the left upper-arm, all of silver lace on
a scarlet ground. (Huen. Courtesy NAM)

174

Trumpeter in campaign dress, Spain, 1811–12. This interesting figure wears a scarlet dolman, faced in sky blue, and sky blue overalls with seams reinforced in scarlet lace. Note the twin chevrons on his left upper-arm which proclaim between sixteen and twenty years' service. He is armed with a 1786-pattern hussar sabre and, tucked into the schabraque strap on his left, a 1763-model pistol. The horse furniture consists of a brown sheepskin schabraque, Hungarian saddle, on an ochre saddle-blanket trimmed in blue, and harness embellished with tassels of mixed threads of yellow, red and blue. (Bucquoy. Courtesy NAM)

1793: Renumbered by Decree of 4 June as the 6eme Régiment de Hussards.

1814: Renamed the Régiment de Hussards de Berry.

1815: Renamed the 6eme Régiment de Hussards and disbanded that same year.

War record:

1805: With the Grande Armée at Ulm and Altenmarkt.

1809: With the Armée d'Italie at La Piave, Raab and Wagram.

1812: With the Grande Armée at Krasnoe, Smolensk and Borodino.

1813: Part of the Grande Armée at Möckern, Lützen, Bautzen, Reichenbach, Dresden and Leipzig.

1814: Fought at La Rothière, Champaubert, Vauchamps, Athies, Reims, La Fére-Champenoise and Paris.

1815: With the Armée de Nord at Ligny and Rocquencourt.

The 7th Hussars

Regimental history:

1792: Formed at Compiègne further to the Convention Decree of 23 November, the regiment was initially dubbed the Hussards de Lamothe before becoming the 8eme Régiment de Hussards.

1793: Renumbered the 7eme Régiment de Hussards following the Decree of 4 June.

1794: Augmented by the cavalry of the Légion de Kellermann (into which the 4th Squadron of the Régiment Saxe-Hussards (No. 4) had been drafted upon the regiment's defection).

1814: Renamed the Régiment de Hussards d'Orléans.

1815: Became the Colonel-Général Hussards prior to being renamed the 7eme Régiment de Hussards. Disbanded in November of that same year.

War record:

1805: Part of the III Corps of the Grande Armée at Mariazell, Afflenz and Austerlitz.

1806–7: With the Grande Armée at Gera, Zehdenick, Prentzlow, Stettin, Lübeck, Czenstowo, Golymin, Eylau, Heilsberg and Königsberg.

1809: With the Armée d'Allemagne at Peising, Ratisbonne, Raab, Wagram and Znaïm.

1812: With the Grande Armée at Vilna, Smolensk, Ostrowno, Borodino, Winkowo and Malojaroslavetz.

1813: Remained with the Grande Armée: Borna, Altenbourg, Leipzig and Hanau.

1814: Fought at Vauchamps, Montereau, Reims, Laon and Paris.

1815: With the Armée du Nord at Fleurus and Waterloo.

The 8th Hussars

Regimental history:

1793: Formed from the Eclaireurs de l'Armée (organised in October 1792 at Nancy by Colonel Fabrefonds) further to the Convention Decree of 26 February, and named the 9eme Régiment de Hussards. Renamed the 8eme Régiment de Hussards by the 4 June decree that same year.

176

1   **Sous-lieutenant, 2nd Hussars, campaign dress, 1805**
2   **Trooper, 2nd Hussars, full dress, 1801-2**
3   **Trumpeter, 4th Hussars, full dress, 1804-5**

A

1 Lieutenant, 1st Hussars, service dress, 1805-7
2 Trooper, 1st Hussars, campaign dress, 1806-8
3 Trumpeter, 5th Hussars, full dress, 1805

1 Major, 8th Hussars, service dress, c.1809
2 Trooper, 9th Hussars, full dress, 1809
3 Trumpeter, 5th Hussars, service dress, 1808-12

1 Lieutenant, 6th Hussars, service dress, c. 1810
2 Brigadier-fourrier, 7th Hussars, campaign dress, 1807-8
3 Trumpet-major, 4th Hussars, campaign dress, c. 1810

1 Captain, 4th Hussars, full dress, 1810
2 Sapper, 5th Hussars, campaign dress, 1813
3 Trumpeter, 6th Hussars, campaign dress, 1812

ANGUS McBRIDE

181

E

1 Chef d'escadron, 5th Hussars, campaign dress, 1810-12
2 Sapper, 1st Hussars, full dress, 1810-12
3 Trumpeter, 9th(bis) Hussars, campaign dress, 1812-13

F

182

ANGUS McBRIDE

1 **Captain, 3rd Hussars, full dress, 1809-13**
2 **Brigadier, 12th Hussars, full dress, 1813-14**
3 **Trumpeter, 1st Hussars, service dress, 1812**

1 Lieutenant, 6th Hussars, service dress, 1814
2 Marechal-des-logis, 4th Hussars, full dress, 1813-14
3 Trumpeter, 2nd Hussars, full dress, 1812-14

1814: Disbanded on 12 May.

War record:

1805: With the Grande Armée at Memmingen, Aicha and Austerlitz.

1806–7: Part of the Grande Armée at Jena, Fakembourg, Eylau and the passage of the Passarge.

1809: With the Armée d'Allemagne at Ratisbonne, Essling, Enzersdorf, Wagram and Znaïm.

1801–11: Attached to the Armée de Brabant in Holland.

1812–13: With the Grande Armée at Ostrowno, Vilna, Borodino, Magdebourg, Altenbourg and Leipzig.

1814: Engaged in the defences of Danzig and Strasbourg and the action at Champaubert.

The 9th Hussars

Regimental history:

1793: Created by the Convention Decree of 25 March as the 10eme Régiment de Hussards from the 2eme Corps of the Hussards de la Liberté (themselves created by the Decree of 2 September 1792). Further to the Convention Decree of 4 June, the regiment was renamed the 9eme Régiment de Hussards.

1814: Disbanded on 12 May.

War record:

1805: With the Grande Armée at Wertingen, Amstetten, Wischau and Austerlitz.

1806–7: Part of the Grande Armée at Saalfeld, Jena, Pultusk, Stettin, Ostrolenka, Danzig, Heilsberg and Friedland.

1809: With the Armée d'Allemagne at Eckmühl, Essling, Raab and Wagram.

1810–13: In Spain: Barbastro and Valencia.

1812–13: With the Grande Armée's 2eme Corps de Réserve at Borodino and Mojaïsk.

1813: With the II Corps of the Grande Armée at Bautzen, Reichenbach, Wachau, Leipzig and Hanau.

1814: Took part in the defence of Schlestadt.

The 10th Hussars

Regimental history:

1793: Formed from the Hussards Noirs (also called the Hussards de la Mort), a freecorps organised in the Nord département, and named the 10eme Régiment de Hussards.

1814: Disbanded at Fontenay on 1 August.

War record:

1805: Part of the V Corps of the Grande Armée at Wertingen, Elchingen, Ulm, Braunau, Amstetten, Vienna, Hollabrünn and Austerlitz.

1806–7: With the Grande Armée at Saalfeld, Jena, Stettin and Pultusk.

1809–11: With the V Corps in Spain: Magalon, Perdiguera, Licinera, Saragossa, Ocaña, Badajoz, Gebora and Albufera.

1813: With the Grande Armée at Weissenfels, Lützen, Bautzen, Dessau, Wachau and Leipzig.

1814: Engaged at La Rothière, Montmirail, Craonne and Laon.

The 11th Hussars

Regimental history:

1793: Formed at Amboise 26 June from various freecorps units including the cuirassiers of the Légion Germanique (created in 1792) and named the 11eme Régiment de Hussards.

1803: Became the 29eme Régiment de Dragons.

Sous-lieutenant in campaign dress, 1811–13. This courier's spring uniform, recorded in Spain, consists of an officers'-pattern 1810-model shako, in theory 220mm tall and 270mm in diameter, standard dolman and scarlet zouave-style overalls. His cartridge-pouch crossbelt is encased in a crimson leather cover and his ornate full-dress sabretache is replaced by a plain leather version bearing an eagle device. His armament comprises an *An XI*-pattern officers' sabre and a brace of pistols. (Benigni. Courtesy NAM)

1810: Recreated from the 2eme Régiment de Hussards Hollandais as the 11eme Régiment de Hussards.
1814: Disbanded.

War record:
1805–11: See Chapter 2, *Dragoons and Lancers*, p. 98.
1812–13: With the Grande Armée at Borodino, Krasnoe, Berezina, Leipzig and Hanau.

The 12th Hussars

Regimental history:
1794: Formed 9 February from the Hussards de la Montagne, a freecorps created at Bayonne in 1793.
1803: Became the 30eme Régiment de Dragons on 20 September.
1813: Re-formed 17 February from the 9eme (bis) Régiment de Hussards. The 9eme (bis) had been created 8 January 1812 from three squadrons of the 9th Hussars detached in Spain.
1814: Disbanded.

War record:
1805–11: See Chapter 2, *Dragoons and Lancers*, pp. 98–99.
1812–13: With the Armée d'Aragon at Barbastro, Diar and Borga.
1813: Three squadrons were with the Grande Armée at Gross-Beeren, Medergersdorf, Leipzig and Hanau.
1814: With the Armée de Lyon at Mâcon, Limonest and Saint-Donat.

The 13th Hussars*

Regimental history:
1795: Formed 1 September from the Hussards des Alpes, a freecorps created on 31 January.
1796: Disbanded.
1813: Re-formed following the Imperial Decree of 28 January with recruits from Rome and Tuscany (*départements* of France at this point). Regiment was

---

* The appellation of 13eme Régiment de Hussards was also applied to the Légion Franche de Cavalerie des Americains et du Midi from its creation on 7 September 1792. The Convention Decree of 21 February 1793 named the unit the 13eme Régiment de Chausseurs à Cheval.

then dissolved on 13 December and the men integrated into the 14eme Régiment de Hussards.
1814: Re-formed 1 January from the Régiment de Hussards Jérôme-Napoléon, created 5 August 1813. The regiment was finally dissolved on 12 August.

War record:
1813: With the Grande Armée at Belzig, Lubnitz and Leipzig.
1813: Part of the Armée d'Italie at Viareggio and Livornia.

188

Colonel Merlin in full dress, 1812–13. Magnificently turned out for dress parade, this colonel has reverted to the shako in place of the fashionable bearskin colpack: it is the *shako rouleau*, or cylindrical shako. Taller still than the 1810-pattern bell-topped shako, it made its appearance in 1812 and, despite being a non-regulation model, it was widely worn throughout the remaining years of the Empire. As we can see, the pelisse was at this point very short indeed, in contrast to the early patterns. The dolman was of correspondingly short cut and the barrel-sash consequently mounted very high on the waist. (Benigni. Courtesy NAM)

1810: Recreated from the 2eme Régiment de Hussards Hollandais as the 11eme Régiment de Hussards.

1814: Disbanded.

War record:

1805–11: See Chapter 2, *Dragoons and Lancers*, p. 98.

1812–13: With the Grande Armée at Borodino, Krasnoe, Berezina, Leipzig and Hanau.

The 12th Hussars

Regimental history:

1794: Formed 9 February from the Hussards de la Montagne, a freecorps created at Bayonne in 1793.

1803: Became the 30eme Régiment de Dragons on 20 September.

1813: Re-formed 17 February from the 9eme (bis) Régiment de Hussards. The 9eme (bis) had been created 8 January 1812 from three squadrons of the 9th Hussars detached in Spain.

1814: Disbanded.

War record:

1805–11: See Chapter 2, *Dragoons and Lancers*, pp. 98–99.

1812–13: With the Armée d'Aragon at Barbastro, Diar and Borga.

1813: Three squadrons were with the Grande Armée at Gross-Beeren, Medergersdorf, Leipzig and Hanau.

1814: With the Armée de Lyon at Mâcon, Limonest and Saint-Donat.

The 13th Hussars*

Regimental history:

1795: Formed 1 September from the Hussards des Alpes, a freecorps created on 31 January.

1796: Disbanded.

1813: Re-formed following the Imperial Decree of 28 January with recruits from Rome and Tuscany (*départements* of France at this point). Regiment was

* The appellation of 13eme Régiment de Hussards was also applied to the Légion Franche de Cavalerie des Americains et du Midi from its creation on 7 September 1792. The Convention Decree of 21 February 1793 named the unit the 13eme Régiment de Chasseurs à Cheval.

Trumpeter in full dress, 1813. This figure illustrates the hussar trumpeters' full-dress uniform as prescribed by the 1812 Regulations. The Imperial Livery he wears was in fact decreed as early as 1810 in an effort to standardise the dress of musicians of all arms, thereby curbing the worst excesses of inter-regimental rivalry for best-dressed heads of column. Needless to say, in the hussars the order was either politely ignored altogether or grudgingly obeyed till the fuss died down, at which point the brand-new livery was deemed worn out and replaced by the colonel's latest creation. Certainly, the trumpet banner illustrated here never got further than the designer's desk; but the Imperial Livery itself is known to have been issued. (Bitry-Boëly. Courtesy NAM)

then dissolved on 13 December and the men integrated into the 14eme Régiment de Hussards.

1814: Re-formed 1 January from the Régiment de Hussards Jérôme-Napoléon, created 5 August 1813. The regiment was finally dissolved on 12 August.

War record:

1813: With the Grande Armée at Belzig, Lubnitz and Leipzig.

1813: Part of the Armée d'Italie at Viareggio and Livornia.

187

P. Benigni.

188

The 14th Hussars

Regimental history:

1813: Raised in Turin further to the Imperial Decree of 28 January and formed of recruits from Genoa and Piedmont. Disbanded on 11 November following the Allies' violation of the capitulation of Dresden. The regiment was then re-formed on 13 December in Turin from dissolved units of the 13th and 14th Hussars.

1814: Disbanded on 16 July.

War record:

1813: Engaged in the defence of Dresden as part of the Grande Armée.

1814: Attached to the Armée d'Italie.

The Plates

A1 *Sous-lieutenant of the 2nd Hussars in campaign dress, 1805*

Recorded by Baron Lejeune, a contemporary of the period, this is an officer in very typical service dress. Although issued a multitude of different uniform and equipment items, hussars were rarely anything like fully accoutred and, even in the instance of an officer personally purchasing his additional uniforms, he would leave all but necessaries behind him at the depot. The figure from which this illustration is drawn is mounted, with a black bearskin schabraque edged in scalloped light blue lace. (Illustration after Benigni)

A2 *Trooper of the 2nd Hussars in full dress, 1801–2*

Formed in 1802, the single elite company of each regiment was accorded a bearskin in imitation of grenadiers of infantry. This interesting early model is literally a fur-covered shako which this regiment retained in use as late as 1805. Only this individual's cords and tassels inform us as to the occasion, he might otherwise be in marching order;

Sapper in service dress, 1814. Retaining his prized colpack in the face of the 1812 Regulations which prescribed an infantry-style grenadier's shako for elite light cavalry, this business-like fellow is armed with the old 1786 hussar-pattern musketoon. His colpack's *flamme* would usually be tucked within the bearskin and covered with a leather top for the march. Note the red-trimmed black sheepskin schabraque instead of the white one reserved for all but musicians. (Benigni. Courtesy NAM)

Hussars in stable dress and overcoat, 1813. The left-hand trooper, in stable-jacket of green wool, wears a light blue fatigue-cap in place of the old *bonnet de police*. Dubbed the 'pokalem' cap, it had the benefit of side flaps which folded down to cover the ears and button under the chin. His companion's greatcoat is equally new in design, consisting of a button-up coat and short shoulder-cape combined, it was far removed from its predecessor, an immense green cloak equipped with a hood. The earlier model would be either wound about the body or left to fall from the shoulders; this looked tolerable on horseback, but on foot the wearer resembled a bundle of laundry. (Benigni. Courtesy NAM)

whole detachments are known to have left for campaign without overalls, waistcoats or dolmans, such being the strain on funds and distribution. His horse's schabraque was of white sheepskin trimmed in sky blue. His lance is a most irregular and unusual form of armament. (Illustration after Rousselot/Cottreau Coll.)

A3 *Trumpeter of the 4th Hussars in full dress, 1804–5*

Drawn from German sources this trumpeter's dress is confirmed by an entry in the Marckolsheim MS for 1807–8 in all respects save the headgear. Unusual for so late a date, we can see that his 1801-model shako retains its *flamme*, an accessory which was universal to the headgear's predecessors but

189

which began to be omitted around 1802. The trumpeter of 1807–8 is similar except that he wears an 1806-model shako, covered in red cloth, bearing a lozenge-shaped shako plate out of which the regimental number has been cut. The trumpeter illustrated is the earliest recorded Empire musician of this regiment. (Illustration after Rousselot)

B1 Lieutenant of the 1st Hussars in service dress, 1805–7
In contrast to the manner in which they are most frequently represented, hussars wore either the dolman or the pelisse except on full dress occasions on which the pelisse would be slung on the left shoulder. Prior to the introduction of chinscales in 1805, a leather strap was looped beneath the queue of the wearer in order to maintain the headgear in position. This individual's horse furniture comprises sky blue schabraque and portmanteau edged in silver lace. (Illustration after Rousselot)

B2 Trooper of the 1st Hussars in campaign dress, 1806–8
The monochrome illustrations in this chapter are all of the 1st Hussars and readers are referred to the illustration on p. 165 for details of this interesting figure's costume and equipment. (Illustration after Benigni)

B3 Trumpeter of the 5th Hussars in full dress, 1805
The 5th Hussars were the ex-Lauzun Hussars to whom, among others, Hoffmann ascribes red facings at their transformation date of 1793 from the 6th Hussars. Thus, although the 5th Hussars are recorded as having sky blue uniform faced in sky blue and white, the red uniform is quite correct and authenticated, being of inverse colours to that of the troopers, in the popular fashion, despite its seeming inaccuracy. The regiment is known to have briefly experimented with a red dolman for troopers around 1802. (Illustration after Jean/Kolbe)

The 14th Hussars

Regimental history:

1813: Raised in Turin further to the Imperial Decree of 28 January and formed of recruits from Genoa and Piedmont. Disbanded on 11 November following the Allies' violation of the capitulation of Dresden. The regiment was then re-formed on 13 December in Turin from dissolved units of the 13th and 14th Hussars.

1814: Disbanded on 16 July.

War record:

1813: Engaged in the defence of Dresden as part of the Grande Armée.

1814: Attached to the Armée d'Italie.

The Plates

A1 Sous-lieutenant of the 2nd Hussars in campaign dress, 1805

Recorded by Baron Lejeune, a contemporary of the period, this is an officer in very typical service dress. Although issued a multitude of different uniform and equipment items, hussars were rarely anything like fully accoutred and, even in the instance of an officer personally purchasing his additional uniforms, he would leave all but necessaries behind him at the depot. The figure from which this illustration is drawn is mounted, with a black bearskin schabraque edged in scalloped light blue lace. (Illustration after Benigni)

A2 Trooper of the 2nd Hussars in full dress, 1801–2

Formed in 1802, the single elite company of each regiment was accorded a bearskin in imitation of grenadiers of infantry. This interesting early model is literally a fur-covered shako which this regiment retained in use as late as 1805. Only this individual's cords and tassels inform us as to the occasion, he might otherwise be in marching order;

Hussars in stable dress and overcoat, 1813. The left-hand trooper, in stable-jacket of green wool, wears a light blue fatigue-cap in place of the old *bonnet de police*. Dubbed the 'pokalem' cap, it had the benefit of side flaps which folded down to cover the ears and button under the chin. His companion's greatcoat is equally new in design, consisting of a button-up coat and short shoulder-cape combined, it was far removed from its predecessor, an immense green cloak equipped with a hood. The earlier model would be either wound about the body or left to fall from the shoulders; this looked tolerable on horseback, but on foot the wearer resembled a bundle of laundry. (Benigni. Courtesy NAM)

whole detachments are known to have left for campaign without overalls, waistcoats or dolmans, such being the strain on funds and distribution. His horse's schabraque was of white sheepskin trimmed in sky blue. His lance is a most irregular and unusual form of armament. (Illustration after Rousselot/Cottreau Coll.)

A3 Trumpeter of the 4th Hussars in full dress, 1804–5

Drawn from German sources this trumpeter's dress is confirmed by an entry in the Marckolsheim MS for 1807–8 in all respects save the headgear. Unusual for so late a date, we can see that his 1801-model shako retains its *flamme*, an accessory which was universal to the headgear's predecessors but

Sapper in service dress, 1814. Retaining his prized colpack in the face of the 1812 Regulations which prescribed an infantry-style grenadier's shako for elite light cavalry, this business-like fellow is armed with the old 1786 hussar-pattern musketoon. His colpack's *flamme* would usually be tucked within the bearskin and covered with a leather top for the march. Note the red-trimmed black sheepskin schabraque instead of the white one reserved for all but musicians. (Benigni. Courtesy NAM)

Trumpeter in service dress, 1814. He wears a scarlet cloth-covered *shako rouleau*, white pelisse and red trousers with a strip of white lace down the outer seams. Initially these were overalls with side openings; trousers had by now become a garment rather than an accessory and had ceased to be fastened along the outer-leg, but rather by means of a button-fly concealed behind a wide flap at the front. The trim on the schabraque is light blue and the red woollen portmanteau is edged in white. The trumpet cords are of mixed red and yellow threads. (Benigni. Courtesy NAM)

which began to be omitted around 1802. The trumpeter of 1807–8 is similar except that he wears an 1806-model shako, covered in red cloth, bearing a lozenge-shaped shako plate out of which the regimental number has been cut. The trumpeter illustrated is the earliest recorded Empire musician of this regiment. (Illustration after Rousselot)

B1 Lieutenant of the 1st Hussars in service dress, 1805–7
In contrast to the manner in which they are most frequently represented, hussars wore either the dolman or the pelisse except on full dress occasions on which the pelisse would be slung on the left shoulder. Prior to the introduction of chinscales in 1805, a leather strap was looped beneath the queue of the wearer in order to maintain the headgear in position. This individual's horse furniture comprises sky blue schabraque and portmanteau edged in silver lace. (Illustration after Rousselot)

B2 Trooper of the 1st Hussars in campaign dress, 1806–8
The monochrome illustrations in this chapter are all of the 1st Hussars and readers are referred to the illustration on p. 165 for details of this interesting figure's costume and equipment. (Illustration after Benigni)

B3 Trumpeter of the 5th Hussars in full dress, 1805
The 5th Hussars were the ex-Lauzun Hussars to whom, among others, Hoffmann ascribes red facings at their transformation date of 1793 from the 6th Hussars. Thus, although the 5th Hussars are recorded as having sky blue uniform faced in sky blue and white, the red uniform is quite correct and authenticated, being of inverse colours to that of the troopers, in the popular fashion, despite its seeming inaccuracy. The regiment is known to have briefly experimented with a red dolman for troopers around 1802. (Illustration after Jean/Kolbe)

Trumpeter of an elite company in service dress, 1814–15. Unusually, his white bearskin colpack bears a sky blue plume in place of the scarlet one we might expect of an elite cavalryman; additionally, the headgear's *flamme* is of the same colour, instead of the familiar red. His pelisse is white with crimson braid. His red trousers are the new kind already described, and were adopted by many regiments for even full dress wear. Some varieties were reinforced with leather on the inside leg in identical manner to the laterally opening overalls, retaining in some instances a small set of buttons at the cuff to facilitate their wear over the tall Hungarian boot; those without leather protection were constructed with a double layer of material to prevent wear and tear. The trumpet cord and tassels are red. (Benigni. Courtesy NAM)

191

C1 Major of the 8th Hussars in service dress, c. 1809

Majors of all branches of the *Grande Armée* were distinguished by a highly individual method: they wore identical insignia to that of the colonel of their regiment, except for the opposite lace colour to that employed by the rest of the regiment. If this figure were, for example, a major of the 7th Hussars (whose uniform was of the same colours but whose lace colour was yellow) we would see gold lace where here we have silver and vice versa. (Reconstruction)

C2 Trooper of the 9th Hussars in full dress, 1809

This rear view allows us the opportunity to describe the barrel-sash's composition: an unravelled total length of 260cm, it consisted of fifty doubled-over lengths of crimson wool, which were divided into two equal groups of 25 doubled lengths, and then threaded in pairs through a total of nine mobile cylindrical barrels, which prevented the lateral opening-out of the threads. Each end of the belt was permanently secured by immovable barrels; to one end was attached a doubled-over length of cord which terminated in a pair of tassels and had a series of four fixed crimson knots along its length, the last being 10cm from the twin tassels; to the other extremity was fixed another, though considerably shorter, doubled-over cord, terminating in a 4cm-long toggle about which the looped end of the long cord was fastened. The free end of the long cord was then knotted loosely about itself after having been slipped through the threads of the front of the sash. (Illustration after Girbal)

C3 Trumpeter of the 5th Hussars in service dress, elite company

This second trumpeter of the 5th Hussars (see B3) probably dates from between 1808 and 1812. He wears a No. 2 dress, long-tailed *surtout*, with the unusual addition of lapels, strongly reminiscent of the infantry officers' pattern 1812 *habit-veste*. His

Colonel Clary in full dress, 1814. The colonel is attired and accoutred in similar style to his predecessors save that the uniform has progressed a stage further, moving away from the classic hussar look, with the inclusion of trousers in the full-dress wardrobe. In the space of less than ten years the costume had developed from a style that had remained unchanged for virtually a century in its rigid conformity to its classical origins, to one that incorporated the comforts and requirements of civilian fashion. (Benigni. Courtesy NAM)

Lieutenant of an elite company in campaign dress, 1814. In place of the prescribed infantry grenadier-pattern shako, with scarlet bands and chevrons, and the cylindrical shako of his troop, this officer favours the non-regulation bearskin colpack. Notice the Morocco leather cover protecting both his crossbelt and cartridge-pouch. On the march, and in action generally, the decorative features of dress such as plume, cords and *raquettes* were packed in the portmanteau. His horse furniture comprises a cloth schabraque embroidered with an Hungarian knot and equipped with a black bearskin cover atop the pistol holsters. (Benigni. Courtesy NAM)

schabraque and portmanteau are sky blue and edged in yellow lace. The blue shako was adopted in 1808 and replaced in 1813 by a scarlet cylindrical pattern. Strange to say, the regiment at this point had trumpeters dressed in both the scarlet-influenced manner shown here and in the modernised inverse-colours: consisting of white dolman, sky blue facings and sky blue pelisse and breeches. (Illustration after Jean/Kolbe)

193

D1 Lieutenant of the 6th Hussars in service dress, c. 1810
Reconstructed from existing garments, among other sources, this officer in marching order typifies the no-nonsense approach to practical campaign dress. His shako is his sole real extravagance and would doubtless be covered in a black oilskin cover at the least sign of inclement weather. Note that the overalls now open by means of a front fly concealed behind a flap in similar manner to the riding breeches, our first indication of the development of trousers as a garment in their own right thus far. (Reconstruction from existing relics, a contemporary portrait and Baldauf)

D2 Brigadier-fourrier of the 7th Hussars in campaign dress, 1807–8
The quarter-master corporal was nominally in charge of the collective quarter-masters of each company of the regiment. Numbering a total of eight in a four-squadron regiment, their rank conferred upon them the organisational responsibilities of distributing food and drink, as well as billets to the members of their respective companies. The status of *fourrier* proper was indicated by a single diagonal strip of metal lace the same colour as the buttons on the left upper arm, subsequent rank was designated by chevrons above the cuff in the normal manner. Note his *charivari* pattern overalls, complete with twin hip-pockets. (Reconstruction)

D3 Trumpet-major of the 4th Hussars in campaign dress in Spain, c. 1810
This trumpet-major, a *maréchal-des-logis* in rank, occupied a highly privileged position next to the regiment's colonel, from whose side he would never stray in order that he might translate the officer's orders instantaneously into trumpet calls that would then be communicated in turn to the troops by the company trumpeters under his command. The role of trumpeter should not be interpreted as 'musician' since they fulfilled a signals role in an era

Hussars in campaign dress, 1814. The leading trooper is armed with the outdated 1786 hussar-pattern musketoon, 103cm in overall length, and the *An XI* light-cavalry sabre, the blade of which was fully 845mm long. Note the fashion of slinging the *manteau-capote 'en sautoir'* about the right shoulder instead of strapping it forward of the saddle's pommel beneath the schabraque; this afforded the wearer some protection from cut and thrust weapons. (Benigni. Courtesy NAM)

Trumpeter in full dress, 1815. This colourful musician's dress comprises a red *shako rouleau* with yellow pompon and white plume, a sky blue dolman with red cuffs and a white pelisse. The shako trim and cords are composed of mixed white and crimson threads, as are the lace and braid on the dolman and pelisse, the colours of the Bourbon livery lace. Further testimony to the brief return of France's monarchy is the fleur-de-lis device on the sabretache. (Benigni. Courtesy NAM)

ignorant of radio waves. Trumpeters received the billets of NCOs and double the pay of a trooper, and it will therefore be appreciated that this individual's rank of sergeant belied his true, considerably higher status. (Illustration after Rousselot/contemporary Spanish illustration)

E1 Captain of the 4th Hussars in full dress, 1810
This high-ranking full-dress figure is of the classic hussar appearance we have endeavoured to avoid, but is no less worthy of comment for that. The alternating chevrons of rank measured 14mm and 23mm respectively, and the bearskin colpack, initially reserved solely for officers of elite companies, was by this time widely adopted by officers generally, irrespective of company. Note the

grenade-shaped plume holder at its top. (Illustration after Hoffmann/Martinet)

E2 Sapper of the 5th Hussars in campaign dress, 1813
The dolman of this colourful figure would have been sky blue with matching collar and white cuffs, and its left upper-arm would bear identical devices to those indicated on the pelisse. His sheepskin schabraque was white with sky blue trim and portmanteau. His most interesting feature is the crossed-axe device on the sabretache; but note also the cuffs on his overalls, cut high in imitation of Hungarian boots. (Illustration after contemporary illustration)

E3 Trumpeter of the 6th Hussars in campaign dress, 1812
The leather reinforcements to his overalls have developed to such an extent that only a tiny area of the base cloth remains visible. A further unusual feature is the white fur of the bearskin and pelisse; relatively common in the early Empire, it was at this period a luxurious rarity. His schabraque is of black sheepskin, trimmed in scarlet, with a portmanteau of light blue, edged in yellow. (Illustration after Hesse/Marckolsheim MS)

F1 Chef d'escadron of the 5th Hussars in campaign dress, 1810–12
Created in 1793, the title of *chef d'escadron* replaced that of lieutenant-colonel and, until the innovation of a major, was second only to the *chef de brigade* or colonel. During the Empire there were supposedly three officers of such rank within each hussar regiment. In summer service uniform, this superior officer's horse furniture would consist of sky blue schabraque and portmanteau, both liberally edged in gold lace of 50mm and 35mm in width respectively. (Illustration after Rousselot)

F2 Sapper of the 1st Hussars in full dress, 1810–12
This elite trooper, his enormous beard and crossed-axe patches defining his status of sapper, would ride at the head of the column along with the regimental eagle, forming with his fellow *sapeurs* a guard of honour about the standard for both parades and battlefield engagements. The fact that hussar regiments rather surprisingly numbered sappers in their ranks, in no way precluded them from counting the more conventional farriers among

Colonel Oudinot in full dress, 1815. The return of Louis XVIII in 1814 heralded the transformation of the leading regiments of each branch of the army into a king's regiment, thus Colonel Oudinot commanded the *Hussards du Roi* at the time of Napoleon's return for the Hundred Days' Campaign. While royalist emblems such as the white cockade were certainly replaced by Imperial equivalents during the unhappy campaign, it is extremely doubtful that such expensive items as officers' accoutrements, emblazoned as here with royal arms and fleur-de-lis, could have been. Uniforms at Waterloo must consequently have frequently borne royalist devices. (Benigni. Courtesy NAM)

Trooper of an elite company and *maréchal-des-logis* of a centre company in full dress, 1815. The dress of the last hussars of the Empire period is a pleasing amalgam of 18th- and 19th-century costume. The higher-waisted and slimmer cut of the uniform, combined with the *shako rouleau's* height and style, lends the dress a modern air which contrasts with the plaited and queued hair and outmoded equipment. (Benigni. Courtesy NAM)

P. Benigni

197

them as well; given the title of *maréchal-ferrant*, their status was indicated by a scarlet horseshoe upon either the upper left or right sleeve. (Illustration after Bucquoy)

F3 Trumpeter of the 9th (bis) Hussars in campaign dress, elite company, 1812–13

The *9eme (bis) Hussards* existed from January 1812 until February 1813, when they became the 12th Hussars. Created from three squadrons of the 9th Hussars in Spain, their uniform was similar in the intervening period. This trumpeter's dolman would have been yellow with scarlet facings. By 1813 the trumpeters were newly equipped with white dolmans and pelisses, with light blue facings and scarlet lace, and light blue breeches ornamented with white lace. (Illustration after Knötel/Bucquoy)

Lieutenant of the *7eme Hussards*, **1815. This splendidly accoutred individual demonstrates the uniform and horse furniture common to junior officers of this period. With the exception of his heavily ornamented** *shako rouleau*, **his dress is as prescribed by the 1812 Regulations, which also laid down very specific instructions as to the embellishment of the** *schabraque* **and the portemanteau: the lace about the former was to be 40mms wide and the regimental number embroidered in the corners to a height of 80mms; for the latter, the lace was 20mms in width and the regimental number no taller than 35mms. (Job. Courtesy of the National Army Museum)**

G1 Captain of the 3rd Hussars in full dress, 1809–13

This extravagantly costumed officer would lead a company of two troops. This uniform would be strictly reserved for full dress occasions and a cheaper, simpler version employed in the field. Such was the enormous expense of these dress uniforms that the Bardin 1812 Regulations were established in order to restrict officially the huge sums sometimes required to kit out officers and heads of column in wasteful and impractical dress. When they came into force they were not totally successful, but they did prevent some of the wilder excesses of the early years being repeated when the Empire was still less able to afford it. (Illustration after Rousselot)

Trooper of the *9eme Hussards* **and** Fourrier **of the** *11eme Hussards*. **The trooper on the left is clad in typical service dress of the 1813–1815 period while the quarter-master on his left is in walking-out or ball dress. They both sport the** *shako rouleau* **which became fashionable in hussar regiments from 1812; note that the trooper's headgear has been covered in scarlet cloth. (Job. Courtesy of the National Army Museum)**

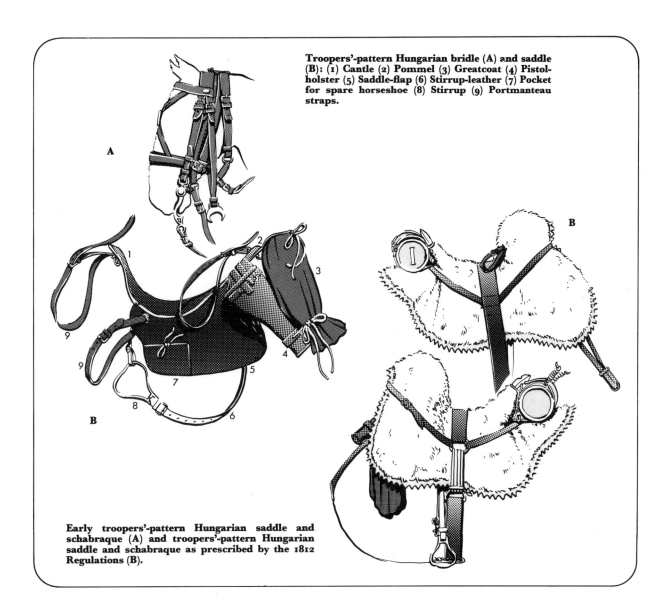

Troopers'-pattern Hungarian bridle (A) and saddle (B): (1) Cantle (2) Pommel (3) Greatcoat (4) Pistol-holster (5) Saddle-flap (6) Stirrup-leather (7) Pocket for spare horseshoe (8) Stirrup (9) Portmanteau straps.

Early troopers'-pattern Hungarian saddle and schabraque (A) and troopers'-pattern Hungarian saddle and schabraque as prescribed by the 1812 Regulations (B).

G2 Brigadier of the 12th Hussars in full dress, 1813–14
By this date overalls as shown here, being of rather better cut than their predecessors, were perfectly acceptable for full dress wear. Although they have buttons down the outer seams, these were by now redundant; the garment opened by means of a concealed button-up fly at the front. On first receipt of the *shakos rouleau*, hussars were inclined to append their old plumes to them, but this practice was soon quashed, leaving only the company-coloured pompon in its stead. A trooper of the elite company differed from this figure only in that his sleeves lacked the twin chevrons of corporals' rank, and his *shako rouleau* was covered in scarlet cloth. (Illustration after Martinet/Carl Coll.)

G3 Trumpeter of the 1st Hussars in service dress, 1812
This trumpeter of a centre company contrasts considerably with those described in the captions to illustrations on pp. 190–191, which describe this regiment's trumpeters in 1814. It could be that those represented in black and white are dressed in uniforms issued under the First Restoration, but it is rather more likely that they simply belonged to different companies or squadrons; for, despite the express specifications of the 1812 Regulations, musicians' uniform persisted in being as varied as before, save that it was now intermingled with elements of the Imperial Livery, confusing the issue still further. (Illustration after Feist)

199

H1 Lieutenant of the 6th Hussars in service dress, 1814
This subaltern is clad in typical end-of-Empire style, the classic silhouette of the hussar uniform all but lost within the practical and civilian-influenced outline of the non-regulation cylindrical shako, slimmer-cut and shorter-than-ever pelisse, and trousers, these last reinforced with a double layer of fabric on the inner leg in place of the cumbersome inset leather. (Illustration after Rousselot)

H2 Maréchal-des-logis of the 4th Hussars in full dress, elite company, 1813–14
This sergeant is dressed and accoutred in the manner prescribed by the 1812 Regulations and it is immediately noticeable, and somewhat ironic, that the regulations devised to modernise and simplify the dress of the Imperial army appear a little to the right side of conservative in contrast to the up-to-the-minute fashions sported by the majority of hussars at this period. Purely for the sake of including it, we have employed a little licence in representing an NCO with the new *An IX/XIII*-pattern musketoon; in fact, neither NCOs or trumpeters were so armed, and nor, for that matter, was a large number of troopers. (Reconstruction)

H3 Trumpeter of the 2nd Hussars in full dress, 1812–14
In similar manner to the previous figure, this trumpeter is illustrated according to the 1812 Regulations, in this instance in the Imperial Livery. Designed to rationalise the dress of musicians throughout the Imperial army, it was only grudgingly accepted by the individual regiments, and often replaced with the regiment's own preferences within a very short time; consequently, it only added to the considerable diversity of musicians' uniforms. (Reconstruction after Bardin/Boisselier)

5

Guard Cavalry

It is the cavalry's task to pursue a victory and forbid a beaten enemy the opportunity to rally.
Without cavalry, battles remain unresolved.

(Napoleon, undated)

The Heavy Cavalry

THE GRENADIERS À CHEVAL

Organisation

1799: Raised as a regiment of light horse on 2 December.

1800: Became *Grenadiers à Cheval* in December and named the *Grenadiers à Cheval de la Garde des Consuls.*

1804: Renamed the *Grenadiers à Cheval de la Garde Impériale* on 18 May. Their strength was 1,018 troopers organised in four squadrons of two companies each.

1805: Squadron of *vélites* added on 17 September, followed by a second squadron later in same year.

1811: *Vélite* squadrons disbanded and the regiment reorganised into five regular squadrons.

1812: Following disastrous Russian campaign, the number of *grenadiers à cheval* recorded in February 1813 being only 127 all told, the regiment was reduced to four squadrons.

1813: Further to the decree of 10 January, a fifth and later a sixth squadron of *vélites* was formed and designated as Young Guard.

1814: With the First Restoration, the regiment was disbanded 23 July and then the original four Old Guard squadrons were re-formed and redesignated the *Corps Royal des Cuirassiers de France.*

1815: Resumed its Imperial title on 8 April for the Hundred Days campaign, at a strength of 1,042 officers and men. Disbanded on 25 November.

Dress and Equipment

The habit: In 1804 the *grenadiers' habits* required the

changing of the buttons to types bearing the Imperial eagle with their passing into the Imperial Guard. The garment was dark blue with like-

Trooper's sabretache, *Chasseurs à Cheval* of the Guard. This pattern was worn throughout the Empire period. On campaign it was covered by a black, waxed and varnished cloth sheath; at first plain, it was later (*c.* 1812) embellished with a painted yellow Imperial eagle and care should be taken not to misinterpret illustrations of this as a second pattern of sabretache constructed of black leather, bearing a copper device. The illustration shows a dark green ground surrounded by aurore lace and piping; a copper Imperial eagle device mounted on the white-lined, scarlet Imperial robes (the lining reveals black Imperial bees), trimmed in gold lace and surmounted by the red-lined, gold Imperial crown. The standards are green, red and blue (from the centre outward), trimmed with gold lace and festooned with white scarfs with gold tassels. The rings are copper and affixed by means of brown leather straps. The outer perimeter of the whole is piped in brown leather. (Hilpert. Courtesy De Gerlache de Gomery Collection)

Chasseur in full dress, 1805–14. Readers are referred to the text for details. The elaborate uniform was worn throughout the Empire period and would be as familiar on the battlefield as on the parade ground. The saddle-cloth and portemanteau are dark green and trimmed in aurore lace. (Toussaint. Courtesy De Gerlache de Gomery Collection)

beginning of the Empire, it closed by means of seven copper buttons, but during 1808 this was augmented to ten. As of 1809, these *surtouts* were distributed solely to NCOs, and the troopers were issued an *habit de petite uniforme* consisting of a replica of the full-dress *habit* but with the plain dark blue cuffs of the *surtout*. The epaulettes and aiguillettes were identical to those described for the *habit* and were probably the self-same articles.

The stable jacket: Worn for all fatigues and off-duty wear, this garment was entirely dark blue and single-breasted, closing by means of nine copper buttons prior to 1809 and eleven thereafter.

The habit-veste: With the First Restoration in 1814, the *grenadiers*, now *cuirassiers*, were issued *habit-vestes* of *cuirassier* pattern. They were dark blue with scarlet cuffs and short turnbacks; the cuff-flaps were white, the grenade ornaments of the turnbacks aurore, and the breast was embellished by a slim scarlet piping. The buttons were copper and bore the *fleur-de-lys*. The complementary cuirasses and helmets were never received and the regiment was therefore obliged to pursue the Hundred Days campaign of 1815 dressed in this rather humble outfit. Epaulettes and aiguillettes remained the same as those worn on the old *surtouts* and *habits*.

Deerskin breeches were worn in full dress and sheep's-hide pairs replaced them for all other duties. White duck-cloth overalls, opening laterally by means of sixteen bone buttons down each outer seam, protected the riding breeches on the march. As of 1813, grey cloth overalls were issued; the inside leg was reinforced by a double layer of the same grey cloth and the outer leg bore a patch of identical cloth to sustain the continual chafing of the sabre and musket. For stable duty, overalls of rough, undyed cloth were adopted, which opened laterally by means of eighteen bone buttons down each outer seam.

The *grenadiers* at first carried the familiar cavalry cape, the *manteau trois-quarts*, cut of white thread mixed lightly with sky-blue. The collar was dark blue and the front opening and rear vent were lined on both sides with scarlet serge. As of 1813, however, the *grenadiers* were issued the *manteau-capote*, a sleeved greatcoat with short shoulder-cape attached. It was of the same colour as its predecessor but embellished with a strip of dark blue lace

coloured collar, scarlet cuffs (with white cuff flaps) and turnbacks, and white lapels. The turnbacks were originally simply folded back and stitched together but, after 1808, they were sewn back and butted-up; they were ornamented with aurore grenade devices mounted on white patches. The shoulders were originally augmented by aurore trefoil epaulettes but, around 1806, these were replaced by the aurore fringeless epaulette variety; both patterns were further embellished by the addition of an aurore aiguillette to the right shoulder. The buttons were copper.

The surtout: A single-breasted *surtout* was worn on all occasions save full dress in a bid to save wear and tear on the *habit*. Constructed of cheaper materials and with plain rounded cuffs of dark blue, it was otherwise identical to the *habit*. At the very

about the shoulder-cape and all other exterior edges. Further ornamentation consisted of aurore lace brandenbergs, complete with fringed tassel and 23mm in width, about the three uniform-pattern buttons of the shoulder-cape. The coat proper fastened by means of six cloth-covered buttons.

The *grenadiers* were shod in a choice of three regulation issue boots: the totally smooth and highly polished rigid, one-piece full-dress pattern; the semi-rigid campaign boot with soft-leather body and stiff knee-section; or the fully soft-leather two-section foot-duty and walking-out-dress variety. Another pattern, non-regulation, frequently employed in walking-out dress was the calf-length Hungarian type which the *grenadiers* purchased privately. *Grenadiers'* spurs were bronzed iron and fastened by means of black leather straps both above and below the foot.

The *grenadiers'* prize headgear was the tall black bearskin, common to the foot *grenadiers* of both the Line and Guard and the mounted Line *carabiniers* prior to 1812. In accordance with the *An X* regulations pertaining to this style of headgear they were supposedly 318mm tall, but it seems likely that, in keeping with the mounted *carabiniers* of the Line, they would have but rarely been under 350mm.

The crown was inset with a patch of scarlet cloth bisected by two strips of aurore lace in the form of a cross. The head-dress was held in place by twin leather chinstraps reinforced with copper scale, and ornamented by an aurore cord, tassel and *raquette*. This ornamental cord pre-dated the chinscales and initially served to keep the head-dress from loss at a time when the headgear was secured by a leather strap hooked beneath the wearer's queue. Finally, the scarlet plume was inserted in a socket hidden behind the tricolour cockade. The cockade was hemispherical and bore an Imperial eagle embroidered in yellow wool at its centre.

In walking-out dress, the *grenadiers* sported a black bicorn *chapeau* complete with tricolour cockade held in position by a loop of aurore lace about a uniform button, vertical aurore piping (although this disappeared post-1811) and scarlet wool pulls in the corners. This bicorn was also the habitual headgear of the *vélites*, who were not issued bearskins.

The *grenadiers'* fatigue-cap (*bonnet de police*) was cut of dark blue cloth with a 35mm wide strip of aurore lace about the turban, including the rear vent, and aurore piping down the seams of the *flamme*, which terminated in an aurore tassel. The front of the turban was ornamented by an aurore wool grenade device.

The webbing included a cartridge-pouch and crossbelt, a swordbelt and bayonet-frog, a musket strap and swordknot. The black leather cartridge-pouch was embellished with a copper grenade device similar to that employed by the mounted *carabiniers* of the Line prior to 1806; thereafter, a

Lieutenant standard-bearer of *Chasseurs* in full dress, 1808. The dress of officers was essentially similar to that of the troop save in quality and detail. Where the troopers' lace, cord and braid was aurore, the officers' was gold; white fur replaced the shoddy black fur trim of the pelisse; a fine white plume adorns the bearskin. The additional strip of lace in chevron about the cuffs of both dolman and pelisse proclaims the wearer's rank, as do the personal touches of decorative sabre and leopardskin saddle-cloth. The saddle-cloth is fringed with dark green cloth and trimmed with gold lace. The standard is a *guidon* presented to each of the chasseur squadrons and carried between 1804 and 1812. (Benigni. Courtesy De Gerlache de Gomery Collection)

Eagle and standard of the *Chasseurs à Cheval*, 1813–14. Further to the decree of 1 July 1813, the *guidons* of the separate chasseur squadrons were abolished and replaced by the above standard to be carried by the first squadron. The silk tricolor measures 55 × 55cm overall and is embellished with gold lace, embroidered Imperial motifs and fringe.

The pole is blue and topped by a gilded eagle, beneath which a tricolor scarf, embroidered in gold thread with Imperial motifs and measuring 16 × 92cm, is tied with gold cord. The gold fringe of the scarf is 5cm long. (Hilpert. Courtesy De Gerlache de Gomery Collection)

lozenge-shaped device bearing a crowned Imperial eagle motif was adopted in its stead. The crossbelt was of wide white buff and stitched along either side of its length; all fittings, from buckles to suspension rings, were of copper.

The waistbelt, sword slings and bayonet-frog were the same variety issued the Empress's Dragoons and the Line *carabiniers* after 1809 (see Chapter 1, *Cuirassiers and Carabiniers*, p. 43). The whole was of white buff with copper fittings, including the large square buckle at the waist which was emblazoned with a grenade device. The waistbelt and bayonet-frog were stitched along their entire exterior edges. The musket strap was of white buff, and the swordknot either white buff or lacquered deerskin.

Although certain German engravings contemporary to the early Empire period illustrate the *grenadiers* with a second crossbelt for the musket, this seems incompatible with its length. Where cavalry are armed with carbines or musketoons, such a

crossbelt would serve to suspend the weapon at waist-height, ready for immediate use; the musket with which both the *grenadiers* and the dragoons of the Guard were armed was so long as to preclude such suspension, save perhaps when mounted, although its length would still prove cumbersome in this position. No trace of this crossbelt can be found in the inventories pertaining to this regiment and French contemporary prints, including the authorities Henschel and Lejeune, certainly do not represent it. It is nonetheless only with reluctance that one dismisses an eye-witness report, however unlikely.

The *grenadiers* were initially armed with the old, straight-bladed *Garde des Consuls* sabre. The hilt was copper and the black leather scabbard encased in a three-section copper sheath. As of 1806, however, they were issued the familiar lightly curved *grenadier à cheval* pattern, with which the Empress's Dragoons were also armed, with a blade *à la Montmorency* 97.5cm long and a copper hilt bearing a grenade

206

device and black leather scabbard sheathed in a protective layer of copper. This copper sheath was composed of three sections held together by the two copper bracelets. The centre section had a cut-out through which the black leather of the scabbard was visible; this substantially reduced the strength of the whole and it was later deemed necessary to replace this large cut-out with two smaller ones in an effort to render the scabbard less flexible.

The musket of the *grenadiers à cheval* is open to some question: it is certain that they carried a pattern 144cm in overall length and with a 106cm barrel, issued in accordance with the First Consul's decree of 14 April 1803 (in which he specifies '. . . a fine musket model, the most attractive possible, of the same length as those issued dragoons, with bayonet, and which will permit fire from a depth of three ranks . . .'). The regimental magazine's inventories reveal 160 muskets in September of 1803 but 150 muskets and bayonets in 1804, and the official inventory of muskets manufactured from the *1er Vendémiaire An XI* through 1820 notes, in 1807, '. . . 50 musketoons of *grenadiers à cheval* pattern'. It is therefore possible that the *grenadiers* received some form of musketoon during the early years of a pattern and date of issue of which we are entirely ignorant: this would justify the German engravings' evidence of a musketoon crossbelt (see above). Alternatively, the loss of ten muskets during 1803/4 may have been natural wastage and the '*grenadier à cheval* pattern' musketoons described in the industrial manifests of 1807 destined for another unit.

The *grenadiers* were also equipped with a brace of pistols of either *An XI* or *An XIII* model.

The Medium Cavalry

THE EMPRESS'S DRAGOONS

Organisation

1806: Created further to the Imperial decree of 15 April from cavalry regiments of the Line (officers culled from the *grenadiers à cheval* and the *chasseurs à cheval* of the Guard) and comprised three squadrons, of which one was of *vélites*. The two regular squadrons numbered 476 men while that of *vélites* counted 296 troopers, commanded by 60 officers in total. Presented by the Emperor to his wife and named the *Régiment de Dragons de l'Impératrice*.

1807: Following the engagements of Eylau and Friedland the regiment was augmented by two squadrons, bringing the total of effectives to 1,269 men.

1808: Service in Spain.

1809: Engaged at Essling and Wagram.

1810: Two squadrons returned to Spain.

1812: On 1 January, squadron of *vélites* disbanded. On 23 January, a sixth squadron of 300 men formed and named the *2eme Dragons de Jeune Garde*; disbanded later in the year and incorporated into existing squadrons. Service in Russia.

1813: Fought at Bautzen, Wachau and Leipzig. Augmented 9 December by a regiment of *éclaireurs*.

1814: Defence of Champagne, engaged at Brienne, Champaubert, Montmirail, Château-Thierry, Vauchamps, Montereau, Rheims, Craonne, Arcis, Saint Dizier and Paris. Disbanded 3 April. Renamed the *Corps Royal des Dragons de France*, 12 May, under First Restoration.

1815: Resumed Imperial title as of 8 April and mustered 935 officers and men. Took part at Ligny and Waterloo, losing a total of 300 men and 25 officers. Dissolved 16 December.

Dress and Equipment

The habit: The full-dress tunic consisted of a dark green *habit*, with dark green collar, white lapels and cuff-slashes, and scarlet cuffs and turnbacks. The skirt was ornamented with pockets simulated by scarlet piping and the turnbacks bore aurore grenade devices mounted on white linen patches. The buttons were copper. The shoulders each bore an aurore fringeless epaulette, while the right shoulder also boasted an aurore aiguillette.

The surtout: This was a plainer and cheaper tunic reserved for everyday wear. It was single-breasted, closing by means of nine copper buttons, with green collar and cuffs. Its simulated pockets, turnbacks

Trumpeter of the *Chasseurs à Cheval* in campaign dress, 1813. Although we might more readily expect a trumpeter in campaign dress to adopt a black bearskin and overalls, we can imagine this fellow immediately prior to joining battle, at which point he would remove his green cape and roll it over his right shoulder as slight protection from edged weapons. His white bearskin colpack has a scarlet *flamme* with gold ornaments and a crimson over sky-blue plume. The trumpet cord is gold mixed with a third of crimson thread. His breeches are sky-blue with mixed gold and crimson lace. His black boots are ornamented with gold lace and tassel, while the saddle-cloth is trimmed with aurore lace. There were six such trumpeters per squadron, mounted on greys, and under the command of a *trompette-major* who formed part of the *Etat-Major*. (Toussaint. Courtesy De Gerlache de Gomery Collection)

discontinued and a grey linen type issued in their stead. For stable dress and general fatigues, rough, undyed overalls, opening laterally by means of eighteen bone buttons, were employed.

Initially, the dragoons were issued the *manteau trois-quarts*, the large cavalry cape with short shoulder-cape of white cloth mixed with blue thread, lined at front and on either side of the rear vent in red and with a green collar. As of 1813, they were equipped with the *manteau-capote*, a sleeved greatcoat with shoulder-cape, of the same colour as the cavalry cape. The short shoulder-cape was fastened by three buttons and these were equipped with aurore wool brandenbergs.

Dragoons' boots were constructed of semi-soft black leather and were of the high riding-boot variety with knee-section. The spurs were detachable and made of blackened iron. In walking-out dress, calf-length boots of Hungarian pattern were adopted, although non-regulation issue.

The dragoons' helmet was of the neo-Grecian *Minerva* style: the copper cap inclined to the rear while the copper-plated crest swept forward. The black horsehair mane passed beneath the copper-plating and was gathered at the tip of the crest into a bulb from which the very tips of the hairs protruded in a form of aigrette; as the years passed, so the horsehair mane emerged from an increasingly low point at rear of the crest. The cap and peak were enveloped in an imitation leopardskin fur turban. Just forward of the copper chinscale rose on the left of the helmet was a copper plume-holder into which the scarlet plume was inserted.

The dragoons employed a plain black bicorn *chapeau* in walking-out dress, of the variety illustrated in Chapter 2, *Dragoons and Lancers*, p. 94. Its sole ornamentation consisted of a tricolour cockade held in place by a loop of aurore lace attached to a copper button of the same pattern as those utilised on the uniform.

The *bonnet de police* was dark green with aurore piping on the seam lines of the *flamme* and aurore lace about the turban. The front was embellished with an embroidered aurore grenade device. Towards the end of the Empire, it would seem that an additional strip of white piping was added to the outside edge of the turban.

Dragoons' webbing comprised a black leather cartridge-pouch and white buff crossbelt; a white

and epaulettes were identical to the *habit*. Around 1809, it was replaced by an *habit de petite uniforme*, sometimes also called a *surtout*, which was identical to the full-dress *habit* but manufactured from cheaper materials and with the plain, round cuffs of the old *surtouts*.

The stable jacket: The *gilet d'écurie* was plain dark green with copper buttons.

The hide riding breeches were reserved for full dress and replaced for the march with overalls of white duck cloth. Around 1811, these overalls were

buff swordbelt, bayonet-frog and slings; and white buff musket strap and swordknot. The cartridge-pouch bore a copper, lozenge-shaped device stamped with a shield bearing an Imperial eagle surmounted by the Imperial crown. The crossbelt was stitched along its sides, in the usual Guard cavalry manner, and had copper fittings.

The swordbelt was designed for use either about the waist or slung over the right shoulder. It was constructed of three separate sections linked by copper rings to which the scabbard slings of the sabre attached. The bayonet-frog was stitched behind the first of these rings. The square copper buckle was stamped with the same device as the cartridge-pouch, although a simpler version, bearing solely an Imperial eagle, was also in service.

Further to instructions from the *Conseil d'Administration* dated 1 December 1812 that '... it is deemed necessary that each NCO and trooper have the lock of his musket sheathed in a leather cover...' an order for 1,000 black leather cases was placed with the master-saddler for issue to the dragoons.

The dragoons' sabre was of the same pattern issued to the *grenadiers à cheval* with a lightly curved *Montmorency* blade mounted in a grenade-ornamented hilt. The scabbard was black leather covered by a brass envelope composed of three sections joined by copper bracelets to which the sword slings attached. The sabre had an overall length of 1.15m.

Dragoons were issued the 1777 model dragoon musket, as modified in *An IX* and *An XI*. Manufactured to a total of 450,000, its characteristics were as follows: length, 141.7cm; weight, 4.275kg; calibre, 17.5mm. They were further equipped with either the *An IX* or *An XIII* model pistols. The *An IX* cavalry pattern pistol replaced the 1766 model which was manufactured and issued until as late as 1802; it had the following characteristics: length, 33cm; weight, 1.3kg; calibre, 17.1mm. A total of 33,000 was manufactured. The *An XIII* model was inspired by the 1786 marine pattern pistol and was a simplified version of the *An IX* pattern with the following specifications: length, 35cm; weight, 1.23kg; calibre, 17.1mm. Both patterns are illustrated in Chapter 1, *Cuirassiers and Carabiniers*, p. 28.

Chasseur on piquet escort duty, foul weather kit, 1806–07. Although, further to the orders dated 11 October 1803, chasseurs on escort duty with the Emperor were required to wear the pelisse and yellow hide riding breeches in order that the Emperor's party might be readily discernible at all times, the rigours of the 1805 campaign were such that the pelisses badly needed attention. The cost of this garment, however, at 59F for the troops and no less than 112.50F for NCOs, was such that it was deemed necessary to conduct the campaigns of 1806 and 1807 in the *habit*, normally reserved for No. 2 dress. Chasseurs on escort duty were further required never to wear their capes or greatcoats, lest it conceal their identity, and were therefore obliged to use only the detachable shoulder-cape in inclement weather. This trooper is so attired and we can go so far as to fix the time of day as between 6pm and 6am, since only between those hours were the escort chasseurs permitted to tuck the *flamme* of their colpacks within the headgear and put on the protective black top (described in the text). (Benigni. Courtesy De Gerlache de Gomery Collection)

The Light Cavalry

THE CHASSEURS À CHEVAL

Organisation

1796: A mixed corps created by General Bonaparte from various units, including the old *Compagnie de Guides à Pied* of the *Armée des Alpes*, and named the *Guides de l'Armée d'Italie*.

1798: Renamed the *Guides de l'Armée d'Orient*.

1800: Became the *Chasseurs à Cheval de la Garde des Consuls*, 13 January. Comprised of one squadron of two companies, 8 September.

1801: Augmented to two squadrons of two companies each, 6 August. Designated a regiment on 14 November.

1802: Raised to a total of four squadrons on 1 October.

1804: Became the *Chasseurs à Cheval de la Garde Impériale* on 18 May.

1805: A squadron of four companies of *vélites* added, 17 September.

1806: *Vélites* formed into a second squadron, 15 April.

1809: December, *vélites* reduced to a single squadron of two companies.

1812: Regiment augmented to a total of five squadrons of *chasseurs* and the *vélites* companies dissolved.

1813: Regiment reorganised into a total of eight squadrons of which the first five were designated Old Guard and the remaining three Young Guard.

1814: Renamed the *Corps Royal des Chasseurs à Cheval de France*, comprising four squadrons, under the First Restoration.

1815: Resumed former Imperial title during the Hundred Days campaign. Under the Second Restoration, the regiment was initially dissolved in October and November but subsequently reconstituted as the *Régiment de Chasseurs de la Garde Royale*.

Chasseur in campaign dress, 1812. The above uniform is known to have been worn without exception throughout the Russian campaign: 'The Chasseurs of the Imperial Guard underwent before my very eyes the entire Russian campaign with only a dolman and a single pair of cloth riding breeches.' (General de Brack, *Avant-postes de cavalerie légère*, Preface p. 24). The riding breeches were undoubtedly the overalls of dark green specified by the *Tarif des effets d'habillement fournis à chaque Chasseur à son arrivée au corps*, dated 15 December 1812, which were double-lined on the inside-leg and about the trouser cuffs with fabric of the same colour, and required 4.10m of aurore lace for their outer seams. The three chevrons of aurore lace on his left upper arm designate between sixteen and twenty years service. Note the sabretache cover of plain black waxed and varnished cloth with its yellow painted symbol. The post-1809 pattern cartridge-pouch is slightly smaller than its predecessor and bears a copper Imperial eagle device. (Benigni. Courtesy De Gerlache de Gomery Collection)

War Record:

1805–1807: With the *Grande Armée* at Nuremberg, Austerlitz, Lopaczyn, Eylau and Guttstadt.

1808: In Spain: Benavente.

1809: Part of the *Armée d'Allemagne* at Wagram.

1811–1812: A detachment in Spain: Elione.

1812: With the *Grande Armée* at Malojaroslawetz.

1813: With the *Grande Armée* at Reichenbach, Dresden, Leipzig, Weimar and Hanau.

1814: Château-Thierry, Craonne and Valcourt.

1815: Courtrai and Waterloo.

Dress and Equipment

The dolman was cut of green cloth, with green collar, scarlet cuffs and aurore lace and braid. It closed by means of eighteen hemispherical copper buttons acting as toggles for the eighteen loops of corresponding braid. The buttons of this central row were larger than those disposed along the four other rows down the breast.

The pelisse was cut of scarlet cloth, the garment was lined in white flannel and trimmed in frizzy black fur. Lace and braid were identical to those of the dolman, as was the copper button arrangement. The collar boasted an aurore lanyard or loop and toggle by means of which the garment was suspended from the shoulder. When worn normally, only the top four buttons could be closed, the jacket falling open thereafter; the loops of the remaining buttons were considerably shorter and purely decorative.

The *habit* was a throwback to the old *Guides* days, but was retained and worn throughout the Empire period. Cut of green cloth, it had green collar and cuffs, lapels and turnbacks, all piped in scarlet. The turnbacks bore aurore hunting-horn devices mounted on a scarlet patch. The left shoulder carried an aurore aiguillette terminating in two brass needles, while the right had a simple aurore trefoil epaulette mounted on green cloth. The hemispherical buttons were copper.

The stable jacket was cut entirely of green cloth, double-breasted, with twin rows of ten copper buttons.

Two patterns of Hungarian breeches were worn, the one of yellow deerskin and the other of green cloth, both of identical cut, very tight-fitting and ending at mid-calf. The former variety were worn for full dress while the latter were reserved for No. 2 dress. Those of green cloth were ornamented along the outer seams by a band of aurore wool lace which also served as decoration for the front flap, describing Hungarian knots.

On the march generally and when on campaign, the *chasseurs* adopted overalls of varying patterns to save these breeches from wear and tear. In the early years green overalls were commonly employed; reinforced with black leather, with a scarlet band of lace down the outer seams, they opened laterally by means of eighteen copper buttons. As of 1808, these were adapted to similar pairs with lace of aurore wool the length of the outer seams. Around 1811 a new variety appeared; no longer reinforced with

Officer of the *Chasseurs à Cheval* in marching order, 1812–14. In common with the rank and file, officers discarded pelisses throughout the campaigns of 1812–14. In the usual manner for campaign dress, this colpack is without the decorative plume and cords and tassels, and the *flamme* is tucked away within the headgear. His expensive green Moroccan-leather crossbelt is protected by a cover of crimson leather, likewise the costly cartridge-pouch. Of considerable interest are his overalls of dark green reinforced about the cuff of the trouser-leg with black leather, a rather rare sight, doubtless with a double thickness of green cloth about the inside leg, and the single strip of gold lace down the outer seam. The saddle-cloth and portemanteau are dark green and trimmed with scarlet piping and gold lace. (Benigni. Courtesy De Gerlache de Gomery Collection)

211

Superior officer of the Polish Lancers in special full dress and trumpeter in full dress, 1809. The memoirs of Joseph Zaluski, a former officer of the regiment, reveal that '. . . At the beginning, when the volunteers had a greater taste for costume than war, we adopted two colours for the uniform: that for full dress was white while that for service dress was dark blue.' The full-dress uniform was therefore envisaged as comprising white *kurtka* and crimson trousers. That this applied only to the officers is borne out by a note from Major Dautancourt to *Chef d'Escadron* Kozietulski dated 21 December 1811 which specifies that crimson trousers were to be worn by all officers. This illustration is based on a sketch by Pierre Hess executed in 1813 during the great parade of the Guard in Dresden. The individual officer is either the *Colonel* or the *Colonel-Major* as only these two officers wore twin fringed epaulettes. The trumpeters' uniform, according to Zaluski, was originally entirely crimson with white facings and lace of mixed silver and crimson thread. This gave way, c. 1809, to that illustrated, comprising white *kurtka* faced in crimson, with crimson trousers laced in white. The lace, epaulettes, aiguillettes and piping were mixed silver and crimson. Note that the trumpeters' webbing was covered in crimson cloth and trimmed in silver lace, and that his *czapska* was covered in white cloth with crimson piping. (Gembarzewski. Courtesy De Gerlache de Gomery Collection)

leather and devoid of lateral buttons, they boasted a double thickness of green cloth on the inside leg and a double band of aurore lace down the outer seams. As of late 1813, a new pattern cut of grey cloth appeared, reinforced with either black or fawn leather on the inner leg and with twin strips of scarlet lace along the outer seams. The First Restoration saw the *chasseurs* issued green overalls, reinforced in black leather with a single band of scarlet lace down the outer leg. Fatigue overalls were of undyed cloth, and closed by means of eighteen bone buttons down each leg.

Initially, the *chasseurs* wore a voluminous cape with short shoulder-cape, both of green cloth. As of 1802, however, their kit was augmented by a longer, detachable shoulder-cape for use over the cape when on the march, and without the cape beneath in two instances: when on foot duty (e.g. guard duty), and for those occasions when the *chasseurs* were acting as escort piquets to the Emperor, for which duty the use of capes was strictly forbidden. As of 1812, a green, sleeved *manteau-capote* (a greatcoat with short shoulder-cape) was issued.

The barrel-sash comprised threads of green wool held together by scarlet barrels. It was passed three times about the waist then tied by means of a loop and toggle of scarlet cord; the ends of the doubled-over cord were slung round to the front of the girdle where they were threaded through the belt proper, knotted, then left to swing free, ending in tassels of scarlet with green fringe.

Chasseurs wore Hungarian-pattern boots of black leather. The heart-shaped top edge was bordered with aurore lace and had a similarly coloured tassel. The spurs, screwed to the heel of the boot, were initially of bronzed iron, but these were replaced as of 1806 with copper-tipped versions owing to the high cost of the bronzed originals.

The *chasseurs* were at first issued a fur-covered shako of the same style as that illustrated previously for the 2nd Hussars (see Chapter 4, *Hussars*). Thereafter, the classic black *colpack* was worn: issued from 1803, it comprised a rigid leather frame covered in bearskin, 25cm tall at front, 27.7cm at rear and 25cm in diameter at top; a scarlet *flamme* piped and tasselled in aurore fell from its top, though this was tucked in and covered with a waxed, black circular cover when on campaign (this rigid cover was attached by means of eight hooks which corresponded to eyes let into the top of the headgear). A green-tipped scarlet plume, about the base of which was festooned a set of short aurore cords and tassels, was inserted above the hemispherical cockade; on the march it would be sheathed in a black, waxed-cloth cover. There was also a pair of leather, copper-scaled chinscales, which might be either tied beneath the wearer's chin or hooked to the back of the headgear by means of a small black leather strap and button.

For off-duty or walking-out dress, *chasseurs* would favour a black, goat's-hair-bordered felt bicorne *chapeau*, dating back to *Guides* days and previously worn for all dress. The cockade loop, corner tassels and slim (from 3 to 5mm) vertical slashes were aurore. The dark green *bonnet de police* was lavishly ornamented with aurore wool lace, scarlet piping and an aurore hunting-horn device. The long *flamme* was piped aurore and terminated in an aurore tassel.

Chasseurs' webbing included a plain black leather cartridge-pouch, cartridge-pouch and musketoon crossbelts, *chasseur*-style swordbelt and swordknot. The plain, black leather cartridge-pouch, gradually replaced post-1809 by a somewhat smaller version bearing a copper Imperial eagle device, was suspended from a white buff leather crossbelt which bore copper buckles and rivets. It was worn beneath a slightly wider musketoon crossbelt, of identical construction, to which it was secured by a spherical copper button. As with all Guard unit webbing, both crossbelts were of finer manufacture than that issued to the Line, significantly so in the finish of the buckles and all metal parts, and embellished with a clearly distinguishable line of stitching along their edges.

The swordbelt was also of white buff leather with twin sword slings and three slings to which the sabretache was attached. The materials and fittings were identical to those employed on the crossbelts. With the introduction of bayonets for their musketoons, the *chasseurs* were supplied separately with bayonet-frogs which were to be stitched immediately behind the first sword-suspension ring. The swordknots were initially made of either white buff leather or lacquered deerskin. Later, these were replaced with varieties constructed of white wool, with white lace tassel.

Kettledrummer of the Polish Lancers, 1811–14. One of ten musicians under the command of a *maréchal-des-logis* recorded by Major Dautancourt as having cost the officers of the regiment 11,675.62F in pay, instruments and dress. It seems likely that the musicians were none other than the trumpeters dressed incognito for the sake of splendid appearance on important occasions. This is borne out by the fact that musicians do not feature on the muster-rolls of the regiment, although this could mean they were simply hired performance by performance. Of interest, and in slight support of the former theory, is the revelation that a deserter trumpeter apprehended by Dautancourt was recorded by him as having made off with, among other valuable property of the Empire, a trombone. (Gembarzewski. Courtesy De Gerlache de Gomery Collection)

Chasseurs were armed with a carbine and a brace of pistols. Originally either a sawn-off musket or musketoon of foreign manufacture, the *chasseurs'* carbine became the 1786 hussar pattern musketoon as of 1803 (see Chapter 3, *Line Chasseurs*, p. 147). The bayonet was that employed with the *An IX* model musketoon, with a blade 48.7cm long. The scabbard was brown leather. As was the lot of all French cavalry, the *chasseurs* were issued pistols of highly diverse patterns and quality, many of foreign origin and with varying calibres. From the end of the Consulate through to that of the Empire, these were slowly replaced by the *An IX* and *An XIII* models (as illustrated in Chapter 1, *Cuirassiers and Carabiniers*, p. 28).

Trooper and trumpeter of the Polish Lancers in marching order, 1808. The lancers are almost invariably represented in their *kurtkas* with plumes flying and epaulettes gleaming; in reality they spent a good three-quarters of their time clad as shown above. This illustration is based on information contained in the archives of the Ministry of War and the correspondence of Dautancourt, and represents their dress on the march from Chantilly to Spain in 1808. They both wear the *gilet d'écurie* and different patterns of overalls: on the left, the trooper wears what are probably his stable overalls; on the right, the trumpeter wears grey overalls, fastened by eighteen pewter buttons mounted on a crimson strip of lace, with flapped hip-pockets bearing three pewter buttons apiece and crimson piping. Note that their *czapskas* are encased in black oilskin and that the saddle-cloth has been folded up under the portemanteau to provide some protection to the white wool Imperial eagle device embroidered thereon. The trumpet-cord is of mixed silver and crimson thread. (Huen. Courtesy De Gerlache de Gomery Collection)

Chasseurs employed a light cavalry pattern sabre specifically designed for the Guard and issued from September 1803. The scabbard was black leather, enveloped by a copper sheath of three sections. The centre section was initially composed of two riveted sheets of copper, but these were later replaced by a single sheet with hollowed-out centre (through which the black leather of the scabbard proper was visible) and welded to the end sections beneath the copper bracelets to which the slings attached.

THE MAMELUKES

Organisation

1799: General Kléber created a mounted company of Syrian Janissaries from Turks who took part in the siege of Acre, 25 September.

1800: Augmented by Mamelukes and formed into three companies of 100 men apiece, 7 July. Renamed the *Mamloucks* [sic] *de la République*, 26 October.

1801: Decree of 13 October orders a single squadron of 250 men to be formed.

1802: Previous decree annulled and a squadron of 150 ordered instead, 7 January. List of effectives dated 21 April reveals 13 officers and 155 men.

1803: Decree of 25 December orders the Mamelukes to form a single company attached to the *chasseurs à cheval* of the Guard. Organisation to comprise: 1 *capitaine-commandant*, French; 1 *adjutant-sous-lieutenant*, French; 1 *chirurgien-major*, French; 1 veterinary surgeon, French; 1 master-saddler, French; 1 master-tailor, French; 1 master-cobbler, French; 1 master-armourer, French; 2 *capitaines*, Mamelukes; 2 *lieutenants*, Mamelukes; 2 *sous-lieutenants*, Mamelukes; 1 *maréchal-des-logis-chef*, French; 8 *maréchaux-des-logis*, of which two French; 1 *fourrier*, French; 10 *brigadiers*, of which two French; 2 trumpeters; 2 *maréchaux-*

ferrants; 85 Mamelukes—a total of 9 officers and 114 men.

1806: Decree of 15 April re-establishes totals as 13 officers and 147 men, including a *porte-étendard*, four *porte-queues*, a *brigadier-trompette* and four French *brigadiers*.

1813: Squadron augmented to 250 men, 29 January. On 6 March, unit becomes tenth squadron of the *chasseurs à cheval* of the Guard. Decree of 17 March establishes second company as belonging to the Young Guard.

1814: Young Guard company detached to the *Armée du Nord*.

Trooper and officer of the Polish Lancers in campaign dress, 1809–14. This illustration serves to convey the far from flamboyant reality behind the glittering full dress. The trooper's cape is white with crimson collar and is of the *manteau trois-quarts* variety. The officer's is dark blue with crimson collar and is the *manteau-capote* pattern. Note that the lance pennant was covered when not in use. (Gembarzewski. Courtesy De Gerlache de Gomery Collection)

1814: With the First Restoration, the company of Mamelukes of the Old Guard were incorporated in the *Corps Royal des Chasseurs de France* (bar seven men who followed Napoleon to Elba); the company of Mamelukes of the Young Guard were incorporated in the *7eme Chasseurs à Cheval*.

At this date, only some eighteen men could be counted true Mamelukes; these retired to the port of Marseilles where they were massacred by the populace.

Despite the Imperial decree of 21 March 1815, in which it is stated that no foreigners could be admitted into the Guard, Napoleon's decree of 24 April prescribed, *inter alia*, that the *chasseurs* of the Guard were to comprise a squadron of two companies of Mamelukes for the Belgian campaign. This is confirmed by the known fact that some ninety-four men who did not serve under the First Restoration re-enlisted for the Hundred Days campaign. No casualties have been recorded, however. Certain Mamelukes who attained officer class continued to serve France after the final abdication and the four remaining in 1830 are known to have accompanied Marshal Clauzel as interpreters for his Algerian campaign.

Of the 583 men who passed through the muster-books over the fifteen-year period, 209 were coloured as against 374 Frenchmen. From 1809 through 1812, three-quarters of the effectives were coloured, but thereafter only about a third were so.

Dress and Equipment

The Mamelukes were originally clad in an oriental costume of Syrian and Turkish Mameluke pattern and they retained this method of dress after passing into French service. The costume comprised: a *cahouk* head-dress, in principal of green further to the 7 January 1802 decree (which sought to demonstrate in this manner the new-found loyalty of these Moslems to France), surrounded by a turban; a sleeved chemise ornamented with lace and piping; an Arab sash; *charoual*-style trousers and boots of either yellow, red or fawn leather.

The weaponry was prescribed by the Consular decree of *11 Germinal An X* (1 April 1802) and included: a carbine; a blunderbuss; a pair of pistols

Officers of the Polish Lancers in undress uniforms, 1808–14. From left to right: an officer in ball dress consisting of white *habit* faced in crimson with silver lace, white waistcoat trimmed in silver lace and braid, white cashmir nankeen breeches, silk stockings and black shoes with silver buttons; an officer in barracks order comprising crimson fatigue-cap with black fur turban, a dark blue *surtout* tunic with crimson piping and silver-plated buttons, and dark blue trousers with twin strips of crimson lace; and finally, an officer in walking-out dress of black felt *chapeau*, dark blue *surtout* with crimson collar and cuffs trimmed in silver lace, plain white waistcoat with silver-plated buttons and white cotton nankeen breeches and stockings. Note that the officers at each side are armed with a gilt-hilted *épée* in lieu of the cumbersome sabre. (Gembarzewski. Courtesy De Gerlache de Gomery Collection)

mace; a lance (for a lancer company which was in fact never formed).

In reality, the blunderbuss was carried and only later replaced with a musketoon. The two pistols were generally both carried in the sash and the saddle-holsters concealed a second pair. Finally, a short hand-axe often replaced the mace.

From 1805 through 1813, the *cahouk* head-dress was either red or crimson with white turban. Its ornaments are open to certain speculation. Although the Würtz Collection indicates only a centrally placed cockade, other authorities show a

(one of which was to be carried in the sash); a *Mameluke* sabre (a Turkish scimitar with a curved blade 77.2cm long, wooden grip and oriental-style brass quillon; a black leather scabbard with brass fittings); a dagger (with 35.5cm blade and wooden hilt, ivory for officers; the sheath was brass); a

Trooper, master-craftsman and NCO of the Polish Lancers in undress uniforms, 1808–14. The trooper is in stable dress of *bonnet de police*, with dark blue *flamme* piped in crimson and crimson turban laced in silver, the entirely dark blue *gilet d'écurie* with pewter buttons and the undyed, bone-buttoned stable overalls. The master-craftsman, in centre, might be tailor, saddler or armourer and is in full dress: a dark blue *habit* with crimson collar and cuffs, all facings trimmed in silver lace, and epaulette and aiguillettes of mixed crimson and silver thread; the dark blue waistcoat is embellished with silver lace and braid of mixed silver and crimson. His breeches are dark blue and laced down the outer leg and on the front flap in the form of Hungarian knots; this lace is the same as that about the top edge of his Hungarian boots and is of mixed silver and crimson thread. The tassels of his boots and swordknot are also of mixed thread. His *chapeau* carries a white plume. The figure on the right is an NCO in dark blue overcoat with crimson piping and silver lace. He wears the regular dark blue breeches with crimson lace and the same style fatigue-cap as the trooper. (Gembarzewski. Courtesy De Gerlache de Gomery Collection)

brass crescent moon surmounted by a brass star; this star is represented as having either five or six points (in which latter case it resembles the Seal of Solomon star commonly borne by Moslem troops); on the other hand, Vanson opts for cockade and star and crescent device. The headgear bore a black aigrette, sometimes gathered into a bulb at the base and in other cases sprouting from amidst a second, shorter and fatter black aigrette.

The jerkin became worn closed with the sash tied on top of it. The variously coloured chemise developed a tall European-style closed collar and, in the case of NCOs, carried French-pattern rank distinctions in the form of either chevrons or stripes, dependent on the style of cuff. The cartridge-pouch and crossbelt were constructed of either red or green Moroccan leather; the Turkish-style sabre cord was usually red and the Mamelukes acquired a red swordknot. In the course of the campaigns, however, French-pattern cartridge-pouches, cross-belts and swordbelts were frequently adopted.

After 1813, the influx of French nationals into the regiment necessitated the creation of a French-style uniform to be worn in conjunction with the oriental dress. The *Tarif des matières employées à la confection des effets d'habillement, d'équipement, etc., à fournir à chaque Mameluk lors de son admission au corps* gives details of both the new oriental and French uniforms. Those already in the ranks were only issued these new effects as and when their old gear was lost or worn out. The list includes:

Oriental dress: A cloth *yaleck* (the chemise) of variable colour, with spherical buttons and wool lace (mixed wool and gold for trumpeters and NCOs); a cloth jerkin of scarlet with spherical buttons and wool lace (wool and gold for trumpeters and NCOs); amaranth *charoual*-style trousers with wool lace (wool and gold for trumpeters and NCOs).

French dress: An indigo *habit* with crimson piping and lace (NCOs to wear an indigo pelisse with gold lace and braid and black fur trim); a scarlet, double-breasted waistcoat; indigo breeches of Hungarian cut; indigo overalls, reinforced with black leather and decorated with crimson lace; an indigo *bonnet de police* with crimson *flamme* and yellow piping, lace and tassel; an indigo stable jacket and grey stable overalls; a grey cloth *manteau-capote*.

Trooper of the Dutch Lancers in marching order, 1811–12. This figure is in typical marching order, with his *czapska* covered in black oilcloth, his *kurtka* buttoned over to protect the dark blue facings, and overalls over his scarlet breeches. The overalls are the undyed cloth stable pattern, which indicates that it is either spring or summer since heavier varieties were employed in poor weather. The saddle-cloth is dark blue and trimmed in yellow lace of two different widths; note that the bottom corner has been tucked up. The portemanteau is scarlet with yellow lace and piping. (Rousselot. Courtesy De Gerlache de Gomery Collection)

It is uncertain but probably unlikely that the French dress was worn on campaign. Instead, both Frenchmen and Mamelukes probably wore oriental dress but with items of equipment borrowed from the French style. Where this 'borrowing' included webbing, it might equally have been of either white buff or black leather.

THE GARDES D'HONNEUR

Returning from the disastrous Russian campaign, the Emperor set about raising a new *Grande Armée* on an empty public purse. One of the most expensive items was cavalry and he therefore conceived of raising a force of 10,000 horse at no expense. He would canvass the nobles and the rich bourgeois to form the *Gardes d'Honneur*, an élite cavalry regiment which would furnish him a personal guard of honour; they would be paid the same as the *chasseurs à cheval* and be assured the rank of *sous-lieutenant* after twelve months' service—in return they would mount, dress and equip themselves at personal expense.

One way or another this was achieved and the 1st Regiment was raised at Versailles, the 2nd at Metz,

Trooper of the Dutch Lancers in marching order, 1812–14. He wears the *manteau-capote* greatcoat cut of sky-blue cloth with scarlet collar. The body of the coat fastened by means of six cloth-covered buttons while the short shoulder-cape bore three similar buttons for the same purpose. The inside legs of the heavy dark blue overalls are reinforced with black leather and scarlet lace ornaments the outer seams. Unlike their British counterparts, the French cavalry only rarely walked their mounts, usually only when steep gradients compelled them, preferring to remain in the saddle for the duration of the march. The usual system was that the horses walked for the first hour after which a ten minute halt was called, during which time the harnessing was adjusted and the pack equipment redistributed; thereafter they walked for a further mile and then alternated with a trot every 100 paces for two hours. As a rule of thumb, their walking-pace was 100yd a minute, their trot 220yd a minute and their gallop 300yd a minute. (Rousselot. Courtesy De Gerlache de Gomery Collection)

the 3rd at Tours and the 4th at Lyon. They included Frenchmen, Dutchmen, Italians and Belgians. These last were the most numerous and totalled twenty-five per cent of the 1st and 2nd Regiments. Unfortunately, the *Gardes d'Honneur* were badly received by the Old Guard, containing as they did green volunteers whose experience did not merit their Guard status, replacements for nobles' sons unwilling to join up (this despite a law specifically drawn up to suppress the practice), plain conscripts paid for with a tax specially levied on childless families, near-mutinous Italians and Dutchmen, and hostile noblemen and pampered bourgeois. They were therefore *in* the Guard but not *of* it.

Desertions were so rife that a special law had to be passed on 7 December 1813 to stem the tide of homeward-bound Dutchmen. Mutiny was not unheard of, and the worst case was doubtless that at Tours which, though suppressed at the outset, culminated in an attempt on the life of *Général de Brigade* the Comte de Segur, the commanding officer of the 3rd Regiment. Once the campaign was under way, however, they acquitted themselves well.

Organisation

1813: By 13 September, 1,000 men of the four regiments had been gathered in the vicinity of Dresden. Fought at Leipzig and Hanau.

1814: The *Gardes* were scattered all over France's eastern border, largely bottled up in such towns as Mayence and Strasbourg. A division of them under General Count Defrance was raised at Rambervilliers on 13 January, and these fought at Rheims. Another contingent, one hundred strong under General Vincent, fought at Dormans and Paris. With the abdication of the Emperor, the regiment was disbanded 14–22 July and most of the men were incorporated in the *Maison du Roi* of Louis XVIII.

1815: Only some eighty-seven men remained of the original corps and these swore allegiance to Napoleon for the Hundred Days campaign.

Dress and Equipment

The four regiments were distinguished from one another by the colour of their plumes: these were dark green with tips of red for the 1st Regiment, indigo for the 2nd, yellow for the 3rd and white for the 4th. Otherwise, they were dressed and equipped in basically the same manner.

The pelisse was of familiar hussar cut and made of dark green cloth, lined in white flannel and trimmed with black fur. The breast bore five rows of eighteen buttons, between which were rows of white braid. The lace about the fur trim was white. The buttons were pewter.

The dolman was also of hussar pattern, cut of dark green cloth with scarlet facings. The breast was ornamented with five rows of eighteen pewter buttons and white braid and lace.

The *Gardes d'Honneur* wore scarlet breeches of Hungarian cut. White lace embellished the outer seams and the front flap in the form of bastion loops, although some varieties bore Hungarian knots in white piping instead. These were generally replaced with riding overalls of dark green woollen cloth, with a strip of scarlet lace down the outer seams, on campaign.

The troopers wore the sleeved *manteau-capote* with both greatcoat and shoulder-cape cut of dark green cloth. The barrel-sash was constructed of crimson threads with white barrels, cords and tassels. The sabretache was of plain black leather bearing a pewter Imperial eagle device and regimental number.

The *Gardes* wore an 1810-pattern shako, 220mm tall by 270mm in diameter. It was covered in scarlet cloth and had upper and lower bands of white. The cords and tassels were also white, and the shako plate and chinscales were of white metal. The *Gardes d'Honneur* took it upon themselves to wear the cords and tassels in affected ways: normally hanging on the right, most wore them on the left, and at least the 3rd Regiment took to hanging both front and rear sets of cord at the front. An existing headgear, part of the Brunon Collection, is clearly the officers' pattern of 1810-model shako, with interlinking rings reinforcing the leather chinstrap and lion's-head roses, but it is uncertain whether this was worn out of dandyism or necessity. Finally, the plumes, described above, had pompons of company colour at their base.

Troopers of the Dutch Lancers in fatigue dress, 1812. The uniforms shown are those reserved for the regimental depot. They wear the *bonnet de police*, the *gilet d'écurie* of sky-blue cloth with scarlet collar, and overalls. The left-hand figure represents winter or foul weather dress, while the right-hand figure is in summer or fine weather uniform; note that the difference involves not only their choice of overalls but also footwear. (Benigni. Courtesy De Gerlache de Gomery Collection)

The webbing comprised a plain black leather cartridge-pouch and plain white buff crossbelt, musketoon crossbelt, swordbelt of light-cavalry pattern and swordknot. Their sabres were the *An XI* light cavalry pattern with copper hilt, 845mm steel blade and iron scabbard. The *Gardes d'Honneur* were equipped with the *An IX/XIII*-pattern light cavalry musketoon.

219

The Light Horse Lancers

THE POLISH LANCERS

Organisation

1807: Raised further to decree of 2 March as the *Régiment de Chevau-Légers Polonais de la Garde*. Organised from Polish volunteers into four squadrons of two companies apiece, 16 April.

Officers of the Dutch Lancers in undress uniforms, 1811. The left-hand figure is a *Capitaine Adjutant-Major* in casual morning dress. This consists of the *bonnet de police* of identical pattern and colour to the troopers' but embellished with gold lace; the *kurtka*, buttoned over, with his rank indicated by aiguillettes on the left shoulder and a heavy gold bullion epaulette on the right; and the regular officers' pattern scarlet trousers with gold lace. The subaltern on the right is clad in the plain dark blue *redingote* popular among lancer officers for foot duty. He wears dark blue *petite tenue* breeches with scarlet lace. Note the *kurtka*-style cut of the top of the overcoat, and his black webbing. (Benigni. Courtesy De Gerlache de Gomery Collection)

1809: Became the *Régiment de Chevau-Légers Lanciers Polonais de la Garde*, with the introduction of the lance following the battle of Wagram.

1811: Renamed the *1er Régiment de Chevau-Légers Lanciers de la Garde*.

1812: Fifth squadron added to regiment. A second regiment, the *3eme Régiment de Chevau-Légers Lanciers* raised on 5 July.

1813: The remains of the second regiment disbanded 22 March and, 11 April, sixth squadron added to the 1st Regiment; first three squadrons designated Old Guard while remaining three categorised as Middle Guard. With the dissolution of the *3eme Régiment de Chevau-Légers Lanciers de la Garde* a seventh squadron was added to the regiment in July and designated Young Guard; composed of Poles and Lithuanians. On 9 December, regiment reduced to four squadrons and a regiment of *éclaireurs-lanciers* attached to the corps.

1814: A single squadron accompanies the Emperor in exile to Elba.

1815: The returned squadron in exile, along with Poles who had remained in France, re-formed the regiment and fought at Ligny and Waterloo.

Dress and Equipment

The Polish lancers wore a *kurtka* of Turkish blue with crimson cuffs, collar, lapels, turnbacks and piping. Although frequently misapplied to additional areas of the facing cloth, silver lace 15mm in width trimmed only the lapels except in the cases of officers, trumpeters and certain NCOs. The lapels were invariably crossed over towards the shoulder bearing the aiguillette when the troops were in any but full dress. This revealed the dark-blue ground colour of the tunic and left but a single strip of crimson piping down the free edge of the lapels to ornament the breast. The aiguillettes were white and worn on the right shoulder until 1809 when, with the introduction of the lance, they were transposed with the white wool fringed epaulette of the left. The buttons were hemispherical and constructed of pewter.

The *gilet d'écurie* was dark blue with shoulder-

220

straps. It was single-breasted, closing by means of nine pewter buttons, and had two buttons at each round cuff.

The lancers' breeches were dark blue and resembled trousers of stovepipe cut. The outer seams were embellished with a slim strip of crimson piping with a strip of crimson lace either side. The lower leg was adjustable about the riding boot by means of five loops of crimson cord. For the march, lancers adopted overalls of dark blue, reinforced about the inner leg with black leather and opening laterally by means of eighteen pewter buttons mounted on a strip of crimson lace down each outer seam. A patch of leather was frequently sewn to the right outer thigh to protect the cloth from the chafing of the slung carbine. In stable dress, lancers employed the standard rough, undyed cloth overalls common to most of the French cavalry.

The lancers at first utilised a plain white cape with crimson collar, the *manteau trois-quarts*, devoid of both sleeves and short shoulder-cape. The adoption of the lance necessitated their exchange for the sleeved *manteau-capote*, constructed of the same cloths and complete with shoulder-cape. The insides of both the front opening and rear vent were lined in crimson. The lancers wore a short, ankle-length, black leather boot.

The Polish lancers wore a *czapska* covered in crimson cloth which varied but little in form during the course of the Empire. Although originally 22cm in 1808, its height was reduced to 20cm by the end of the era. White piping ornamented the crown, while a strip of white lace covered the join between the top and the black leather cap itself. The peak was black leather lined in green and trimmed in silver. The front of the headgear was emblazoned with a stamped rising-sun plate with brass rays and silver centre, bearing a brass Imperial 'N' cypher. The chinstrap roses were embossed lions' heads bearing hooks and were silver-plated. The chinstrap itself was leather, in a crimson cloth sheath with protective interlinking rings of silver. In full dress, the *czapska* would be embellished with white cords and tassels and a white plume 47cm tall. In marching order the cords, tassels and plume would be packed in the portemanteau and the *czapska* enveloped in a cloth cover—usually constructed of waxed black cloth or oilskin.

The equipment comprised swordbelt and slings,

Officers of the Dutch Lancers in undress uniforms, 1811. The left-hand figure is clad in walking-out or ball dress consisting of black felt *chapeau*, with white plume and gold ornaments; scarlet *frac* tunic, with dark blue cuffs and piping about the lapels and collar; plain linen waistcoat; white cotton breeches and stockings, and black shoes with gilded buckles. The right-hand figure is in informal dress reserved for quarters. It comprises a Polish bonnet, the *confederatka*, of scarlet cloth with gold lace and piping; a dark blue *surtout* tunic with scarlet collar, cuffs and piping down the breast and about the turnbacks; a plain white waistcoat, and dark blue undress breeches with scarlet lace. Note the preference for black webbing with these breeches. His sabre is the officers' pattern of the *An XI* light cavalry model. (Rousselot. Courtesy De Gerlache de Gomery Collection)

swordknot, cartridge-pouch and crossbelt, musketoon crossbelt and sling, and musketoon lock-cover. The swordbelt was of white buff leather, with brass fittings and a large square brass buckle stamped with a crowned Imperial eagle device. The swordknot was either of white buff or lacquered deerskin. The cartridge-pouch was of highly polished black leather and bore a brass crowned Imperial eagle device. It was suspended from a white buff crossbelt with brass buckle and

Trumpeters of the Dutch Lancers in full dress, 1813. Trumpeters' full-dress uniform consisted of a white *czapska* and *kurtka* with scarlet breeches. The facings were scarlet. The gold lace about the collar, cuffs and lapels was 11mm in width and both the epaulettes and the aiguillettes were of mixed scarlet and gold thread. The gold lace of the breeches was 22mm in width. The *czapska* was of identical pattern to that of the troopers, but with the piping, cords and tassels of mixed scarlet and gold in the proportions of two-thirds and one-third respectively. The plume is here shown as scarlet with white tip, but this is open to some doubt and white plumes with scarlet tips were equally possible. (Toussaint. Courtesy De Gerlache de Gomery Collection)

fittings. The musketoon crossbelt was constructed of these same materials but with the addition of a steel musket clip complete with slim white buff strap. The musketoon's lock cover was also of white buff and all the buff leathers were stitched along both sides of their entire length in common with the other units of Guard cavalry.

The steel-bladed lance introduced in December of 1809 had a blackened wood staff and steel ferrule. The wrist-strap was of Hungarian leather. The overall length was 2.75m. The pennant which attached to the top was crimson over white and measured 487mm in depth, 487mm in length from V-cut to the staff and 73cm in overall length. The lancers received rather poor quality Prussian sabres

when the regiment was raised in Poland and these were replaced upon their arrival in France, in March 1809, by either the *An XI* light cavalry pattern sabre, with iron scabbard, or earlier patterns of hussar variety, with brass fittings and hilt. These 'hussar' style sabres might either have been the variety we associate with Line hussars or those with which the *chasseurs à cheval* were issued. The weight of the *An XI*-pattern light cavalry sabre's iron scabbard was such as to provoke complaints to the Ministry of War that copper- or brass-fitted scabbards were preferred.

Trumpet-banner of the Dutch Lancers, 1811. This illustration is based on a photograph of an existing model exhibited at the Kazan cathedral in St. Petersburg. It measures 40 × 30cm; for colours, see Plate E1. (Rousselot. Courtesy De Gerlache de Gomery Collection)

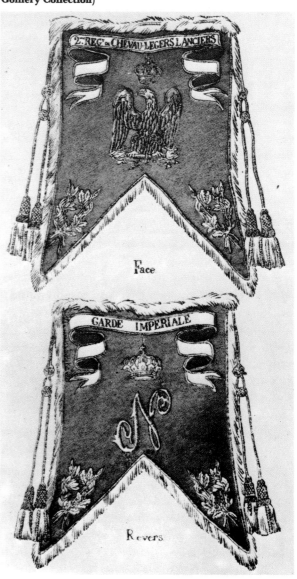

Trumpeter of the Dutch Lancers in campaign dress, 1813. The full dress white *kurtka* of the trumpeters was reserved solely for the most formal occasions and a second full dress *kurtka* of sky-blue replaced it on most occasions. The trumpeter illustrated is so clad, with the lapels buttoned over; the tunic has scarlet collar, cuffs and turnbacks with gold lace, and epaulettes and aiguillette of mixed gold and scarlet thread. (Rousselot. Courtesy De Gerlache de Gomery Collection)

The lancers also received musketoons of dubious foreign origin and these were duly replaced by the *An IX*-pattern musketoon of Imperial manufacture. Their pistols were initially of Prussian origin, but these were found to be too long for their holsters and were exchanged for either the *An IX* or *XIII* pattern.

THE DUTCH LANCERS

Organisation

1810: Further to the decree of 13 September, the Dutch *Régiment de Hussards de la Garde à Cheval du Roi* became the *2eme Régiment de Chevau-Légers Lanciers de la Garde*. The regiment comprised 58 officers, 881 men and 865 horses divided into four squadrons. Reorganisation of 1 October raised the existing *Etat-Major* from eleven to twenty officers, including: 1 *colonel*, 2 *majors*, 4 *chefs d'escadrons*, 1 *quartier-maître*, 1 *capitaine-instructeur*, 2 *capitaines-adjutants-majors*, 4 *lieutenants-sous-adjutants-majors*, 1 *porte-aigle*, 2 *chirurgiens-majors*, 2 *chirurgiens-aides-majors*, and 12 troopers.

The decree further instructed that officer-class vacancies should be filled with officers from other Dutch cavalry units, while trooper vacancies should be filled from the *3eme Régiment de Hussards Hollandais* and the *Garde du Corps Hollandaise*.

1812: Regiment augmented to five squadrons 11 March, the fifth comprising men culled from some thirty cavalry depots and a single squadron of the Dutch *Garde Royale* retrieved from the 1st Hussars stationed in Spain. Totals of 1 September include 1,406 troopers, including 58 *vélites*.

1813: Decree of 10 January reorganised the regiment into eight squadrons of 250 men apiece, the numbers made up with Frenchmen. On 22 February, a squadron of the *Garde à Cheval de Paris* was assimilated into the regiment (official decree of 6 March), bringing it to a total of ten squadrons. On 17 March, the first five squadrons designated Old Guard and the remaining five *Jeune Garde*.

1814: Royal Ordnance of 12 May turned Old Guard squadrons into the *Corps Royal des Chevau-Légers Lanciers de France*, comprising 42 officers and 601 men. *Jeune Garde* squadrons dissolved. Marshal Ney's review of 2 August lists 32 officers and 482 men.

1815: With the return of Napoleon, the regiment resumed Imperial service, incorporating the single remaining squadron of Polish lancers which accompanied the Emperor to Elba, 8 April, under the name of the *Régiment de Chevau-Légers de la Garde Impériale*.

With the Second Restoration, the Polish squadron entered Russian service (1 October) while the remainder were

Syrian horseman, 1799. The Mamelukes were originally formed from cavalry such as this. His headgear is brick red with a white turban, striped in red; the chemise is white with vertical red pinstripe; the waistcoat is dark green with yellow half-sleeves and lace; the sash is cobalt, and the breeches are brick red. The sabre and scabbard are gold, as are the pistol holsters, stirrups, false-martingale and balter. The saddle-cloth is scarlet with gold lace trim. The stirrup-leather is brown and the fringe on the bridle and false-martingale is mixed scarlet and brick red. (Huen. Courtesy De Gerlache de Gomery Collection)

disposed of by Royal decree of 5 September: the 3rd Squadron at Castel-Sarrazin (9 November); the 4th Squadron at Grenade (16 November); the *Etat-Major* and 1st Squadron at Gignac (16 December); and the 2nd Squadron at Agen (20 December).

Dress and Equipment

The Dutch lancers' *kurtkas* were cut of scarlet cloth and had dark blue collar, cuffs, lapels, turnbacks and piping. In their case, the aiguillettes were always worn on the left shoulder while the right bore a fringed epaulette; both forms of shoulder ornament were made of yellow wool save for the crescent of the fringed epaulette, which was dark

blue. Buttons were copper and the *kurtka* was usually buttoned over to the left, towards the aiguillettes, hiding the dark blue lapels save for a dark blue piping which trimmed the open edge. The lancers' *gilet d'écurie* consisted of a sky-blue tunic with scarlet collar. It was double-breasted and closed by parallel rows of nine copper buttons. Like their Polish contemporaries, the Dutch Lancers also employed this tunic widely in marching order and as general campaign dress wear.

The lancers wore similar trousers to their Polish counterparts but cut of scarlet cloth and with twin strips of dark blue lace down the seams of the outer leg. The pattern of overall generally employed was dark blue, reinforced with black leather about the inside leg and opening laterally by means of eighteen copper buttons set on scarlet lace down each outer seam. These same overalls were frequently embellished with hip-pockets with button-down flaps; the flaps ended in three points and bore either three or five copper buttons. The off-white stable overalls were also occasionally adopted in marching order dependent on the weather. The Dutch Lancers employed a sleeved *manteau-capote* of sky-blue with scarlet collar.

Both Polish and Dutch Lancers were shod in a black leather, ankle-length boot described as the Mameluke pattern. The spurs were copper-plated except for the iron rowel.

The Dutch Lancers' *czapska* was modelled, as indeed was their entire costume, on their Polish comrades' pattern. It was covered in scarlet cloth and had yellow piping along the crown seams, and in the form of a cross on the top, and a wide strip of yellow lace disguised the join with the black leather cap. The front plate was identical to the Poles' version, as were the other smaller details of the headgear. The plume, however, was white and the cords and tassels yellow; these ornaments were reserved for full dress and the hat was usually worn without accessories; in marching order the whole was encased in black oilcloth.

The *bonnet de police* consisted of a dark blue turban, trimmed in yellow lace, and a scarlet *flamme*, trimmed along its seams with yellow piping and terminated by a yellow tassel.

The webbing of the Dutch Lancers was in all respects identical to that issued the Polish Lancers. Readers are referred to the appropriate section.

1 Trooper, Empress's Dragoons, marching order, 1806–1809
2 Trumpeter, Empress's Dragoons, marching order, 1810–1814
3 Officer, Empress's Dragoons, cape, 1806–1813

1 Trooper, *Grenadiers à Cheval*, service dress, 1806–1807
2 Trumpeter, *Grenadiers à Cheval*, full dress and cape, 1806–1807
3 Officer, *Grenadiers à Cheval*, service dress, 1809–1814

1 **Officer,** *Chasseurs à Cheval,* **full dress, 1804–1808**
2 **Trooper,** *Chasseurs à Cheval,* **campaign dress, 1804–1808**
3 **Trumpeter,** *Chasseurs à Cheval,* **campaign dress, 1812**

1 *Brigadier-trompette*, Polish Lancers, service dress, 1810–1814
2 Subaltern, Polish Lancers, campaign dress, 1810–1814
3 Trooper, Polish Lancers, service dress, 1810–1814

ANGUS McBRIDE

1 **Trumpet-major, Dutch Lancers, full dress,** 1811
2 **Lieutenant** *Sous-adjutant-major,* **Dutch Lancers, campaign dress,** 1812
3 *Brigadier,* **Dutch Lancers, summer marching order,** 1812–1814

1 Trooper, German Light Horse, service full dress, 1807
2 Trumpeter, German Light Horse, campaign dress, 1808–1809
3 Officer, élite squadron *(Garde du Corps)*, German Light Horse, 1807–1809

1 Trooper, 1st Regt. of *Gardes d'Honneur*, full dress, 1813–1814
2 Trumpeter, 3rd Regt. of *Gardes d'Honneur*, 1814
3 Officer, 3rd Regt. of *Gardes d'Honneur*, 1814

1 Trooper, Lithuanian Tartars, 1812–1813
2 Trooper, Lithuanian Tartars, 1812–1814
3 Trooper, Mamelukes, 1808–1813

ANGUS McBRIDE

They were originally issued the same pattern of sabre as that reserved for the *Chasseurs à Cheval* of the Guard, with copper hilt and copper-sheathed black leather scabbard. As of 1813, however, these were replaced by the *An XI* light cavalry pattern sabre with copper hilt and iron scabbard.

Their lance measured a total of 2.268m with an iron blade of 216mm. It was mounted on a staff of blackened wood and this bore a white over scarlet serge pennant of the same dimensions as those given for the Polish Lancers; this pennant was replaced for full dress by a replica in silk. The pennant was enveloped in a black taffeta cover on the march. With the introduction of the musketoon, the lancers found themselves hopelessly overloaded with weaponry and, during the course of the Russian campaign, generally disposed of their unfamiliar lances at the earliest opportunity. After 1813, the armament of the troops was rationalised in the same manner as that described for the Polish Lancers.

The lancers were issued carbines during the course of 1811. They were the *An XIII* pattern light cavalry musketoon (see Chapter 3, *Line Chasseurs*, p.147), with an overall length of 115cm. Although described as carbines, the musketoons of Napoleon's cavalry in fact never had the benefit of rifled barrels. The lancers' pistols were either the *An IX* or *XIII* model.

THE GERMAN LANCERS

The Grand Duchy of Clèves-Berg had been conquered by revolutionary France and was presented to Marshal Murat by Napoleon in 1806. On 12 July it entered into the alliance of satellite states of the Empire, the Confederation of the Rhine. The State was to supply a 5,000-strong contingent for the *Grande Armée* including a regiment of cavalry which Murat, in 1807, named the *Régiment de Hussards du Grand-Duc de Berg*. He canvassed the colonels of the *Grande Armée*'s cavalry regiments to furnish him with trained, experienced, German-speaking NCOs and proposed that each regiment should also furnish him with a trooper to swell the ranks. Murat also envisaged a 100-strong corps of *Gardes d'Honneur Polonais*. Neither project proved too successful and the single resulting corps was in turn named the *Régiment du Grand-Duc de*

Officer of Mamelukes, 1804–05. His red headgear is striped with gold with a sky-blue pompon, and white plume in a gold holder. His tunic is apple-green with silver lace, the waistcoat ochre with gold lace. The crossbelt is gold and the sash is white. His trousers are red as are his pistol-holsters and cartridge-pouch, this last trimmed gold, while the holsters have gold ornaments. He wears cream gloves. The saddle-cloth is sky-blue with gold ornaments; the saddle proper is apple-green as are the bridle and false-martingale, with gold ornaments. The stirrups are silver. A black-handled steel-headed axe is strapped to the saddle. His scimitar is gilt-hilted and the scabbard is black leather with gilt fittings. (Rousselot after Hoffmann. Courtesy De Gerlache de Gomery Collection)

Clèves, the *Chevau-Légers de la Grande Duchesse* and, finally, the *Régiment de Chevau-Légers du Grand-Duc de Berg*. The unit was formed at Münster and comprised six companies divided into three squadrons and a seventh company of élite *Garde du Corps*.

Organisation

1808: September saw the regiment raised to four squadrons of two companies each. The first squadron was admitted into the Imperial Guard and despatched to accompany King Joseph on his ill-fated journey to Madrid. The second squadron joined Murat in Naples. The two

Mameluke trooper, 1807–08. His crimson head-dress has a black aigrette, white turban, tricolour cockade and gold ornaments. His tunic is grass-green with black piping; the waistcoat is indigo with black piping. The crossbelt is scarlet while the pistol holster is crimson with gold ornaments. The black-scabbarded gilt-hilted scimitar is suspended from a scarlet cord in the Turkish fashion. His sash is sky-blue with gold fringe; his trousers are brick-red and his boots brown. (Rousselot after Vanson. Courtesy De Gerlache de Gomery Collection)

remaining squadrons stayed in Münster, and, on 29 August, were incorporated into the newly raised *Régiment de Chasseurs à Cheval du Grand-Duc de Berg*.

1809: On 11 January, the *Chevau-Légers* of Berg were disbanded and their men divided between the Guard cavalry regiments and the new *Chasseurs à Cheval* of Berg. Towards the end of the year, the troopers were issued lances, renamed the *Chevau-Légers Lanciers de Berg* and, on 17 December, admitted to the Guard.

1810–1811: The regiment was on service in Spain.

1812: In March a second regiment of light-horse lancers was raised.

1813: With the dissolution of the Confederation of the Rhine in October, the two regiments passed into Prussian service.

Dress and Equipment

The original uniform consisted of a Polish lancer-style cream *kurtka*, faced in amaranth (a form of pink), with white wool epaulettes and pewter buttons. The *czapska* was of the usual style, covered in amaranth cloth and bedecked with a white plume with amaranth tip. The élite company was distinguished by white loops about the lapel buttons and a white aiguillette. The existence of this uniform was short-lived and the troops leaving for Spain were dressed in a similar manner, but with white cloth replacing the cream. In conjunction with this uniform was a *petite tenue* replica constructed of grey/sky-blue cloth, reserved for day-to-day wear and marching order.

The *chasseur* regiment, created in 1808, wore a dark green *kurtka* faced in amaranth and dark green Hungarian breeches, trimmed in amaranth piping and lace. Their shako was covered in amaranth cloth. The shoulder-straps were dark green trimmed in amaranth piping. Upon their receiving the lance, the uniform remained largely the same, save that the shako bands were now white, and white wool epaulettes were added to the *kurtka*.

In 1812, the uniform reverted to lancer-style, cut in dark green with amaranth facings and white epaulettes. The *czapska* was amaranth trimmed in white piping. The élite company was distinguished by a black colpack and scarlet plume and epaul-

234

ettes. The 2nd Regiment, created in March 1812, was clad in identical manner save that their *czapskas* were covered in dark green cloth. The élite company of this second regiment did not receive the colpack but was distinguished by a scarlet plume and epaulettes.

Their webbing was of French pattern and constructed of white buff. The black leather cartridge-pouch of the *chasseurs* bore the initials 'CLB' in brass. The lance pennant was amaranth over white for the duration of the 1809–1813 period.

Mameluke trooper, 1807–08. His scarlet head-dress has a white turban with gold clasp, tricolour cockade and dark green aigrette. His tunic is dark green with black lace and his waistcoat is sky-blue with black lace. His sash, crossbelt and trousers are scarlet. The pistol holster is brown leather with gold ornaments. His scimitar has a black scabbard with gold fittings and is suspended by a scarlet cord. The saddle-cloth is dark green with white piping and crimson lace; the fringe is composed of alternating white and crimson strands. The portemanteau is dark green and piped in white with crimson lace. The stirrups are iron. (Rousselot after Würtz. Courtesy De Gerlache de Gomery Collection)

Chef d'Escadron of the Mamelukes, 1809–10. His scarlet headgear has a white turban and plume, gold ornaments and plume holder. His tunic is white with gold lace. His waistcoat is scarlet with gold lace. His sash is gold with intermittent threads of red and dark green. His trousers are brick red as is the trim to his leopardskin saddle. The pistol holster is crimson with gold ornaments. The saddle-cloth is dark green with gold ornaments and lace. The leathers are brown with gold ornaments and scarlet flounce. (Tanconville after Bockenheim. Courtesy De Gerlache de Gomery Collection)

THE LITHUANIAN TARTARS

The Lithuanian Tartars were the Moslem descendants of the Tartars who had settled in Lithuania during the Middle Ages.

Organisation

1812: Mustapha Achmatowicz, a lieutenant-colonel of Polish cavalry, charged with raising a regiment of cavalry in July. Only one squadron was in fact formed and was given the rôle of scouts attached to the *3eme Régiment de Chevau-Légers (Lithuaniens)* of the Guard. This regiment was wiped out at Slonim on 19

235

The standard-bearer and *portes-queues* of the Mamelukes, 1807. The eagle-bearer and his guard were established further to the Imperial Decree of 15 April 1806 which also determined that the Mamelukes were to total thirteen officers and 147 troopers and NCOs. The standard itself was awarded the Mamelukes after the battle of Austerlitz, at which the company had particularly distinguished themselves. It was of 1804 pattern and was inscribed: L'EMPEREUR DES FRANCAIS/A LA COMPAGNIE DES MAMELUKS (sic)/DE LA GARDE IMPERIALE, and, on the reverse: VALEUR ET DISCIPLINE. The *portes-queues* bore copper poles 2·70m in height, on top of which were horse tails of which two were black while those of the remaining poles were red and yellow respectively.

Dress and Equipment

The dress and equipment of the Lithuanian Tartars is as complicated as that of their fellow Moslems, the Mamelukes. Although the subject is open to considerable conjecture and controversy, it seems possible to discern two overlapping periods of costume: the first dating from 1812 through 1813 and the second from 1813 through 1814. This is borne out by Dautancourt who, in a letter dated 11 July 1813, mentions that, of a troop of twenty-six Tartars, six still wear their *old* uniforms. Both types of uniform were based on the oriental pattern and the detail is as follows:

1812–1813: The headgear was a black, peaked shako with a dark green *flamme* ornamented with scarlet piping and tassel. About its base was wound a yellow turban and its front carried a star and crescent device in brass. The chemise was dark green with scarlet collar and cuffs, trimmed in yellow lace and with yellow shoulder-straps. The jerkin was scarlet and edged in yellow lace. The trousers were dark green, of *charoual* shape, with scarlet lace down the outer seams. The ankle-boots

October, but the surviving Tartars participated in the defence of Vilna.

1813: Only one company remained, consisting of fifty men and three officers, and this became the 15th company of the Polish Lancers with whom they fought at Dresden, Leipzig and Hanau. On 9 December, those who remained were incorporated along with some Poles and 230 Frenchmen into the *3eme Eclaireurs* of the Guard.

1814: The regiment was disbanded and the Tartars returned to Lithuania in June.

236

were black leather, although officers favoured yellow ones. The equipment included a French sabre or Turkish scimitar (certainly for officers); a brace of pistols; webbing of French pattern; a dagger and a lance. The lance pennant was red over either white or dark green.

1813–1814: The headgear was a black fur colpack without a peak. The *flamme* was dark green with white cords and tassels and scarlet plume. The chemise was scarlet. The jerkin was yellow with black piping. The *charoual*-style trousers were indigo. Equipment remained the same but the lance pennant became crimson over white.

All references above to scarlet or crimson are open to the same vagaries as with the Mamelukes, and we are uncertain as to whether both colours were interchangeable or whether the fading crimson led witnesses to record the colour as scarlet.

The Mameluke heads of column, 1810. This illustration represents the heads of column as we might have expected to see them on parade. Their dress is based on the paper soldiers of the *Collections Alsaciennes* and we can discern the kettle-drummer, followed by the *brigadier-trompette* with four trumpeters and six musicians in tail, including two cymbalists, two *chapeau-chinois* players ('Jingling Johnnies') and two timpani drummers. Although the relative positions of the different musicians are open to question, we see here a qualified consensus of opinion. (Rousselot. Courtesy De Gerlache de Gomery Collection)

The Plates

A1 Trooper of the Empress's Dragoons in marching order, 1806–1809

Although dragoons are most frequently illustrated in the lapelled *habit*, this garment was in fact reserved solely for full-dress functions and was replaced by the *surtout* tunic shown here for all other duties. Single-breasted, closing by means of nine copper buttons, and with plain, rounded cuffs, it was otherwise identical to the *habit* but cut from less expensive cloth. Post-1809, it was replaced by a replica of the full-dress tunic called the *habit de petite uniforme*, again manufactured from cheaper materials. He carries a heavy cavalry pattern sabre identical to that borne by the *Grenadiers à Cheval* and would also be armed with the 1777-pattern dragoon musket, as modified in *An IX* (see Chapter 2, *Dragoons and Lancers*, p. 96). By their very nature, dragoons were trained to serve either mounted or on foot; in the latter case, the swordbelt would be hung over the right shoulder rather than worn about the waist.

237

*A2 Trumpeter of the Empress's Dragoons in marching
order, 1810–1814*

In the same manner as the troopers, trumpeters
wore the plain *surtout* tunic for all occasions other
than full dress. Prior to 1810, the garment was
similar to the one shown but with sky-blue cuffs and
collar and scarlet turnbacks. The collar and cuffs of
both garments were edged with gold lace 22mm in
width, and the turnbacks were ornamented with
gold embroidered grenade devices. The epaulettes
were gold with a central stripe of sky-blue, while the
aiguillettes were one-third gold and two-thirds sky-
blue. The full-dress tunic was originally of sky-blue
cloth cut in the same manner as the troopers' *habits*,
with the sky-blue replacing the dark green; the
collar, cuffs, cuff-flaps, lapels and turnbacks
remained identical to those of the troopers save that
a total of 6.2m of 23mm lace embellished them,
including the formation of lace brandenbergs on
the lapels. After 1810, this full-dress *habit* became
white with sky-blue collar, cuffs, lapels and
turnbacks, all trimmed with lace 34mm in width.
The epaulettes worn with these full-dress tunics
were identical to those shown but the aiguillettes
were mixed in the proportions of two-thirds gold to
one-third sky-blue. The trumpeters were commanded by a trumpet-major and three *brigadiers-
trompettes*. Their dress was the same as the trumpeters with the addition of rank distinctions
consisting of the twin gold stripes of a *maréchal-
des-logis-chef* for the *trompette-major* and the single
gold stripe of a *maréchal-des-logis* for the *brigadiers-
trompettes*.

*A3 Officer of the Empress's Dragoons in cape,
1806–1813.*

The uniform of officers was precisely the same as
that of the men but cut of finer cloth and with gold
buttons and epaulettes. We see here an officer in the
voluminous *manteau trois-quarts* similar to that of the
rank and file but cut of dark green cloth and with
gold lace trim to the short shoulder-cape. As of
1813, this would be exchanged for the sleeved
manteau-capote, an identically coloured greatcoat
with gilded buttons. Both the *manteau trois-quarts*
and the *manteau-capote* were reserved for riding and
a double-breasted *redingote* or greatcoat adopted for
foot duty. The officers' helmet was of the same
pattern as that of the men but with browned gold

Kettle-drummer of Mamelukes, 1810–12. Pink headgear with
gold ornaments, white turban and plume and pink ostrich
feathers. White tunic with sky-blue cuffs and wings, pink
collar and gold lace. The waistcoat, saddle- and kettle-drum
cloth are green with gold lace and ornaments. The trousers
and crossbelt are pink with gold lace. The ribbons on the
kettle-drum cloth, the horse's leathers and ostrich plumes are
pink. The tassels are mixed gilt and pink thread. His sash is
white, as is the horse's plume, and the stirrups are gilt.
(Rousselot after Dubois de l'Estang. Courtesy De Gerlache de
Gomery Collection)

plate and greater embellishment. The plume, safely
packed away in the portemanteau in bad weather,
would be scarlet for the company officers and white
for those attached to the *Etat-Major* (regimental
staff).

*B1 Trooper of the Grenadiers à Cheval in service dress,
1806–1807*

The dress and equipment of the *Grenadiers à Cheval*
was largely that prescribed for the mounted *Garde
des Consuls* and was little modified, save by use,
during the Empire; this accounts for their rather
old-fashioned look until 1814, when the First
Restoration turned the regiment into cuirassiers
and they were issued the *cuirassier habit-veste* of more

modern appearance. The individual illustrated wears the *surtout* tunic commonly adopted in all but full dress, for which the *habit* was reserved. After 1809, the *surtout* was replaced by a cheap replica of the full-dress *habit*, although NCOs persisted in the use of the garment until 1814. The ornaments of the *surtout* were identical to those of the *habit* and this rule extended to the NCOs, whose rank distinctions were as follows: *brigadiers* (corporals) were distinguished by twin stripes of aurore lace on a scarlet ground above each cuff; the *maréchaux-des-logis* (sergeants) wore a single gold stripe mounted on scarlet ground above the cuff and, in addition, the cord and tassel of the bearskin, the trefoil and fringeless epaulette, the aiguillette, the piping and tassel of the *bonnet de police*, and the swordknot were all of thread mixed one-third gold and two-thirds scarlet; finally, the *maréchaux-des-logis-chefs* (sergeant-majors) had twin gold stripes on scarlet ground above the cuff and the same additional details as the *maréchaux-des-logis* but manufactured in the proportions of two-thirds gold and one-third scarlet.

B2 Trumpeter of the Grenadiers à Cheval in full dress and cape, 1806–1807

In common with the troopers, the trumpeters wore the *surtout* for the campaigns of 1806 and 1807, leaving their full dress *habits* in storage at their depot. The *surtout* illustrated closed by means of either seven or ten copper buttons, dependent upon its age; and had gold grenade devices on the turnbacks, and gold lace 22mm in width about the collar and cuffs. On both the *surtout* and the full dress *habit*, the trumpeters wore epaulettes and aiguillettes of mixed gold and crimson thread in the proportions of one-third and two-thirds respectively prior to 1809 and one-seventh and six-sevenths thereafter. His cape is of the same cut as the troopers' *manteau trois-quarts* and this pattern was probably worn until 1814 and not replaced by a sky-blue *manteau-capote* in 1813.

B3 Officer of the Grenadiers à Cheval in service dress, 1809–1814

The officers were dressed in the same manner as the men but in finer uniforms of superior cut and gilded buttons. Their *habits* bore gold aiguillettes and gold epaulettes appropriate to their rank (see Chapter 3,

Line Chasseurs, p. 142). In full dress they would add a scarlet plume and gold cords and tassels to the bearskin; staff officers wore white plumes. In the same manner as their men, officers would adopt overalls in place of hide or linen breeches when in marching order; these were generally of grey cloth, closing by means of cloth-covered buttons, but dark blue overalls were not unknown.

C1 Officer of the Chasseurs à Cheval in full dress, 1804–1808

This officer represents the classic *chasseur* of the Guard, frequently seen in contemporary paintings

Trooper of the *Corps Royal des Dragons de France* in full dress, 1815. With the First Restoration, the Empress's Dragoons were renamed the *Corps Royal des Dragons de France* by Louis XVIII. The dragoons retained their old uniforms and equipment with the substitution, where possible, of all Imperial emblems for Royal ones: the buttons, belt-buckles and cartridge-pouch plates now bore *fleur-de-lys* insignia, while the Imperial crown which had ornamented the front of the helmet crest was replaced by a Gorgon's head symbol. Following the re-formation of the regiment in 1815, after the Hundred Days campaign, the dress was further modified by the issue of a black-maned crested helmet, shown above, with white plume in lieu of scarlet. Note also that the Imperial crown device normally embroidered in the angle of the cloth schabraque has been replaced by the élite grenade device, and that his aiguillettes have been moved to the left shoulder. (Job. Author's Collection)

French NCO of the Mamelukes, late Empire. His scarlet headgear has gold ornaments, white turban and black aigrette. His tunic is sky-blue with black lace and gold rank and service chevrons. His waistcoat and trousers are scarlet with black piping. His sash is indigo with scarlet tassel and gold fringe. His black-scabbarded scimitar has gold fittings and is suspended on a scarlet cord. (Rousselot after Vanson. Courtesy De Gerlache de Gomery Collection)

and prints, complete with full ornaments and pelisse. In fact, such costume was the exception rather than the rule. The pelisse immediately dates this individual to before 1809, whereafter the *chasseurs* campaigned with dolmans alone. Even previously, we know that the pelisses of all ranks were so damaged during the 1805 campaign that the campaigns of both 1806 and 1807 were made without them, such was the expense of repairing them. Naturally, we might expect those of officers to have either lasted longer or to have been replaced out of private funds, unlike those of the rank and file. The gold chevrons on his cuffs indicate his officer status and their number and width further designate his precise rank in the hierarchy (see Chapter 3, *Line Chasseurs*, p. 142, for specific detail on this). His sabre is typical of the extremely ornate patterns affected by those of rank and the scabbard is constructed of gilded bronze. (The sabretache is illustrated artificially caught up and turned forwards by the scabbard in order to show detail.)

C2 Trooper of the Chasseurs à Cheval in campaign dress, 1804–1808

Although the battle of Austerlitz is known to have been fought in full dress by this regiment, this outfit is typical of the *chasseurs* on the march between Ulm and Somosierra. His hide breeches have been replaced by overalls, he wears the warm pelisse in lieu of dolman, his headgear is devoid of ornament and has its *flamme* tucked into its top, and his cape is conveniently slung over his right shoulder, in anticipation of either rain or battle, in which latter case it would provide sufficient protection to turn a sword or bayonet thrust. In point of fact this practice was employed at Austerlitz despite the troops' full dress uniform. Note the sabretache cover of stiff, varnished black cloth; a hand-painted yellow Imperial eagle motif was frequently added.

C3 Trumpeter of the Chasseurs à Cheval in campaign dress, 1812

The reorganisation of 1802 raised the number of trumpeters from two to three per company (i.e. six per squadron) creating a total of twelve under the command of a trumpet-major and two *brigadiers-trompettes*. By 1811, they numbered thirty, while in 1813, with the formation of four Young Guard

Trooper of the Mamelukes, 1808–10. This Mameluke wears a crimson *cahouk* head-dress with black aigrette. His chemise is yellow with black wool lace; the waistcoat is indigo with black lace and piping; the sash is sky-blue and the *charoual* trousers are scarlet. This rear-view affords us the opportunity to note that both cartridge-pouch crossbelt and carbine crossbelt are of French light cavalry pattern, as indeed is the cartridge-pouch itself, a developing trend as the campaigns rolled by and the possibilities of replacing worn equipment with oriental patterns decreased. The portemanteau is cut of dark green cloth and has crimson lace with a strip of white piping on either side of the rounded ends. (Rousselot after Bance. Courtesy De Gerlache de Gomery Collection)

squadrons, they totalled fifty-four. The last five campaigns, including that of 1812 in Russia, were undertaken without pelisses and this trumpeter is therefore typical of the post-1808 period. Trumpet-majors and *brigadiers-trompettes* were clothed in the same manner but with the addition of gold rank chevrons above the cuffs: two for the *trompette-major* and one for the *brigadiers-trompettes*.

D1 Brigadier-trompette of the Polish Lancers in service dress, 1810–1814

The white full-dress *kurtkas* were so easily soiled and damaged that the pattern shown here was issued as a service-dress replacement. It was distributed along with trousers of like colour, deep sky-blue, and the trumpeters therefore most frequently looked precisely like the troopers save for the ground cloth and the additional lace about the collar and cuffs. The *brigadier's* rank is indicated by a silver lace chevron above each cuff. His epaulette and aiguillettes are composed of two-thirds crimson and one-third silver thread. We have taken the liberty of illustrating the *czapska* without its protective cover, the better to display the white pattern issued musicians, and the typical campaign overalls of the period in lieu of the sky-blue trousers.

D2 Subaltern of the Polish Lancers in campaign dress, 1810–1814

The dress of officers of the Polish Lancers followed the general rule of Napoleonic cavalry in that the officers were clad and equipped in similar fashion to the troopers, but in clothing of better quality and with silver replacing all pewter and white wool. For the sake of showing the *czapska* detail, we have not shown it encased in the protective cover we might expect in marching order. In similar fashion, the lapels are illustrated folded back, rather than crossed over in the direction of the aiguillettes to

reveal the dark-blue ground cloth. His expensively ornamented crossbelt has been sheathed in a cover of crimson leather to save it from wear and tear. He carries the officers' pattern of the *An XI* light cavalry model sabre, although hussar patterns were certainly not unknown.

D3 Trooper of the Polish Lancers in service dress, 1810–1814

This figure illustrates the transposition of the aiguillettes with the fringed wool epaulette which took place after the adoption of the lance in 1809. When the lancers received their lances they also retained all their previous armaments, including musketoon, sabre and brace of pistols, and it was so

241

equipped that they took part in the Russian campaign of 1812. Aside from the enormous encumbrance of this veritable arsenal, it was pointed out that the second rank of lancers would scarcely require a lance, and in April 1813 the weaponry was redistributed among the ranks in the following manner: in each company of 125 men, the first row comprised two *maréchaux-des-logis* with sabre and two pistols; four *brigadiers* with sabre, musketoon and bayonet, single pistol and lance; and forty-four troopers with sabre, single pistol and lance. The second rank would consist of four *brigadiers* and forty-four men equipped with sabre, single pistol, musketoon and bayonet. Thereafter would come three trumpeters with sabre and two pistols; two farriers with sabre and single pistol; eighteen troopers, half of whom were armed with sabre and carbine and the remainder with sabre and lance; and a *maréchal-des-logis-chef*, two *maréchaux-des-logis* and a farrier armed with sabre and two pistols. As a consequence, the webbing of the troopers was modified and the musketoon crossbelt only issued to those so armed.

E1 Trumpet-major of the Dutch Lancers in full dress, 1811

This special full-dress uniform was introduced on 15 August 1811. The trumpet-major and the three *brigadiers-trompettes* were equipped with the white colpack shown here at a cost of 51F apiece; the trumpet-major's headgear was further embellished with a sumptuous gold and scarlet cord and tassels at a cost of 36F. The trumpet-major's rank distinctions were those of a *maréchal-des-logis-chef*, a single gold chevron mounted on scarlet ground above the cuff, and, in addition, two strips of gold lace on the collar as shown in our illustration. With the existing gold lace which trimmed the facings, the lace therefore formed a depth of three on the collar and two at the cuff. The *brigadiers-trompettes* had the twin gold chevrons of a *maréchal-des-logis* and an additional single stripe of gold lace on the collar: the lace would therefore have a visual depth of two at the collar and three at the cuff. Note also this *trompette-major*'s webbing, consisting of five strips of gold lace on a scarlet ground. The trumpet-banner is that reproduced in black and white on another page, and readers are referred to its caption for further detail.

Trooper of the Empress's Dragoons in *petite tenue à pied*, 1808. The dragoons were trained to fight both mounted and on foot, and were consequently armed with the long 1777-model dragoon musket, as modified in *An IX*. His *petite tenue* consists of a *surtout* tunic in place of his full-dress *habit*. Note that the swordbelt was slung over the right shoulder when on foot. (Detaillé. Author's Collection)

242

E2 Lieutenant Sous-adjutant-major of the Dutch Lancers in campaign dress, 1812

This officer was one of four of identical rank attached to the *Etat-Major* of the regiment. Officers' dress was basically the same as the troopers with gold in place of yellow, but the Dutch Lancers were permitted the latitude common to light cavalry regiments and their officers sported personalised costumes of many varieties. The black and white illustrations furnish several examples of this trait and we here represent a fairly typical example of campaign dress. The white ostrich or heron feather plume of his *czapska* has been removed and the costly headgear encased in a protective cloth with only a gold cord pompon to designate its wearer's status. His crossbelt is likewise protected in a sheath of Moroccan leather. Other types of overalls included a dark blue pattern with leather reinforcement to the inside leg and a scarlet strip of lace down the outer leg.

E3 Brigadier of the Dutch Lancers in summer marching order, 1812–1814

We have illustrated this figure without the normal cloth campaign cover in order to display the detail of his *czapska*. The scarlet headgear was otherwise similar to that worn by the Polish Lancers. He wears his *kurtka* buttoned towards the aiguillettes, which were always on the left side for the Dutch

Lancers. His rank is indicated by twin chevrons of yellow lace; a *maréchal-des-logis* would have a single chevron of gold lace above the cuffs and, in addition, *czapska* cords, epaulette and aiguillettes of one-third gold and two-thirds scarlet; a *maréchal-des-logis-chef* would be identical to the sergeant, save for two gold chevrons above each cuff. For full dress, this individual would add yellow cords and tassels and a white plume to his *czapska*, and replace the *pantalon d'écurie* shown here with scarlet breeches with twin strips of dark blue lace down the seam. The *pantalon d'écurie* (stable overalls) were frequently authorised in lieu of the heavy, dark blue overalls in fine weather.

F1 Trooper of the German Light Horse in service full dress, 1807

We have taken the liberty of illustrating this figure in the corps' original uniform of cream with amaranth facings. In fact, this uniform was dropped shortly before the 1st Squadron departed for Spain to support King Joseph's 'triumphant' entry into Madrid in 1808; thereafter it differed solely in being made of white in lieu of cream cloth. Upon the reversion of this regiment to lancer-style

A cannonball explodes among a troop of *Grenadiers à Cheval*. The cavalry charged in successive rows and were particularly vulnerable to the hurtling iron of the artillery which, if the ground was dry, would rend and bounce its way throughout the depth of the regiment. (Detaillé. Author's Collection)

243

dress in 1812, after the *chasseur*-style of the intervening years, the uniform was similar to that shown except that both *kurtka* and breeches were cut of dark green cloth, and the waist sash was dropped in favour of the wide waistbelt shown on figure F2. In full dress, this figure would add white cords and tassels to his *czapska* along with a white plume tipped with amaranth.

F2 *Trumpeter of the German Light Horse in campaign dress, 1808–1809*

This figure is reconstructed as we might imagine his dress in Spain. He retains the *kurtka* of the same pattern as that worn by the troopers but with reversed colours and the addition of silver lace to the facings to designate his rôle and status. His

czapska is protected by a typical cover and he wears overalls in place of the easily soiled amaranth breeches.

F3 *Officer of the élite squadron, the Gardes du Corps, of the German Light Horse, 1807–1809*

Initially a company, the élite section of the Berg Light Horse was augmented to squadron strength in 1808 and became the *Gardes du Corps* who originally accompanied King Joseph to Spain. They were distinguished from the balance of the regiment by the button-hole loops on their lapels and by their aiguillettes. A trooper of this same squadron would be identically clad save that all ornaments illustrated here in silver would be of white wool. Note that both the *czapska* plate and the belt-buckle bear the initial 'J' rather than an Imperial device.

A regiment of *Gardes d'Honneur* engage a swarm of Russian cossacks, 1813–14. Although a motley bunch, the *Gardes d'Honneur* distinguished themselves at the battles of Hanau, Leipzig and Rheims, despite inauspicious beginnings which included not only numerous mutinies and desertions, but also conspiracy to murder their commanding officer. (Job. Author's Collection)

G1 Trooper of the 1st Regiment of Gardes d'Honneur in full dress, 1813–1814

The hussar-style uniform illustrated here is taken directly from a surviving uniform: see body of text for details.

G2 Trumpeter of the 3rd Regiment of Gardes d'Honneur, 1814

The dress of trumpeters of these regiments is uncertain and several solutions are possible. That shown is the hussar style, with inverted colours to the troopers', and is highly likely for at least one of the regiments. Another possibility is the regulation Imperial Livery in which all trumpeters of the *Grande Armée* were supposedly clad, comprising dark green tunic with the specially designed Imperial lace about all the facings and in loops

about the breast buttons. The Alsatian Collections show them in sky-blue pelisses and dolmans, scarlet breeches and black fur bearskin colpacks. All of the above solutions are plausible and it is quite possible that they are all correct in one regiment or another.

G3 Officer of the 3rd Regiment of Gardes d'Honneur, 1814

The dress of officers was essentially the same as that of the men save that all white areas of the men's dress became silver. Rank distinctions were also silver and followed those accorded officers of *chasseurs* and hussars of the Line. Their headgear was either the scarlet shako shown here or a black bearskin colpack with scarlet *flamme* and silver ornaments. Their plumes would be identical to their men's except for staff officers whose plumes were white. Their webbing was red Moroccan leather trimmed in silver lace.

H1 Trooper of the Lithuanian Tartars, 1812–1813

The oriental dress of the Lithuanian Tartars is open to considerable controversy and this illustration is based on the representations of Genbarzevski,

246

Timbalier of the *Grenadiers à Cheval*. **Although based on a contemporary illustration conserved in the Cottreau Collection, this magnificent individual's dress and trappings are the subject of some controversy. Some authorities maintain that it dates either to the very early years of the Empire or possibly as late as 1809, when the marriage of Napoleon to the Arch-Duchess Maria-Louise of Austria occasioned considerable expenditure on both Court and household troops'** **uniforms. These possibilities, however, clash with two other contemporary recordings of drummers' dress, by Hoffmann and Garnier, which indicate a hussar-style dress until as late as 1810. This fact leads other authorities to conclude that the costume was devised at the earliest in 1813, by which date such extravagant expense was highly unlikely and the design never actually implemented. (Job. Courtesy of the National Army Museum)**

Malibran and Chelminski. We have shown the costume associated with the creation of the corps, worn throughout 1812 and to a lesser extent in 1813. Although the costume is Eastern, the equipment is undoubtedly French, the sabre being identical to those issued the Guard lancers. The lance pennant is variously recorded as red over dark green or white, or even white over red.

H2 Trooper of the Lithuanian Tartars, 1813–1814

This costume is reconstructed from information supplied by such authorities as Vernet, Knötel, Noirmon and Marbot. It was supposedly the new dress issued in 1813, but troopers undoubtedly continued to wear their old uniforms where these had been previously issued. Another source, the *Bourgeois de Freyberg* MS of 1813, records a costume comprising the old-style shako (see figure H1) with white turban; scarlet chemise; indigo jerkin with red lace; a wide sash into which the pistols have been tucked; and grey overalls of French cut with dark green lace down the outer seams.

H3 Trooper of the Mamelukes, 1808–1813

This figure is based on an existing costume in the Brunon Collection with the sole major change of a green *cahouk* head-dress in place of the yellow model included in the collection. This green pattern was ordered by Consular decree of 7 January 1802 to indicate the new allegiance of the Moslem warriors to France. Although most contemporary illustrations depict the Mamelukes in red or crimson *cahouks*, these green varieties were certainly also worn, as attested by records made by Hendschell in 1806–07 and Geissler in 1809–10.

Officer of the Polish Lancers in the white gala tunic faced crimson, and crimson trousers, characteristic of the early period; the *czapska* is fully dressed. It is possible that trumpeters and senior NCOs may also have acquired this second parade uniform.